Effective Schools

Volume 6 in
Research on Sociocultural Influences on
Motivation and Learning

Series Editors:
Dennis M. McInerney, *University of Western Sydney*
Shawn Van Etten, *State University of New York, Cortland*

Research on Sociocultural Influences on Motivation and Learning

Dennis M. McInerney and Shawn Van Etten, Series Editors

Effective Schools

edited by

Dennis M. McInerney
University of Western Sydney

Martin Dowson
University of Western Sydney

and

Shawn Van Etten
State University of New York, Cortland

INFORMATION AGE
PUBLISHING

Greenwich, Connecticut • www.infoagepub.com

Library of Congress Cataloging-in-Publication Data

Effective schools / edited by Dennis M. McInerney, Martin Dowson, Shawn Van Etten.
    p. cm. — (Research on sociocultural influences on motivation and learning)
  Includes bibliographical references.
  ISBN 1-59311-491-5 (pbk.) — ISBN 1-59311-492-3 (hardcover)
  1. Educational sociology—United States. 2. Academic achievement—United
States. 3. Minorities—Education—United States. 4. Pluralism (Social
sciences)—United States. 5. Teachers—United States. I. McInerney, D. M.
(Dennis M.), 1948- II. Dowson, Martin. III. Van Etten, Shawn. IV.
Series.
  LC191.4.E44 2006
  306.43'2—dc22

                                                                2006007219

Printed in the United States of America

CONTENTS

PREFACE

Students arrive in our classrooms with complex sociocultural histories comprised of family, cultural, physical, social, emotional, and prior learning experiences. In order to be effective, schools must address sociocultural issues arising from these complex histories. However, the imperative to address complex sociocultural histories has not always been as clearly evident as it is at present. In many countries around the world the majority-dominated culture has often dictated both the framework and the criteria for education success: success to be achieved not only by students but also by teachers, schools, districts, and the countries themselves. The aim of this volume is to examine current research related to effective schooling from a range of social and cultural perspectives that have clear implications for students' motivation, learning, and ultimately their success, in diverse contexts.

In addressing school effectiveness, Michael Apple captured the need to take a holistic, integrated, relational perspective on education, one that does not view education as a group of "separate compartments" but as a comprehensive, multidimensional, and interactive whole. In order for education to be successful, Apple (1988) argued that education must accept seeing

> subjects having a specific class, race, and gender, students whose biographies are intimately linked to the economic, political, and ideological trajectories of their families and communities; to the political economies of their neighborhoods; and—in an identifiable set of connections—to the exploitative relations of the larger society. As I shall claim, these same things must be said about teachers as well as "learners," for teachers' work cannot be divorced from these conditions. (p. 60)

The claims of Apple (1988) were revisited by Marilyn Cochran-Smith in her 2005 Presidential address for the American Educational Research Association as she laid out three concerns impacting, for better or for worse, the future of teacher education: (1) teacher education as a policy problem; (2) teacher education based on research and evidence; and (3) teacher education driven by outcomes (Cochran-Smith, 2005). A primary claim by Cochran-Smith is that teacher education has been "guided more by tradition, fashion, or ideology than by cutting-edge research and solid evidence" (p. 8). But now, more than ever, the education enterprise involves "teacher educators working with colleagues in economics, measurement, sociology, psychology, and anthropology to invent mixed methods for studying the meaning and impact of teacher preparation variations" in order that teachers are able to accommodate and harness the diversity of student motivation and learning needs in research-oriented and evidence-based ways (p. 8).

The issues highlighted by Apple (1988) and Cochran-Smith (2005) are highly relevant for school effectiveness research and practice, and reverberate strongly throughout this volume. In particular, the authors highlight the need for a renewed emphasis on the empirical investigation of socioculturally relevant pedagogies, and socioculturally sensitive approaches to policy and reform, in order to accommodate the diverse motivation and learning needs of students in defensible ways. Also woven throughout this volume is the identified need to incorporate diverse view points and perceptions as part of the essence of the education enterprise—to shape schools not from a majority standpoint but from integrated majority-minority perspectives that take into consideration the diverse needs and values of students, teachers, and communities in specific contexts and across the globe.

Dennis M McInerney
Martin Dowson
Shawn Van Etten

REFERENCES

Apple, M. (1988). *Teachers and texts: A political economy of class and gender relations in education.* New York: Routledge

Cochran-Smith, M. (2005). The new teacher education: For better or for worse? *Educational Researcher, 34*(7), 3-17.

ABSTRACTS

Sociocultural Perspectives on Effective Schooling: Voices from Some of the Leading Authorities in the Field

The authors in this volume make an exciting and substantial contribution to our understanding of educational effectiveness from a sociocultural perspective. In doing so, the authors address salient issues concerning *Research* (Section 1: chapters 2 and 3), *Pedagogy* (Section 2: chapters 4, 5, and 6), *Teachers* (Section 3: chapters 7 and 8), and *Learning Environments* (Section 4: chapters 9, 10, and 11). Each of these issues is dealt with in novel, insightful, and practical ways by the authors.

Overview

In chapter 1, Martin Dowson, Dennis McInerney, and Shawn Van Etten begin by noting that "effective schools" and "effective schooling" have been educational buzzwords for nearly 2 decades. Research emanating from the "effective schooling" paradigm has identified key features of schools and schooling that are said to provide students with a "high-performance" education, that is, an education that makes a tangible difference to students' academic and life outcomes—particularly the outcomes of students from diverse groups. This chapter focuses on some of the key features identified in the effective schools research, and discusses these features from a sociocultural perspective. The aim of this discussion is to highlight the relevance and applicability of effective schooling practices for those researchers and practitioners particularly interested in promoting the academic and life outcomes of students from socially, culturally, and linguistically diverse backgrounds.

On Research

In chapter 2, Leon Kyriakides and Bert Creemers propose a novel and dynamic model of educational effectiveness that explains variation in student achievement by defining relations amongst important effectiveness factors which operate at different levels in school contexts. This model is based on the key understanding that flexibility and specificity in school effectiveness measures (what they label "differentiated effectiveness") often determines the impact of these measures on student learning outcomes. One of the most directly researched areas of differentiated effectiveness concerns whether different teacher behaviors and curricula are necessary for pupils exhibiting different background characteristics. The Dynamic Model focuses, in particular, on how differentiation in teacher behaviors and curricula can contribute to effective teaching and enhanced learning outcomes. The authors also make specific suggestions concerning how the model may be used to introduce policies promoting the provision of equal opportunities to students of different social groups.

In chapter 3, Daniel Muijs discusses the impact of important sociocultural changes impacting research into educational effectiveness. These changes, Muijs forcefully argues, render highly problematic the traditional emphasis of researchers in the field of educational effectiveness on self-contained, state-funded public schools. Specifically, the marketization processes, public sector reform and globalization are driving new forms of school organization. The new forms of school organization are characterized by, among other factors, a competitive focus, expanded educational functions, and increased connectivity—especially through the use of communications technology. So far, however, school effectiveness research has largely ignored these important changes, and researchers in the field have tended to act as if the traditional school can be examined in isolation from these trends. To the contrary, Muijs argues that new forms of school effectiveness research are required to meet the demands of rapidly changing educational environments.

On Pedagogy

In chapter 4, Kenneth Tyler, R. Trent Haines, and Eric Anderman seek to better understand the role that motivation plays in the association between culturally relevant pedagogy and school performance. Culturally relevant pedagogy is championed as one way to effectively address achievement difficulties faced by many ethnic minority students. However, the empirical links between relevant pedagogy, the psychological characteristics of such instruction, and students' academic outcomes have not been made clear. In order to make these links clearer and more amenable to empirical research, Tyler, Haines, and Anderman propose a new conceptual model of school performance with specific application to ethnic minority students exposed to culturally relevant instruction. The authors also show how the model implicates specific and tangible learning activities and strategies for minority students. thus making a timely, thoughtful, and practical contribution to a theme of increasing importance in school effectiveness research.

In chapter 5, Richard Walker and Mike Horsley note that research into effective teaching and schooling has tended to ignore the key issue of textbook pedagogy. Walker and Horsley's chapter clearly explains the notion of textbook pedagogy and analyses its complementarity with another important aspect of effective teaching—pedagogical content knowledge. The chapter then presents an insightful sociocultural analysis of teachers' use of textbooks and other learning resources in the classroom. Two empirical studies, conducted by members of the Teaching Resources and Textbook Research Unit (TREAT) at the University of Sydney, are then examined to indicate how teachers adapt and use textbooks and other resources in their classrooms. A further Australian national study explores the use of photocopied materials in primary and secondary classrooms, and investigates the way that teachers utilized these materials in their classrooms.

In chapter 6, Robert Rueda, notes that reading instruction has been a major focus in attempts to improve academic achievement among students in the United States, especially amongst Latino and African American students in low SES schools in urban settings. Complementing Tyler, Anderman, and Haines (chapter 3), Rueda focuses on *culturally accommodated instruction*, noting that these approaches to instruction attempt to reduce presumed mismatches between students and the sociocultural features of classrooms with a goal of improving learning and achievement. Yet, like Tyler et al., he also notes that there are no clear models which attempt to explain how such accommodations might impact learning. Rueda addresses this deficit in the literature by addressing possible cognitive and motivational routes through which cultural accommodations might work, thus providing a coherent framework for a more systematic examination of these factors with a specific focus on the area of reading comprehension.

On Teachers

In chapter 7, La Tefy Schoen discusses three sources of social and cultural influences over teacher behavior: those internal to individual teachers, those internal to the school culture, and those derived from the larger societal context. Using specific examples, Schoen asserts that the most pervasive and controlling forces acting on teachers are those emanating from the culture of the school at which they work. School culture is subsequently described as being comprised of four dimensions: the professional orientation of the faculty, the overall organizational structure of the school, the quality of the learning environments, and the extent of student-centered focus. Through these collective dimensions, the school culture acts as a tacit and covert controlling force that strongly influences the way in which teachers perform their work. Suggestions are made for increasing teacher efficacy for change, and altering each dimension of school culture in ways most likely to enhance teacher and school effectiveness.

In chapter 8, David Watkins and Qunying Zhang, explore common views concerning the qualities a teacher should posses in one particular sociocultural context: The People's Republic of China. They note that Chinese views of what constitutes a good teacher emphasize the teachers' commitment to the holistic development of students both within and outside the classroom. However, Watkins and Zhang are not content to accept these views without question and, as a result, ask some provocative questions about these views: Do Chinese teachers really hold these views? Do other cultures share their opinions? Do these views vary at different levels of education and in different subject areas? Why is it important to try to answer such questions anyway? A further relatively neglected question is whether students and their teachers share a common view of "the good teacher." The authors address these questions in a way that sheds considerable light on socioculturally accepted notions of "the good teacher."

On Learning Environments

In chapter 9, Deborah Lowther, Steven Ross, Fethi Inan, and J. Daniel Strahl discusses how educational technology may be used to change the culture and professional practice of teaching, particularly in high poverty schools. They argue that, even with increased access to technology, students in low-income schools have performed substantially below average on recent assessments. The authors propose that the central reason for this underperformance is ineffective use of computers in the classroom. Visits to over 1,000 classrooms revealed that computers are infrequently used, or used primarily for simple, noncritical thinking activities. These activities do not enhance students' ability to perform on standardized assessments requiring higher-level thinking skills. The authors' research demonstrates, in contrast, that if technology is used in an active and engaging, student-centered learning environment, it can have a positive impact on the student outcomes—especially within high poverty schools. In order to achieve these outcomes, however, teachers must be prepared to implement effective technology integration approaches and must be provided with embedded support to do so.

In chapter 10, Mimi Bong and Sung-il Kim focus on the significant influence of actual and perceived school and classroom climates on various aspects of student functioning in school. Their chapter begins with a brief review of the literature concerning the impact of perceived learning environments on students' motivation, affect, and learning. The authors then introduce empirical findings from their own research on predictive relations between perceived school mastery and performance goal structures, parental expectations, teacher-student relationships and students' academic confidence, reasons for studying in school, positive emotions, and sense of belonging while at school. In particular, the authors identify the unique role played by parental expectations on these Korean girls' motivation as well as the mediating role of teacher-student relationships between perceived school environment and student motivation.

In chapter 11, Jan Heysek begins by noting that effective discipline is a key contributor to effective education more generally, and effective schools in particular. In the sociocultural context of the "new" South Africa, this chapter analyses disciplinary issues in two new multicultural schools in South Africa in the context of underlying potential racism evident in both these schools. The two schools were selected for the research project because they represent two different points on the continuum from "good" discipline" to "poor" discipline. They also represent two different points on the continuum between, on the one hand, being opposed to social and cultural change and, on the other hand, accepting the profound social, political, and cultural changes occurring in broader South African society. The analysis indicates that racism still exists in some schools. However, a deeper understanding of the attitudes of individuals involved provides an important context for the racism and its associated disciplinary issues.

Together, these chapters form a diverse yet integrated volume which will be of substantial interest to researchers and practitioners pursuing the critical issue of enhancing school effectiveness in diverse sociocultural contexts. We trust your own research and practice will benefit substantially from the insightful contributions of the authors to this work.

CHAPTER 1

WHAT WE KNOW ABOUT EFFECTIVE SCHOOLS AND EFFECTIVE SCHOOLING FROM A SOCIOCULTURAL PERSPECTIVE

Martin Dowson, Dennis M. McInerney, and Shawn Van Etten

"Effective schools" and effective schooling" have been educational buzz-words for nearly 2 decades (Herman, 1999; Taylor, Pearson, Clark, & Walpole, 2000). Research emanating from the "effective schooling" paradigm has identified key features of schools and schooling that are said to provide students with a "high-performance" education, that is, an education that makes a tangible difference to students' academic and life outcomes—particularly the outcomes of students from diverse groups. This chapter focuses on some of the key features identified in the effective schools research, and discusses these features from a sociocultural perspective. The aim of this discussion is to highlight the relevance and applicability of effective schooling practices for those researchers and practitioners particularly interested in promoting the academic and life outcomes of students from socially, culturally, and linguistically diverse backgrounds.

Effective Schools, 1–13
Copyright © 2006 by Information Age Publishing
All rights of reproduction in any form reserved.

From a sociocultural perspective, effective schools or "high perfor-mance schools" or "high performance learning communities" (see Ber-man et al., 1992) focus intentionally and explicitly on the social, cultural, and linguistic diversity evident among their student populations. In doing so, socioculturally effective schools consider both the theoretical and practical issues relevant to ensuring educational success for all stu-dents. These schools address issues of diversity "head-on" in order to maximize the educational achievement and life potential of their stu-dents, and in order to sustain substantial educational improvements over time. This "head on" approach includes:

(a) framing and supporting a whole-school vision that values social, linguistic and cultural diversity;
(b) developing classroom practitioners who willingly focus on educa-tional issues pertaining to diversity;
(c) valuing collaboration with the community and flexibility in address-ing community needs; and
(d) eliminating policies and procedures that limit or detract from the quality of educational experiences of linguistically, socially and cul-turally diverse students.

On a somewhat more specific level, optimal learning conditions that support socially, linguistically, and culturally diverse student populations, leading to high academic performance among these students, include:

Leadership Issues

(a) a supportive school-wide climate that results in low staff turnover, and extensive student bonding opportunities;
(b) resource allocation that clearly reflects and communicates adminis-trative, institutional, and political support;
(c) school leadership that is focused on catering for diversity and allows time for monitoring, reflection, and change implementa-tion;

Pedagogical Issues

(d) a balanced curriculum that includes both basic and higher-order thinking skills, explicit skill instruction, and opportunities for stu-dent-directed instruction;

(e) a commitment to curricula flexibility, including one-on-one and small-group instruction tailored to students' specific developmental levels;

(f) carefully managed educational transitions (e.g., between elementary and high school, and high school and university), accompanied by a strong focus on continuity across systems and issues;

(g) the use of instructional strategies that enhance understanding and provide extensive opportunities for practice, including carefully scaffolded instruction, the use of native/indigenous languages and cultures in instruction, and regular informational/performance feedback;

(h) systematic student assessment, including the careful alignment of instructional and assessment activities;

Relational Issues

(i) staff development focused on enhancing the cultural skills and sensitivities of teachers; and

(j) extensive home-school and school-community connections.

Other features of socioculturally effective schools commonly cited in the literature include policies, programs, and strategies that support the development of the ethnic identity and indigenous/native languages and cultures of diverse students, and programs that support cross-cultural understanding among students (e.g., August & Hakuta, 1997; Cummins, 1989).

FOCUSING THE ENQUIRY

As the brief overview above suggests, it would be easy for school effectiveness research to degenerate into a "wish-list" of school characteristics desired by students, teachers, parents, and researchers. We hasten to add that we do not think this criticism applies to the research reviewed above! However, we are aware of the need, in this review, to focus on a limited range of the most salient aspects of school effectiveness—especially as these apply to socioculturally diverse students. Without argument (but see Langer, 1991; Lucas, Henze, & Donato, 1990; Rogoff, 1994; Taylor, Pearson, Clark, & Walpole, 2000; for some supportive literature), we state that these characteristics include shared beliefs, strong partnerships, responsive curricula, high expectations, focused leadership, and mentoring and relationships. We also state that specific strategies deployed in the classroom have a marked impact on the learning and achievement of diverse students. These strategies substantially enhance the sociocultural impact of educational provision in effective schools.

Shared Beliefs

Socioculturally effective schools share a common set of beliefs that allow them to act in coordinated ways to enhance student learning. These beliefs include:

(a) the "core" belief that sociocultural diversity is something to be cherished, supported and promoted;
(b) a recognition of the close relationship between low levels of educational achievement and poverty, poor health, inadequate housing, and other measures of socioeconomic disadvantage;
(c) an understanding that addressing socioeconomic disadvantage requires the adoption of evidence-based approaches to the teaching and learning of diverse students; and
(d) an acceptance of the need to develop systematic links with the home, previous schools, other service providers and the wider community in order to provide a holistic and integrated educational experience for all students,

Socioculturally effective schools not only hold shared beliefs, but consistently convey these beliefs to students in practical terms. Effective schools may, for example, show their commitment to sociocultural diversity by encouraging and supporting the development of students' native languages and cultures through the employment of bilingual staff who share students' language and cultural backgrounds. Schools may also provide language and cultural development through formal classes, and/or through less formal means such as the use of instructional aides, peer tutoring, and the deployment of community resources. These programs encourage an empowering, value-added orientation to students' language and cultural backgrounds, while communicating to students that they, and their sociocultural heritage and identities, are valued and respected. (Penuel & Wertsch, 1995).

Strong Partnerships

Shared beliefs facilitate the formation of strong partnerships between schools, parents and caregivers, and the wider community. These partnerships, in turn, allow the school and its parent and community partners to jointly progress standards of education for all students. The partnerships also provide the framework within which parents/caregivers and the community is able to be, and to become, actively involved in educational decision-making processes, including planning for the introduction of new programs designed to meet the needs of students from diverse social, cultural and linguistic backgrounds. Partners who share common understandings about why decisions have been taken and how decisions are to be implemented are more likely to promote proposed changes, and to accept the accountability measures required for effective educational change (including monitoring and reporting back to the community).

Family involvement is a key outcome of effective parent-school partnerships, and is recognized as an important contributor to school effectiveness for all students. For example, strong partnerships between schools and the parents and caregivers of diverse students will often be reflected in improvements in diverse students' academic achievement and in their more regular school attendance (Ortiz, Parker, & Tempes, 2001). It is quite common, however, for cultural and linguistic minority parents to be isolated from school activities due to a cultural differences in understandings concerning the role parents should play in schooling, the failure of school to communicate to parents in a language they can understand and with which they are comfortable, or a lack of access to staff at a school who speak the parent's language. Schools that are linguistically and culturally effective deliberately seek to overcome obstacles to the participation of parents and actively encourage and facilitate parents' involvement in their children's schooling. Such involvement may include involvement in school committees, school festivals and celebrations, student field trips, and other curricula and extracurricular activities. Parent participation may also be evident in school governance. Moreover, whatever the mode of parental involvement, this involvement will be enhanced through regular communication to parents—especially in various home languages.

Responsive Curriculum

Effective schools focus on the implementation of a dynamic, flexible, and responsive curriculum that contributes to the development of essential knowledge, skills, and attitudes in all students. Such a curriculum builds on students' capacities to view the world critically and to live and act in the world in an independent yet cooperative and responsible manner.

Within the overall sweep of effective curricula, socioculturally effective school curricula provide specific means to meet the diverse needs of heterogeneous linguistic, cultural, and social minorities. In designing curricula, educators in socioculturally successful schools keep diversity front-of-mind, but are also cognizant of the need to avoid streaming students from linguistic, cultural, and social minorities into basic-content classes alone. Thus, socioculturally effective curricula provide for various degrees of difficulty and sophistication across the classes available to diverse students, and emphasize diverse approaches to teaching content at various levels (including formal school instruction in languages other than English—or whatever is the dominant language in the given country). Moreover, schools that successfully address diverse-group needs provide targeted means through which these students can, in particular, develop their skills and abilities in English (or the dominant language) across different content areas.

In somewhat more specific terms, responsive curricula addressing social, cultural, and linguistic diversity:

(a) make explicit attempts to integrate home culture and practices in school based learning activities;
(b) focus on maximizing student interactions across differing levels of English/dominant language proficiency, academic performance, and recency of immigration;
(c) consistently attempt to elicit ideas from students when planning units, themes, and activities;
(d) utilize thematic approaches to learning activities, where the integration of various skills, events, and learning opportunities is emphasized; and
(e) employ an appropriate mix of explicit teaching and self-directed learning activities within the context of emerging information and communication technologies.

High Expectations and Standards for Achievement

The importance of holding high expectations for all students is critical. Often, however, students from diverse backgrounds, and in particular minority cultural groups, are given the implicit message that less is expected of them than of dominant-group students (Berman et al., 1992; Kozol, 1991). In effective schools, students from diverse language, social, and cultural groups are expected to demonstrate learning and achievement equal to that of majority/dominant groups, and concrete steps are put in place to challenge and to support and ensure diverse-group learning.

An agreed framework of standards is a precondition for improving learning outcomes for students from diverse backgrounds. Within such a framework, high expectations are made explicit and are translated into specific targets for both the school and the student. These targets then form the basis for monitoring, assessment, and reporting across the school community. In turn, effective monitoring, assessment, and reporting require the collection and dissemination of comprehensive and accurate information. In particular, current and comprehensive information needs to be provided to students, their families and other stakeholders in order to sequentially track educational progress and ensure continued learning and development. Importantly, performance measurement will be seen within the context of a systemic approach to monitoring improvement against a clearly defined standards framework. This framework will include national (and perhaps even international) literacy and numeracy benchmarks and goals.

Continuous monitoring and recording of student progress and achievement in academic and social areas is also vital in determining future directions for school organization and curriculum delivery to serve the needs of students from diverse backgrounds. Moreover, planning towards future directions will be strengthened where students, parents, and community members reflect upon, and then provide input into, current and future assessment and reporting processes.

Focused Leadership

Socioculturally effective school leaders do not treat diverse-group education as a peripheral concern to be addressed by subgroups of staff members. Rather, catering for students from diverse backgrounds is considered a central concern of the school and its leadership. Principals show their support for diverse groups and diverse-group programs through such actions as promoting staff development focused on sociocultural and sociolinguistic diversity, including issues relevant to linguistic and cultural education on meeting agendas, working directly and closely with diverse-group support staff, finding ways to bring diverse students' family members into the school community, and advocating for students from diverse backgrounds in the school and in the community.

The integration into mainstream school programs of evidence-based approaches to the teaching and learning of students from diverse backgrounds relies heavily on the commitment of school leaders and leadership teams. In the most effective schools, school leaders take direct responsibility for the introduction of new programs and approaches and/ or strongly support colleagues who have been given the responsibility for introducing new initiatives. Another fundamental requirement of school leadership is that it assists everyone in the school community affected by the introduction of new approaches to teaching and learning to deal positively and effectively with the changes. This assistance does, however, require a collective understanding of the importance of change in schools characterized by diversity. It is also essential that leadership effectively plans and coordinates the introduction change so that any change is both welcomed and made sustainable.

In socioculturally effective schools, staff in specialized diverse-group programs (e.g., English as a second language (ESL) classes, transition programs, etc.) participates fully in school activities and decision making, and the health of these special programs is seen as central to school planning and decision making. Other school staff show their support for linguistic, social, and cultural diversity by seeking out professional development opportunities that enable them to be more knowledgeable and effective with diverse students in their classes, by attending activities sponsored by diverse groups in the school and community, and by acting as advocates for diverse-groups and diverse-group programs in the school and the wider community.

As suggested above, professional development is critical to the provision of leadership in any school (Harvey & Dowson, 2003 Harvey, Sinclair, & Dowson, 2005). In socioculturally effective schools, professional development is explicitly designed to help teaching, support, and administrative staff to serve language minority students more effectively. Effective schools may also offer incentives and compensation to encourage staff to participate in staff development activities focusing on student diversity. As a result of these professional development practices, socioculturally effective schools become staffed by people who are knowledgeable of key factors and strategies facilitating effective education in diverse contexts. Moreover, as indicated above, the team leader needs to be the focal point for the professional development of staff. However, in the most effective schools, team members assume responsibility for each other's growth in sociocultural and sociolinguistic interest and expertise.

Mentors and Relationships

Student engagement is regarded as a critical benchmark of school effectiveness. Integral to engagement, however, are relationships: teachers with students, teachers with each other, teachers with parents, the school with the community, and students with students. A safe and supportive school/community environment, that is, an environment characterized by stable, caring relationships provides the best chance for facilitating student engagement. Ideally, this environment will reflect respect and concern for the diverse needs of students, embedded in the everyday relational practices of students, educators, and administrators. In particular, teacher and/or student mentors can exert a critical influence on students' present and future attitudes to, and experiences of, schooling and learning. Socioculturally effective schools provide mentors who understand the complex factors influencing diverse students' behavior and learning and who communicate effectively with these students. These mentors may speak students' native languages or ensure that someone facilitates their communication with students who are not fluent in English (or whatever is the dominant language if not English). Mentors are knowledgeable about students' cultural values and experiences, and of issues in cross-cultural communication and counseling. In socioculturally effective schools, students from diverse cultural backgrounds are provided with consistent access to mentors with appropriate skills and knowledge rather than being randomly assigned to mentors who may not possess the skills and knowledge necessary to provide effective and consistent care to students.

In the Classroom

Socioculturally effective schools provide multiple creative opportunities for students from diverse social and cultural backgrounds to learn, achieve, and reflect on their own learning in supportive environments where truth, honesty, and a respect for diversity are valued and encouraged. Establishing this type of educational environment is, obviously, easier said than done. In particular, a major challenge for socioculturally effective schools is to provide structured teaching and learning programs that are simultaneously responsive to diverse developmental needs. Also of key importance are educators who know, understand and can work collaboratively with their diverse students, who have high expectations and standards, and who are flexible, risk-taking facilitators receptive to educational innovation. Moreover, in socioculturally effective schools there is recognition that even with the best teaching, some students will need additional support to achieve success. Thus, interventions for students at risk becomes an important consideration, and a range of strategies, including one-on-one and small group teaching, individualized learning programs, mentoring programs, and parent/community support options must be considered. Finally, classroom organization should recognize socially- and culturally-based differences in learning styles, emotional needs, areas of interest, and general capacities and capabilities.

SPECIFIC TEACHING STRATEGIES

The more general points made in the paragraph above implicate a variety of specific teaching strategies that will be evident in socioculturally effective schools.

Fostering English/Dominant Language acquisition and the development of mature English/Dominant Language literacy. Socioculturally effective schools utilize students' indigenous/native language capacities and abilities to facilitate English/dominant language literacy development. Effective programs in these schools do not rush students English/dominant language development but, rather, focus on the mature development of English/dominant language skills over time. The focus is on slow but sustained improvement in English/dominant language literacy to the point where native/indigenous language speakers become independent learners of, and in, English/dominant language.

Organize Instruction in Innovative Ways

Innovation is a critical component of socioculturally effective education because student diversity often demands creative, innovative solutions to complex instructional problems. Examples of effective innovations include: (a) "schools-within-schools" to more responsively deal with diverse language and social needs of the students, (b) "families" of students who stay together for major parts of the school day, (c) "continuum classes" in which teachers remain with their students for 2 to 3 years, helping teachers to become highly familiar with, and responsive to, students and their needs, and (d) grouping and regrouping students on a continuous basis so as to respond to developmental, cultural, and other important differences between students. These innovations rely on schools being committed to catering for the needs of diverse students because implementing multiple, innovative approaches to education does require organizational, administrative, and curricula effort.

Protect and Extend Instructional Time

There is considerable evidence (e.g., Minicucci, & Olsen, 1992) that instructional time is positively related to student learning and achievement. Implicitly or otherwise, effective schools recognize the links between instructional time and student outcomes, and so strive to protect instructional time as far as possible. Protecting instructional time may be critical for socioculturally diverse students because these students may require additional learning time over and above that which is provided to "mainstream" students in order to master curriculum content. In order to protect and extend instructional time schools may, for example, deliberately reduce extracurricular activities offered by the school, rationalize teachers administrative workloads (especially teachers working with diverse students), and utilize after-school programs, computer assisted learning in the home as well as in the school, and voluntary weekend schools and summer schools. Such school activities multiply the opportunities for students to engage in academic learning.

Expand Teachers' Roles and Responsibilities

Expanding teachers' roles and responsibilities does not mean giving teacher more work! It does mean devolving to teachers as much *instructional* authority as possible so that teachers can make instructional decisions most likely to positively impact on student learning and achievement. Such devolvement is especially critical with students from diverse social, cultural, and linguistic backgrounds who typically require curriculum modification on an ongoing basis. In socioculturally effective schools, therefore, teachers are assigned extensive roles in curricula and instructional decision making. Decision making will, however, also be highly collegial in order to ensure within- and across-grade articulation and coordination. Devolvement and collegiality ensure that teachers form active partnerships in instructional design, including in the design of "authentic" assessments that extensively inform future instruction.

Focusing on the Future

A series of recent studies by the authors (McInerney & Dowson, 2003; McInerney, Dowson, & Yeung, 2005) have indicted the importance of a "future focus" when dealing with students from diverse minority cultural backgrounds in particular. Often these students have higher absenteeism rates, report a decreased interest in learning, leave school early, and so forth, because they do not have a clearly articulated sense of the future. Socioculturally effective school and classrooms, therefore, focus students attention on the future, for example, on the utility of schooling for future valued employment, and the desirability of going on to further education, on students' goals and how these goals can be achieved with the aid of "a good education," and so forth. This future focus helps students navigate potential present obstacles in their schoolwork (e.g., hard schoolwork, or negative peer, parent or teacher influence) and provides the motivation to continue along an academic pathway most likely to result in enhanced educational and life outcomes.

CONCLUSION

This chapter has focused on a relatively restricted range of characteristics of school and classes that are particularly relevant when considering the learning and motivational needs of socioculturally diverse students. These features are, of course, also applicable to effective schooling with mainstream students. However, using many practical examples, we have endeavored to show how these characteristics directly address the needs of diverse students. It is unlikely, and probably unwarranted, that any particular school (no matter how effective) will display all of the characteristics identified in this chapter. However, we suggest that effective schools are likely to display several of these characteristics, and that effective schools are very unlikely to display few or none of these characteristics. Moreover, we suggest that schools wishing to improve their effectiveness with students from diverse social and cultural backgrounds could profit from adopting strategies identified in this chapter that are particularly suited to their unique contexts of diversity.

REFERENCES

August, D., & Hakuta, K. (Eds.). (1997). *Improving schooling for language-minority children: A research agenda*. Washington, DC: National Academy Press.

Berman, P., Chambers, J., Gandara, P., McLaughlin, B., Minicucci, C., Nelson, B., et al. (1992). *Meeting the challenge of diversity: An evaluation of programs for pupils with limited proficiency in English*. Berkeley, CA: BW Associates.

Cummins, J. (1989). *Empowering minority students*. Sacramento: California Association for Bilingual Education.

Harvey, P., & Dowson, M. (2003). Transitional experiences of new teachers in Christian schools: A case study. *Journal of Research in Christian Education, 12,* 217-243.

Harvey, P., Sinclair, C., & Dowson, M. (2005). Teacher motivations for postgraduate study: Development of a psychometric scale for Christian higher education. *Christian Higher Education: A Journal of Applied Research and Practice, 4*(4), 241-264.

Herman, P. (1999). *An educator's guide to school-wide reform.* Washington, DC: American Institutes for Research.

Kozol, J. (1991). *Savage inequalities: Children in America's schools.* New York: Crown.

Langer, J. A. (1991). Literacy and schooling: A sociocognitive perspective. In E. H. Hiebert (Ed.), *Literacy for a diverse society: Perspectives, practices, and policies* (pp. 7-27). New York: Teachers College Press.

Lucas, T., Henze, R., & Donato, R. (1990). Promoting the success of Latino language-minority students: An exploratory study of six high schools. *Harvard Educational Review, 60*(3), 315-340.

McInerney, D. M., & Dowson, M. (2003). Thoughts about school: Does culture, sex, neither or both make a difference? *Aboriginal Studies Association Journal, 12*, 34-43.

McInerney, D. M., Dowson, M., & Yeung, A. S. (2005). Facilitating conditions for school motivation: Construct validity and applicability. *Educational and Psychological Measurement, 65*, 1046-1066.

Minicucci, C., & Olsen, L. (1992). *Programs for secondary limited English proficient students: A California study.* Washington, DC: National Clearinghouse for Bilingual Education.

Ortiz, M., Parker, D., & Tempes, F. (Eds.). (2001). *Schooling and language minority students: A theoretical framework.* Los Angeles: California State University, Evaluation, Dissemination and Assessment Center.

Penuel, W. R., & Wertsch, J. V. (1995). Vygotsky and identity formation: A sociocultural approach. *Educational Psychologist, 30*(2), 83-92.

Rogoff, B. (1994). Developing understanding of the idea of communities of learners. *Mind, Culture, and Activity, 1*, 209-229.

Taylor, B. M., Pearson, P. D., Clark, K., & Walpole, S. (2000). Effective schools and accomplished teachers: Lessons about primary grade reading instruction in low-income schools. *Elementary School Journal, 101*, 121-166.

Part I

ON RESEARCH

CHAPTER 2

USING THE DYNAMIC MODEL OF EDUCATIONAL EFFECTIVENESS TO INTRODUCE A POLICY PROMOTING THE PROVISION OF EQUAL OPPORTUNITIES TO STUDENTS OF DIFFERENT SOCIAL GROUPS

L. Kyriakides and B. P. M. Creemers

In this chapter, we propose a novel and dynamic model of educational effectiveness that explains variation in student achievement by defining relations among important effectiveness factors which operate at different levels in school contexts. We then make specific suggestions concerning how the model may be used to introduce a policy promoting the provision of equal opportunities to students of different social groups.

Effective Schools, 17–41

THE PROPOSED DYNAMIC MODEL OF
EDUCATIONAL EFFECTIVENESS

The comprehensive model of educational effectiveness introduced here (Creemers, 1994), which is considered as the most influential theoretical model in the field (Teddlie & Reynolds, 2000), refers to factors operating at different levels (i.e., student, classroom, school, system) and at the same time it is based on the assumption that there are direct and indirect relations between these levels and specific school outcomes (e.g., achievement scores). Recently, four studies have been conducted in order to test the validity of Creemers' model (de Jong, Westerhof, & Kruiter, 2005; Kyriakides, 2005; Kyriakides, Campbell, & Gagatsis, 2000; Kyriakides & Tsangaridou, 2004). All of them used multiple methodologies and all provided empirical support for the model. However, the dynamic model also assumes that relations in the model may not be linear, and that factors at the same level also may be related to each other.

In principle each factor in the dynamic model is measured by taking into account five dimensions: *frequency, focus, stage, quality* and *differentiation*. First, the *frequency* dimension refers to the quantity that an activity associated with an effectiveness factor is present in a system, school or classroom. This dimension represents probably the easiest way to measure the effect of a factor on student achievement and most effectiveness studies used this dimension to define effectiveness factors. For example, personal monitoring at school level can be measured by taking into account how often the principals use a monitoring system to supervise their teachers. Educational Effectiveness Research (EER) could attempt to identify whether this dimension of measuring personal monitoring is related not only directly to student outcomes but also indirectly through teacher behavior in the classroom. Further, it is questionable that there is a linear relation between frequency of personal monitoring and both types of outcomes. It can be assumed that after an optimal value of using a monitoring system it may not have an additional effect on outcomes but even can lead to negative effect in teacher behavior and ultimately in student outcomes.

Second, the factors are measured by taking into account the *focus* of the activities which reveals the function of the factor at classroom, school, and system level. Two aspects of the focus of a factor can be measured. The first aspect refers to the specificity of the activities which can range from specific to general. For example, in the case of school policy on parental involvement, the policy could either be more specific in terms of concrete activities that are expected to take place (e.g., it refers to specific hours that parents can visit the school) or more general (e.g., it informs parents that they are welcome to the school but without giving them specific information about what, how, and when). The second aspect addresses the purpose for which an activity takes place. An activity may be expected to achieve single or multiple purposes. In the case of policy on parental involvement, the activities might be restricted to a single purpose (e.g., parents visit schools to get information about student progress) or address more than one purpose (e.g., parents visit the school to exchange information about children progress and to assist teachers in and outside the classroom). It is expected that the measurement of the focus of an activity either in terms of its specificity or in terms of its purposes may be related in a curvilinear way with student outcomes. For example, the guidelines on parental involvement which are very general may not be helpful for parents or teachers in establishing good relations which can result in supported student learning. On the other hand, a school policy which is very specific in defining activities may restrict teachers and parents in creating productive ways for implementing school policy. Similarly, if all activities are expected to achieve a single purpose then the chance to achieve the purpose is high. However, the effect of the factor might be small due to the fact that other purposes are not achieved and/or synergy may not exist since the activities are isolated. On the other hand, if all the activities are expected to achieve multiple purposes there is a danger that specific purposes are not successfully addressed.

Third, the activities associated with a factor can be measured by taking into account the *stage* at which they take place. It is assumed that the factors need to be in place over a long period of time to ensure that they have a continuous direct or indirect effect on student learning. This assumption is partly based on the fact that evaluations of programs aiming to improve educational practice reveal that the extent to which these intervention programs have any impact on educational practice is partly a function of period of time that the programs are implemented in a school. This assumption is also in line with one of the principles of the comprehensive model of educational effectiveness, namely constancy. Creemers (1994) argues that there should be constancy, meaning that effective instruction is provided throughout the school career of the student. For example, school policy on quantity of teaching, which refers to policy on cancellation of lessons and absenteeism, is expected to be implemented throughout the year and not only through specific regulations announced at a specific point of time (e.g., only at the beginning of the school year). Measuring the stage dimension gives information about the continuity of the existence of a factor but the activities associated with the factor may not necessarily be the same.

Fourth, the dimension *quality* can be discerned in two different ways. The first way refers to the properties of the specific factor itself. For instance, school policy on assessment can be measured by looking at the mechanisms which have been developed in order to establish instruments which meet defined psychometric standards (i.e., validity, reliability, representativeness, and comprehensiveness). At the same time, assessment policy can be examined on the basis of whether or not this policy makes clear that teachers are expected to make use of assessment information for formative rather than summative reasons (Black & Wiliam, 1998; Harlen & James, 1997; Kyriakides et al., 2000). This evaluation implies the second aspect of measuring the quality of a factor which has to do with its impact on the subjects which are addressed by the factor. In the case of school policy on assessment, the subjects are the teachers who are expected to implement the policy whereas when we measure the effect of the factor within the EER framework the impact that the factor has on student learning outcomes is examined.

Finally, the dimension *differentiation* refers to the extent to which activities associated with a factor are implemented in the same way for all the subjects involved with it (e.g., students, teachers, schools). It is expected that adaptation to specific needs of each subject or group of subjects will increase the successful implementation of a factor and ultimately maximize its effect on student learning outcomes. Although differentiation could be considered as a property of an effectiveness factor, it was decided to treat differentiation as a separate dimension of measuring each effectiveness factor rather than to incorporate it into the quality dimension. In this way, the importance of taking into account the special needs of each subject or group of subjects is recognized. The dynamic model is, therefore, based on the assumption that it is difficult to deny that persons of all ages, learn, think, and process information differently. Thus, effective teachers are expected to acknowledge, honor, cultivate individuality, support the concept of differentiated instruction and build on the premise that learners differ in important ways (Tomlinson, 1999).

Summary So Far

The dynamic model is based on the assumption that the relations of some effectiveness factors with student achievement may not necessarily be linear. Moreover, effectiveness factors are not considered to be unidimensional constructs but, rather, the five dimensions described above are used to define them. Table 2.1 illustrates the operational definition of these five dimensions, which reveal the importance of collecting both quantity and quality information about the functioning of each factor. Moreover, treating differentiation as a separate dimension of measuring each effectiveness factor reveals the importance of differentiation in

**Table 2.1.   Operational Definitions of the Five Dimensions of
Measuring Each Effectiveness Factor and
Ways of Measuring Each Dimension**

Dimensions	Operational Definitions	Ways of Measuring
Frequency	It refers to the *quantity* that an activity associated with an effectiveness factor is present in a system, school or classroom.	Two indicators are used: (a) How many tasks are used? (b) How long each task takes place?
Focus	It reveals the function of the factor at classroom, school and system level. The following two aspects of focus of each factor are measured: (a) Specificity (b) The number of purpose for which an activity takes place	(a) Specificity is measured by investigating the extent to which activities are too specific to too general. (b) How many purposes are expected to be achieved?
Stage	It refers to the *period* at which they take place. It is assumed that the factors need to take place over a long period of time to ensure that they have a continuous direct or indirect effect on student learning.	(a) When does the task take place? (Based on the data emerged from the above question, data about the continuity of the existence of a factor are collected.)
Quality	It refers to the properties of the specific factor itself, as these are discussed in the literature.	(a) What are the properties of tasks associated with a factor which reveal the functioning of each factor? (b) To what extent the function of each task is in line with the literature?
Differentiation	It refers to the extent to which activities associated with a factor are implemented in the same way for all the subjects involved with it.	To what extent different tasks associated with each factor are provided to different groups of subjects involved with this factor?

teaching and helps us incorporate research on differentiated effectiveness into the theoretical framework of EER.

However, research investigating the validity of the proposed dynamic model of EER is needed. In this context, a longitudinal study currently being conducted in Cyprus is attempting to generate evidence concerning the validity of the dynamic model. Specifically, a specialized type of confirmatory factor analytic model (i.e., the Correlated Trait Correlated Method model) is being used to examine the extent to which each effectiveness factor can be measured by taking into account data which emerge from different sources (i.e., observations and student questionnaires) and refer to each of the five dimensions of the model presented above (Kline, 1998). Moreover, both the effect of the various explanatory variables concerning teacher behavior in the classroom (X_i) and the effect of the second power of these variables (i.e., X_i^2 values) upon student achievement are examined in order to find out whether some variables have inverted-U curvilinear relationships with student outcomes (Goldstein, 2003). Furthermore, multilevel path analytic methods (Heck & Thomas, 2000) are being used in order to examine whether factors operating at the same level are interrelated. The results of this study may help us empirically support the framework used to measure each effectiveness factor. In addition, the importance of searching for nonlinear relations of effectiveness factors with student achievement will be examined.

EFFECTIVENESS FACTORS AT THE CLASSROOM LEVEL: THE MEASUREMENT OF TEACHER'S INSTRUCTIONAL ROLE

Above we have described in a more general way the five dimensions of the proposed dynamic model of EER which can be used to measure each effectiveness factor. However, in order to explain better how these five dimensions can be used to establish such a model, this section refers to the specific measurement of eight factors concerning teacher behavior *in classrooms*, which according to the dynamic model are related to student achievement gains. The choice made for the classroom level is based on the fact that studies on EER show that this level is more significant than the school and the system level (e.g., Hextall & Mahony, 1998; Kyriakides et al., 2000; Yair, 1997), and defining factors at the classroom level can be seen as a prerequisite for defining the school and the system level (Creemers, 1994).

Our dynamic model refers to eight effectiveness factors which describe teacher's instructional role: orientation, structuring, questioning, teaching modeling, applications, management of time, teacher role in making classroom a learning environment, and assessment. These eight factors are briefly described below and help us identify the importance of using the model to differentiate teaching practice and provide equal opportunities to pupils of different sociocultural groups.

Orientation

Orientation refers to teacher behavior in providing the objectives for which a specific task or lesson or series of lessons take(s) place and/or challenging students to identify the reason for which an activity takes place in the lesson. It is expected that the engagement of students with orientation tasks might encourage them to actively participate in the classroom since the tasks that then take place become meaningful for them (Creemers, 1994). In this context, the measurement of the dimension frequency is based on an examination of the number of orientations tasks that take place in a typical lesson as well as how long each orientation task takes place. The second aspect of focus which refers to the purpose of the activity can be measured by examining the extent to which an orientation task is restricted to finding one single reason for doing a task or finding the multiple reasons for doing a task. The measurement of this dimension of orientation reveals the extent to which teachers help their students understand the importance of finding the meanings of each task in which they are expected to be involved. The third dimension of measuring orientation refers to the stage at which an activity takes place. It is expected that orientation tasks will take place in different parts of a lesson or series of lessons (e.g., introduction, core, ending of the lesson) and in lessons that are expected to achieve different objectives. Further, it is expected that the teacher will be able to take other perspectives into account during these orientation tasks. For example, students may come with suggestions for the reasons of doing a specific task which an effective teacher is expected to take into account. As far as the focus dimension is concerned, it is possible that an orientation task may refer to a part of a lesson or to the whole lesson or even to a series of lessons (e.g., a lesson unit). This classification designates the specificity of the orientation task.

The measurement of the dimension quality refers to the properties of the orientation task and especially whether it is clear for the students and to the impact that the task has on student engagement in learning process. For example, teachers may present the reasons for doing a task in a perfunctory manner without having much effect on student participation. Other teachers may encourage students to identify the purposes that can be achieved by doing a task and therefore increase their motivation towards a specific task/lesson/series of lessons. Finally, differentiation is measured in a similar way for each of the eight factors. In the case of orientation, it is assumed that effective teachers are those who provide different types of orientation tasks to students by taking into account differences in the: (a) personal and background characteristics of their students, (b) teaching objectives, and (c) organizational and cultural context of their school/classroom. Research into differentiated teacher effectiveness reveals the importance of adapting teaching by taking into account these three dimensions of differences.

Structuring

Rosenshine and Stevens (1986) point out that achievement is maximized when teachers not only actively present materials but structure it by: (a) beginning with overviews and/or review of objectives; (b) outlining the content to be covered and signaling transitions between lesson parts; (c) calling attention to main ideas; and (d) reviewing main ideas at the end. Summary reviews are also important since they integrate and reinforce the learning of major points (Brophy & Good, 1986). It can be claimed that these structuring elements not only facilitate memorization of the information but allow for its apprehension as an integrated whole with recognition of the relationships between parts. Moreover, achievement is higher when information is presented with a degree of redundancy, particularly in the form of repeating and reviewing general views and key concepts.

Structuring is measured as follows. First, frequency is measured by taking into account the number of structuring tasks that take place in a typical lesson as well as how long each task takes place (e.g., the percentage of teaching time spent on structuring). Second, focus is measured by investigating whether a structuring task refers to a part of a lesson or to the whole lesson or even to a series of lessons (e.g., a lesson unit). As far as the second aspect of focus is concerned, a structuring task may refer to the achievement of a single objective or to the relation of the elements of the lesson in relation to multiple objectives. It is expected that the structuring tasks which have strong impact on student behavior are those which refer to the achievement of multiple objectives since the tasks which refer to a single objective may increase the fragmentation of learning process. The third dimension of measuring structuring, which refers to the stage at which an activity takes place, is measured in the same way as in the case of orientation. It is, therefore, taken into account that structuring tasks may take place in different parts of a lesson or series of lessons (e.g., introduction, core, ending of the lesson).

Fourth, the dimension of quality is measured by examining the impact that the task has on student learning. It is expected that structuring tasks are not only clear for the students but also help them understand the structure of the lesson. For this reason, clarity is not seen as a property of structuring or as an independent factor of teacher effectiveness. Clarity is seen as a condition for helping students to understand the structure and the content of a lesson/series of lessons. On the contrary, the aspect of quality which refers to the properties of a structuring task has to do with the extent to which teachers organize their lessons/series of lessons so as to move from easier tasks to more complicated ones. This aspect of quality is embedded in research on teacher effectiveness that reveals that students learn more when the information is not only well structured but it is also sufficiently redundant and well sequenced (Armento, 1977; Nuthall & Church, 1973; Smith & Sanders, 1981). Finally, in the case of structuring, differentiation is measured by investigating the extent to which teachers provide different types of structuring tasks to students according to their learning needs. Teachers are also expected to take into account the objectives of their lessons in providing structuring tasks.

Questioning Techniques

Muijs and Reynolds (2000) indicate that effective teachers ask a lot of questions and attempt to involve students in class discussion. Although data on the cognitive level of question yield inconsistent results (Redfield & Rousseau, 1981), the developmental level of students defines, to a large extent, the optimal question difficulty. It seems clear that most questions (almost 75%) should elicit correct answers (Anderson, Evertson, & Brophy, 1979; Brophy & Evertson, 1976) and that most of the rest should elicit overt, substantive responses (incorrect or incomplete answers) rather than failures to respond at all (Anderson et al.; Brophy & Good, 1986). Optimal question difficulty should also vary with context. For example, basic skills instruction requires a great deal of drill and practice and thus frequent fast-paced review in which most questions are answered rapidly and correctly. However, when teaching complex cognitive content or trying to get students to generalize, evaluate, or apply their learning, effective teachers usually raise questions that few students can answer correctly or that have no single correct answer at all.

Brophy (1986) argues that issues surrounding the cognitive level of questions cannot be reduced to frequency norms. Researchers should take into account the teacher's objectives, the quality of the questions and their timing appropriateness. As far as their timing appropriateness is concerned, Bennett, Desforges, Cockburn, and Wilkenson (1981) pointed out that not only the frequency of errors is important but also their timing and quality. Early in a unit, when new learning is occurring, relatively frequent errors may be expected. Later, when mastery levels should have been achieved, errors should be minimal. It has been also shown that there should be a mix of product questions (i.e., expecting a single response from students) and process questions (i.e., expecting students to provide explanations) and that effective teachers ask more process questions (Askew & William, 1995; Everston, Anderson, Anderson, & Brophy, 1980).

The frequency dimension of questioning is, therefore, measured by taking into account not only the total number of questions but also the ratio between process and product questions. Another way of measuring the frequency dimension of questioning has to do with the length of pause following questions which is expected to vary according to the difficulty level of questions. Brophy and Good (1986) point out that a question calling for application of abstract principles should require a longer pause than a factual question.

The focus dimension of this factor is measured by looking at the type of each question and especially its relation with the tasks that take place during a lesson (i.e., specificity) as well as with the objectives that are expected to be achieved through asking the question. Stage is measured by taking into account that teachers may raise questions at different parts of the lesson and for different reasons. For example, teachers may ask questions in the introduction of a lesson in order to link the new lesson with previous lessons and during the core of the lesson in order to discover problem(s) that students have with the content of the lesson or identify need(s) for further clarifications. Questions may also be raised at the end of the lesson as part of the attempt of teacher to assess students for formative reasons. Thus, the measurement of this dimension requires shifting from the individual question to the question sequences as the unit of analysis.

Quality is measured by taking into account the clarity of a question and especially the extent to which students understand what they are expected to find out. Sometimes questions are vague or the teacher asks two or more questions without stopping to get an answer. Another property that is also measured is the appropriateness of the difficulty level of the question since it is possible that students may understand the question and still do not answer because it is too difficult for them.

Finally, differentiation is measured by looking at the extent to which teachers direct questions to specific students or take answers from specific students. It is also expected that the pauses following questions vary with their complexity or cognitive level. Moreover, the feedback that teachers give to student answers varies according to the learning needs of students and their personal characteristics (i.e., personality type and thinking styles). Furthermore, the types of questions that are used by the teacher depend on his/her teaching objectives and the characteristics of his/her students. Effective teachers are expected to take into account the goals of each lesson when asking questions. For example, sometimes teachers may begin with a higher level question and then proceed with several lower level follow-up questions since this is an appropriate approach for some objectives (e.g., asking students to suggest an application of idea and then probing for details). A different objective (e.g., stimulating students to integrate certain facts and draw a conclusion from them) may require a series of lower level questions (to call attention to the relevant facts) followed by higher level questions.

Teaching Modeling

EER has shown that effective teachers help pupils to use strategies and/ or develop their own strategies which can help them solve different types of problems (Creemers & Kyriakides, 2005). As a result of this teaching, it is more likely that students will develop skills that help them organize their own learning (e.g., self-regulation, active learning).

The frequency dimension of teaching modeling can be measured by looking at the number of teaching modeling tasks that take place in a lesson and the teaching time devoted to them. With respect to *focus*, teaching modeling tasks can be examined in relation to the extent to which they refer to strategies which can be used to solve problems under various conditions (e.g., problems of different subjects). This measure refers to the specificity aspect of this dimension. Moreover, focus can be seen in relation to the extent to which teachers provide opportunities to students to use/develop more than one strategy to solve specific problems/types of problems. Third, the stage dimension is concerned with the sequence under which a teaching-modeling task is offered. It is possible that initially students are faced with a problem and then are expected to use/ develop a particular strategy to solve it. On the other hand, teachers may teach a strategy or different strategies to students and then students are asked to use these strategies in order to solve a problem.

Fourth, the measure of the quality deals with the properties of teaching-modeling tasks and especially with the role that the teacher is expected to play in order to help students use a strategy to solve their problems. Effective teachers may either present a strategy with clarity or invite students to explain how they solve a problem and use that information for promoting the idea of modeling. The latter approach may encourage students not only to use but also to develop their own strategies for solving problems. Quality is also measured by looking at the impact that an activity has on student behavior. Students may either become able to use a strategy in an effective way (i.e., finding the solution of the problem) or the use of the strategy may become an obstacle in dealing with a problem (e.g., causes more confusion about the problem). Finally, differentiation can be seen in terms of adapting teaching modeling to specific needs of group of students. These might result in more emphasis on applying a single strategy for a group of students to solve problems or more emphasis on using multiple strategies for a group of strategies or even develop different strategies for different groups of students. Effective teachers are also expected to take into account the different thinking style of their students in presenting strategies for problem solving (Kyriakides, 2005; Sternberg, 1988).

Application

Effective teachers also use seatwork or small group tasks since they provide needed practice and application opportunities (Borich, 1992) and can be linked to a direct teaching model (Rosenshine, 1983), which emphasizes immediate exercise of topics taught during the lesson. Thus, the frequency can be measured by looking at the total time devoted to application tasks (e.g., percentage of teaching time). Focus can be measured by investigating the specificity of the application tasks that students are expected to perform. Specifically, we can examine the extent to which the application tasks refer to some parts of the lesson or to the whole lesson or even to a series of lessons. This means of measurement is also related to the second aspect of focus since it enables us to examine the number of purposes that are expected to be achieved by each application task.

Stage is measured by looking at the phase of the lesson in which each application task takes place. The quality of application tasks is measured by looking at the extent to which students are simply asked to repeat what they have already covered with their teacher or the application task is more complex than the content covered in the lesson or even it is used as a starting point for the next step of teaching and learning. The extent to which application tasks are used as starting points of learning can also be seen as an indication of the impact that application tasks have on students. Finally, differentiation refers to the extent to which teachers give more opportunities for application to students who need them (e.g., low achieving students). It also refers to teacher behavior in monitoring, supervising, and giving corrective feedback during application activities. Brophy and Good (1986) argue that once the students are released to work independently effective teachers circulate to monitor progress and provide help and feedback. But as it has been mentioned above, effective teachers should provide to low socioeconomic and low achieving students more frequent encouragement for their efforts and praise for their successes.

The Classroom as a Learning Environment:
The Contribution of the Teacher

Classroom climate is a factor that teacher effectiveness research has found to be significant (e.g., Creemers & Reezigt, 1996; Kyriakides, Campbell, & Christofidou, 2002; Muijs & Reynolds, 2000). The climate is usually seen as associated with the behavior of the stakeholders, whereas culture is seen as measuring the values and norms of the organization (Heck & Marcoulides, 1996; Hoy, 1990). It is supported that a healthy organization deals effectively with outside forces while directing its energies towards its goals. Classroom climate research is described as the stepchild of psychological and classroom research (Creemers & Reezigt). The classroom effects research tradition initially focused on climate factors defined as managerial techniques (e.g., Doyle, 1986). Management is necessary to create conditions for learning and instruction, but management itself is not sufficient for student results (Creemers, 1994). On the other hand, the psychological tradition of classroom environment research paid a lot of attention to instruments for the measuring of students' perceptions of climate. Many studies report on their psychometric characteristics (Fraser, 1991) but climate factors (such as the way a teacher behaves towards the students) and effectiveness factors (e.g., quality of teaching) were studied as isolated constructs (Johnson & Johnson, 1993; Wubbels, Brekelmans, & Hooymayers, 1991). In this context, EER has to take the first steps to integrate elements of different research traditions. Thus, the dynamic model refers to teacher contribution in creating a learning environment in his/her classroom and five elements of classroom as a learning environment are taken into account: teacher-student interaction, student-student interaction, students' treatment by the teacher, competition between students, and classroom disorder. The first two elements are important components of measuring classroom climate as classroom environment research has shown (Cazden, 1986; den Brok, Brekelmans, & Wubels, 2004; Fraser, 1991). However, the dynamic model refers to the type of interactions that exist in a classroom rather than on how students perceive teacher interpersonal behavior. The other three elements refer to the attempt of teachers to create a businesslike and supportive environment for learning (Walberg, 1986). The ways used to measure these five elements are briefly described below.

Interactions are measured by taking into account the role of the teacher in establishing interaction between students and between students and himself/herself. The dimension frequency refers to the number of interactions between students and between students and the teacher which take place. Focus is measured by classifying each interaction according to the purpose(s) each interaction is expected to serve (e.g., managerial reasons, learning, social encounter). As far as the stage is concerned, interactions are seen in relation to the phase of the lesson in which they take place. Quality is measured by investigating the immediate impact that teacher initiatives have on establishing relevant interactions. We are mainly interested to identify the extent to which the teacher is able to establish on task behavior through the interactions she/he promotes since several studies (e.g., de Jong et al., 2004; Kyriakides, 2005; Teddlie & Reynolds, 2000) as well as the comprehensive model of effectiveness (Creemers, 1994) emphasize the importance of keeping students on task. Finally, differentiation is measured by looking at the different strategies the teacher is able to use in order to keep different groups of students involved in the classroom interactions which promote student learning.

The other three elements of this classroom-level factor are measured by taking into account the teacher's ability to establish rules, persuade students to respect and use the rules, and maintain them in order to create a learning environment in their classroom. The first element refers to more general problems that can arise when students do not believe that they are treated fairly and are respected as individual persons by their teacher whereas the other two deal with specific situations in the classroom which might create difficulties in promoting learning (i.e., competition between students, classroom disorder) Thus, frequency is measured by looking at the number of problems that arise in the classroom (e.g., classroom disorder: fight between two students) and the various ways that teachers use to deal with them. Focus is measured by looking at the specificity of the problem that is observed (e.g., incidental or a continuous one that takes the classroom back to problems that were not solved successfully) as well as to the reaction of the teacher in terms of the purpose(s) that he/she attempts to achieve (e.g., solving only the specific problem or creating an atmosphere that avoids the further existence of similar problems). For example, in the case of investigating the way teachers deal with negative effects of competition, the teacher can either deal with the specific problem that arises or put the problem in a more general perspective and help students see the positive aspects of competition and avoid the negative ones. Stage is measured by looking at the phase of the lesson at which the problem arises.

Quality is seen in relation to the impact that the teacher behavior has on solving the problem(s) that arise as measured through students' behavior. For example, a teacher may not use any strategy at all to deal with a classroom disorder problem or may use a strategy but the problem is only temporarily solved or may use a strategy that has a long-lasting effect. Finally, differentiation is measured by looking at the extent to which teachers use different strategies to deal with problems caused by different groups of students. For example, individual student(s) might cause a problem in order to get attention from classroom mates and/or the teacher. It is probably a better strategy not to pay attention when the problem is small since any reaction from the teacher may promote the continuation of causing problems. Similarly, effective teachers attempt to change the classroom participation rules if they found out that classroom disorder problems are caused by a group of students due to the fact that the existing rules are not sensitive to the difference between participation rules common in some cultural groups and those typical of conventional schools.

Management of Time

The comprehensive model of educational effectiveness (Creemers, 1994) considers opportunity to learn and time on task as two of the most significant effectiveness factors which operate at different levels. Moreover, opportunity to learn is related to student engagement and time on task (Emmer & Everston, 1981). Therefore, effective teachers are expected to organize and manage the classroom environment as an efficient learning environment and thereby to maximize engagement rates (Creemers & Reezigt, 1996). In this context, the dynamic model supports the argument that management of time is one of the most important indicators of teachers' ability to manage classrooms in an effective way. Thus, frequency is measured by taking into account how much time is used for teaching per lesson and how much time is covered within the time framework. Focus dimension is not measured separately since the main interest of this factor is whether students are on task or off task. Stage is measured by taking into account time attribution to different phases of the lesson. The quality dimension is measured through the data collected in relation to the role of teacher in creating a learning environment in his/her classroom. Finally, differentiation is measured by looking at the allocation of time for different groups of students.

Assessment

Assessment is seen as an integral part of teaching (Stenmark, 1992) and especially formative assessment is one of the most important factors associated with effectiveness at all levels and especially at the classroom level (de Jong et al., 2004; Kyriakides, 2005; Shepard, 1989). Information gathered from student assessment should enable teachers to identify their students' needs as well as to evaluate their own teaching practice. In this study, frequency is measured in terms of the number of assessment tasks and the time that they take place. It is expected that there is a curvilinear relation between the frequency of teacher evaluation and student outcomes since an overemphasis to evaluation might reduce the actual time spent on teaching and learning. On the other hand, teachers who do not collect any information are not able to adapt their teaching to student needs. Focus is measured by looking at the ability of the teacher to use different ways of measuring student skills rather than using only one technique (e.g., written tests). It is also important to examine whether the teacher makes more than one use of the information that she/he collects (e.g., identify needs of students, conducting self-evaluation, adopting his/her long-term planning, using evaluation tasks as a starting point for teaching). Stage is measured by investigating the period at which the evaluation tasks take place (e.g., at the beginning, during, and at the end of a lesson/unit of lessons) and the time lack between collecting information, recording the results, reporting the results to students and parents and using them for planning his/her lessons.

Quality is measured by looking at the properties of the evaluation instruments used by the teacher such as the validity, the reliability, the practicality and the extent to which the instruments cover the teaching content. The impact of evaluation activities can be examined by measuring the type of feedback that the teacher gives to his/her students and the way students use the teacher feedback. Effective teachers are expected to provide constructive feedback which has positive implications to teaching and learning (Muijs & Reynolds, 2001). Finally, differentiation is examined in relation to the extent to which teachers use different techniques for measuring student needs and/or different ways to provide feedback to different groups of students by taking into account their background and personal characteristics such as their thinking style (Kyriakides, 2005). It is also considered important for teachers to take into account the fact that students' perceptions of the importance of testing may vary due to their differences in their background characteristics and this variation in perceptions may explain variation in achievement. For example, some Native American cultures value cooperation rather than independent achievement. Therefore, teaching and assessment that relies on or encourages a high need for achievement may be maladaptive for some Native American children. In addition, ability and achievement tests that assume a high need for achievement may result in underestimates for such groups of students.

SUGGESTIONS FOR POSSIBLE USES OF THE DYNAMIC MODEL: PROVIDING EQUAL OPPORTUNITIES TO STUDENTS OF DIFFERENT SOCIAL GROUPS

Historically, EER is concerned with two dimensions of measuring educational effectiveness that emerge from different perceptions about the ultimate goals of schooling and are concerned with quality and equity in education. Generally in society, quality in education is seen in relation to the extent to which schools can achieve the preferable high results in various learning domains and subject areas. Therefore, the criteria for educational effectiveness are seen at the level to be obtained by individual students, classes and schools with respect to the objectives of education. However, it is also possible to look from a different angle at the effectiveness of a school. Specifically, the sociocultural perspective of EER is concerned with the extent to which schools are able to reduce the variance in achievement between students (i.e., equity). Such an approach results in educational objectives and criteria for educational effectiveness which are not related to the achievement of specific objectives by a group of students but are concerned with the achievement of various groups of students in relation to each other. The idea behind this approach is that education should contribute to social justice and democracy by reducing the gap between groups of students with regards to their background characteristics such as gender, prior abilities, and sociocultural status of their family. It can, therefore, be argued that findings of research into differentiated educational effectiveness (see Campbell, Kyriakides, Muijs, & Robinson, 2004) are partly associated with the ability of education to provide equal opportunities to students.

A sociocultural perspective of EER also draws attention to process variables emerging from organizational theories such as the school climate, culture, and structure and for contextual variables. It has been shown that the differentiated effect of teachers and schools can partly be explained by process variables. Moreover, research into differentiated effectiveness gives more attention to the different behaviors or characteristics needed for teacher and school effectiveness in different contexts. For example, Teddlie and Stringfield (1993) suggested that effective schools in different social class contexts displayed different characteristics depending on the socioeconomic context in which they operated. Likewise, Brophy (1992) concluded that different classroom behavior in low and high social class contexts were needed for teachers to be effective. It can be claimed that the proposed dynamic model of EER incorporates what Hopkins and Reynolds (2001) call "context specificity." This section is an attempt o show how the dynamic model of EER can be used in providing equal opportunities to students of different sociocultural groups.

Despite the contribution of EER in providing answers regarding the differentiated effects of teachers and schools on student outcomes, there have been many critics of EER who argue that EER has created more problems than it had generated solutions (Slee & Weiner, 2001; Slee & Weiner with Tomlinson, 1998; Thrupp, 2001a). Critics see a conservative orientation to effectiveness research. It is argued that there are really no grounds for thinking that EER can overcome the effects of social inequality. It also is pointed out that while greater effectiveness may somewhat improve the absolute performance of disadvantaged groups; it will not improve their relative performance against more advantaged groups (Thrupp, 2001b, p. 446). However, Reynolds and Teddlie (2001, p. 112) claim that: "With their pessimism, passivity and inability to do anything more than talk about change, it is the critics that are the true conservatives now as in the 1960s." Nevertheless, researchers of educational effectiveness may have to examine further issues dealing with equality in education.

It can be claimed that the dynamic model of EER may provide a new perspective in the discussion about educational equality and answers could be provided to the critics of EER who argue that EER has not given consideration to equity and justice. Fielding (1997, p. 141) acknowledges the early work of EER as "a necessary corrective to an overly pessimistic, even deterministic, view of the influence of social and political factors on the efficacy of schools." Findings concerning differentiated teacher and school effects support the conclusion that teachers and schools matter most for underprivileged and/or initially low-achieving students. This observation implies that school choice is a critical issue for students from disadvantaged backgrounds and policy-makers should provide relevant information to their parents who are very likely not to take this issue as much into account as parents of privileged students. It can also be argued that the dynamic model of EER could help us improve educational practice in terms of the two dimensions of measuring effectiveness, which emerged from the sociocultural perspective of educational effectiveness, concerning quality and equity. In order to support our argument four possible uses of the dynamic model in providing equal opportunities to students of different social groups are mentioned.

First, the dynamic model of EER takes into account results of research into differentiated effectiveness and this is reflected in the fact that differentiation is seen as one dimension of measuring each effectiveness factor. Therefore, the model can be seen as a useful tool for teacher and school self-evaluation by considering not only quality but also equity in measuring their own effectiveness. Since school and teacher self-evaluation is considered as the key to improvement (Macbeath, 1999), teachers and schools may attempt to improve their practice by providing differential support to the various groups of their students based on their background and personal characteristics. Moreover, teachers and headteachers could be encouraged to draw their own meanings of what makes schools and teachers effective in terms of both efficiency and equity by considering the knowledge-base of effective teaching practice provided by the model. Special attention on the extent to which their practices take into account the different needs of each subject or group of subjects could also emerge.

Second, based on the five dimensions of each effectiveness factor presented in the model, different teaching profiles, which affect in different ways the achievement of each social group of students, can be produced. Teachers may, therefore, identify the extent to which their classroom behavior is similar to any of these profiles and whether specific changes to their practices are needed in order to adopt a more effective profile and respond to the needs of students of different background and personal characteristics. It is important to note that the dynamic model may reveal more than one weaknesses in teaching practice. Although such a finding may not be helpful for identifying specific avenues of professional development, different *priorities* for professional development for each teacher can be identified. These priorities will be based on the fact that the effects of the improvement of effectiveness factors on student outcomes depend on the stage at which each individual teacher is at the moment. Thus, one teacher who attempts to improve his/her orientation skills may result in improving student outcomes more than attempting to improve his/her skills in teaching modeling. A completely different interpretation can be drawn for another teacher by looking at the situation at which he/she is at the moment.

Third, using the dynamic model of EER, policymakers could conduct large-scale evaluation studies. Since some of the effectiveness factors are expected to have a curvilinear relation with student achievement, the impact of an intervention program attempting to improve a specific aspect of teaching practice (e.g., questioning techniques, teacher evaluation) will depend on what the current situation is. Therefore, data collected through these studies may help policy-makers identify those dimensions that constitute the major weaknesses of the system and therefore design relevant intervention programs for improving teaching practice and making the system not only more effective in terms of its quality but also able to provide equal opportunities to students of different socio-cultural groups.

Finally, using the dynamic model of EER, policy makers could evaluate national and school policy on equality of opportunities in education. Mostly school improvement and school change are not concerned with the outcomes themselves so much as with the inputs, the processes and the context of the school and of education in general and the elements within that (Fullan, 1991). But the success and the failure of school change are affected by the influence that all of these factors have on student outcomes (Hargreaves, 1995; Hopkins, 1996; Reynolds, Hopkins, & Stoll, 1993). Even when the effectiveness of different components is improved, the question remains as to whether or not that change induces higher pupil outcomes. Therefore, the evaluation of any policy promoting equality of opportunities can be based on investigating its impact on promoting educational progress of socially disadvantaged pupils and on reducing unjustifiable gender differences at the school level (Kyriakides, 2004). Moreover, the effectiveness of microlevel policies on equality of opportunities in education can be evaluated by examining whether there is any association between the effectiveness of the school and the implementation of such policy. Research is, however, needed to investigate the impact that the use of the model may have on improving teaching practice at teacher-level through building self-evaluation mechanisms and at national level through establishing an "evidence-based" approach on introducing educational policy promoting the provision of equal opportunities. Generally, it can be claimed that since the dynamic model draws from research into differentiated effectiveness and illustrates ample opportunities for promoting differentiation in practice, policymakers and teachers can use the model as a framework for defining their roles and professional activities. However further research is needed to investigate the validity of the model and identify whether using the model results in more effectiveness in terms of both quality and equity.

CONCLUSIONS

Despite the fact that educational practice remained basically fixed and non adaptive in most countries, findings of research into differentiated effectiveness reveal that teachers and schools are differentially effective in promoting the learning of different groups of students. It has also been shown that characteristics of effective teaching vary according to student background characteristics such as socioeconomic status and ability (see Brophy, 1992; Campbell et al., 2004). These findings suggest that relying on the development and use of differentiated textbooks and curriculum may be necessary, but it is not sufficient, for promoting equity at the school level. The most critical factor is the teacher's ability to respond to the different learning and affective needs of their students. It is, therefore, argued that theoretical models of EER incorporating the results of research into differentiated teacher and school effectiveness should be developed. Current models are generic in nature and are based on the assumption that effective teachers and schools are effective with all students, in all contexts, in all aspects of their subjects and so on.

In this context, a dynamic model of EER, which is not only multilevel in nature but also demonstrates the complexity of improving educational effectiveness by taking into account the major findings of research into differentiated effectiveness, is presented in this chapter. The main characteristics of the model are provided in the third section of this chapter. Specifically, interaction effects between effectiveness factors and student individual differences are taken into account. For this reason, the proposed model is based on the assumption that the relation of some effectiveness factors with achievement are curvilinear and their effects may vary according to the personal and background characteristics of the subjects which are addressed by these factors, and the cultural and organizational context in which they are expected to perform. Moreover, it is claimed that the current models of EER do not explicitly refer to the measurement of each effectiveness factor and are, therefore, not in a position to demonstrate the complexity of improving educational effectiveness. As a consequence, it is supported that, in principle, each factor, which refers to the classroom, school and system level, can be measured by taking into account five dimensions: frequency, focus, stage, quality and differentiation.

It is emphasized that although differentiation could be considered as a property of an effectiveness factor, differentiation is treated as a separate dimension of measuring each effectiveness factor. In this way, the importance of taking into account the special needs of each subject or group of subjects is strongly supported. It is also made explicit that adaptation to specific needs of each subject or group of subjects will increase the successful implementation of a factor and ultimately maximize its effect on student learning outcomes. Moreover, the description of the effectiveness factors at the classroom level, provided in the fourth section of this chapter, may help teachers to identify ways to differentiate their instruction and provide equal opportunities to the different sociocultural groups of students.

Four ways of using the dynamic model for promoting the provision of equal opportunities to students of different groups are also given in the last section of this chapter. Although further research investigating the validity of the proposed model is needed, it is expected that teachers and policy makers will make use of the effectiveness knowledge base upon which the dynamic model is based and design relevant programs for providing equal opportunities to students of different social groups. Moreover, based on the proposed model, a framework for evaluating the effectiveness of the national policy on providing equal opportunities to students of different sociocultural groups can be established. It can, therefore, be claimed that using the proposed dynamic model of EER, we can improve the effectiveness of teaching practice both in terms of its quality and equity.

REFERENCES

Anderson, L., Evertson, C., & Brophy, J. (1979). An experimental study of effective teaching in first-grade reading groups. *Elementary School Journal, 79,* 193-223.

Armento, B. (1977). Teacher behaviors related to student achievement on a social science concept test. *Journal of Teacher Education, 28,* 46-52.

Askew, M., & William, D. (1995). *Recent research in mathematics education, 53,* 5-16. London: Office for Standards in Education.

Bennett, N., Desforges, C., Cockburn, A., & Wilkenson, B. (1981). *The quality of pupil learning experiences* (Interim report). Lancaster, England: University of Lancaster, Centre for Educational Research and Development.

Black, P., & Wiliam, D. (1998). *Inside the Black Box: Raising standards through classroom assessment.* London: King's College London School of Education.

Borich, G. D. (1992). *Effective teaching methods* (2nd ed.). New York: Macmillan.

Brophy, J. (1986). Teacher influence on student achievement. *American Psychologist, 41*(10), 1069-1077.

Brophy, J. (1992). Probing the subtleties of subject matter teaching. *Educational Leadership, 49,* 4–8.

Brophy, J., & Evertson, C. (1976). *Learning from teaching: A developmental perspective.* Boston: Allyn & Bacon.

Brophy, J., & Good, T. L. (1986). Teacher behaviour and student achievement. In M. C. Wittrock (Ed.), *Handbook of research on teaching* (pp. 328-375). New York: MacMillan.

Campbell, R. J., Kyriakides, L., Muijs, R. D., & Robinson, W. (2004). *Assessing teacher effectiveness: A differentiated model.* London: RoutledgeFalmer.

Cazden, C. B. (1986). Classroom discourse. In M. C. Wittrock (Ed.), *Handbook of research on teaching* (pp. 432-463). New York: MacMillan.

Creemers, B. P. M. (1994). *The effective classroom.* London: Cassell.

Creemers, B. P. M., & Kyriakides, L. (2005, April). *Establishing links between Educational Effectiveness Research and improvement practices through the development of a dynamic model of educational effectiveness.* Paper presented at the 86th annual meeting of the American Educational Research Association, Montreal, Canada.

Creemers, B. P. M., & Reezigt, G. J. (1996). School level conditions affecting the effectiveness of instruction. *School Effectiveness and School Improvement, 7*(3), 197–228.

de Jong, R., Westerhof, K. J., & Kruiter, J. H. (2004). Empirical evidence of a comprehensive model of school effectiveness: A multilevel study in mathematics in the first year of junior general education in the Netherlands. *School Effectiveness and School Improvement, 15*(1), 3-31.

den Brok, P., Brekelmans, M., & Wubbels, T. (2004). Interpersonal teacher behaviour and student outcomes. *School Effectiveness and School Improvement, 15*(3-4), 407–442.

Doyle, W. (1986). Classroom organization and management. In M. C. Wittrock (Ed.), *Handbook of research on teaching* (pp. 392-431). New York: MacMillan.

Emmer, E. T., & Everston, C. M. (1981). Synthesis of research on classroom management. *Educational Leadership, 38*(4), 342-347.

Everston, C. M., Anderson, C., Anderson, L., & Brophy, J. (1980). Relationships between classroom behaviour and student outcomes in junior high math and English classes. *American Educational Research Journal, 17,* 43-60.

Fielding, M. (1997). Beyond school effectiveness and school improvement: Lighting the slow fuse of possibility. In J. White & M. Barber (Eds.), *Perspectives on school effectiveness and school improvement, 137-160.* London: Institute of Education.

Fraser, B. J. (1991). Two decades of classroom environment research. In B. J. Fraser & H. J. Walberg (Eds.), *Educational environments: Evaluation, antecedents and consequences*, (pp. 3-29). Oxford, England: Pergamon.

Fullan, M. (1991). *The new meaning of educational change.* London: Cassell.

Goldstein, H. (2003). *Multilevel statistical models* (3rd ed.). London: Edward Arnold.

Hargreaves, D. H. (1995). School culture, school effectiveness and school improvement. *School Effectiveness and School Improvement, 6*(1), 23-46.

Harlen, W., & James, M. (1997). Assessment and learning: Differences and relationships between formative and summative assessment. *Assessment in Education, 4*(3), 365-379.

Heck, R. A., & Marcoulides, G. A. (1996). School culture and performance: Testing the invariance of an organizational model. *School Effectiveness and School Improvement, 7*(1), 76–106.

Heck, R. H., & Thomas, S. L. (2000). *An introduction to multilevel modeling techniques.* Mahwah, NJ: Erlbaum.

Hextall, I., & Mahony, P. (1998). *Effective teachers effective schools.* London: Biddles.

Hopkins, D. (1996). Towards a theory for school improvement. In J. Gray, D. Reynolds, C. Fitz-Gibbon, & D. Jesson (Eds.), *Merging traditions: The future of research on school effectiveness and school improvement* (pp. 30- 50). London: Cassell.

Hopkins, D., & Reynolds, D. (2002). *The past, present and future of school improvement.* London: DfES.

Hoy, W. K. (1990). Organisational climate and culture: A conceptual analysis of the school workplace. *Journal of Educational and Psychological Consultation, 1*(2), 149-168.

Johnson, D. W., & Johnson, R. T. (1993). Cooperative learning and classroom and school climate. In B. J. Fraser & H. J. Walberg (Eds.), *Educational environments: evaluation, amendments and consequences* (pp. 55-75). Oxford, England: Pergamon.

Kline, R. H. (1998). *Principles and practice of structural equation modeling.* London: Gilford Press.

Kyriakides, L. (2004). Differential school effectiveness in relation o sex and social class: Some implications for policy evaluation. *Educational Research and Evaluation, 10*(2), 141-161.

Kyriakides, L. (2005). Extending the comprehensive model of educational effectiveness by an empirical investigation. *School Effectiveness and School Improvement, 16*(2), 103-152.

Kyriakides, L., Campbell, R. J., & Christofidou, E. (2002). Generating criteria for measuring teacher effectiveness through a self-evaluation approach: A complementary way of measuring teacher effectiveness. *School Effectiveness and School Improvement, 13*(3), 291-325.

Kyriakides, L., Campbell, R. J., & Gagatsis, A. (2000). The significance of the classroom effect in primary schools: An application of Creemers comprehensive model of educational effectiveness. *School Effectiveness and School Improvement, 11*(4), 501-529.

Kyriakides, L., & Tsangaridou, N. (2004, April). *School effectiveness and teacher effectiveness in physical education.* Paper presented at the 85th annual meeting of the American Educational Research Association, Chicago.

MacBeath, J. (1999). *Schools must speak for themselves: The case for school self-evaluation.* London: Routledge.

Muijs, D., & Reynolds, D. (2000). School effectiveness and teacher effectiveness in mathematics: Some preliminary findings from the evaluation of the Mathematics Enhancement Programme (Primary). *School Effectiveness and School Improvement, 11*(3), 273-303.

Muijs, D., & Reynolds, D. (2001). *Effective teaching: evidence and practice.* London: Sage.

Nuthall, G., & Church, J. (1973). Experimental studies of teaching behaviour. In G. Chanan (Ed.), *Towards a science of teaching* (pp. 9-25). London: National Foundation for Educational Research.

Redfield, D., & Rousseau, E. (1981). A meta-analysis of experimental research on teacher questioning behaviour. *Review of Educational Research, 51*, 237-245.

Reynolds, D., Hopkins, D., & Stoll, L. (1993). Linking school effectiveness knowledge and school improvement practice: Towards a synergy. *School Effectiveness and School Improvement, 4*(1), 37-58.

Reynolds, D., & Teddlie, C. (2001). Reflections on the critics and beyond them. *School Effectiveness and School Improvement, 12*(1), 99-113.

Rosenshine, B. (1983). Teaching functions in instructional programs. *Elementary School Journal, 89*, 421-439.

Rosenshine, B., & Stevens, R. (1986). Teaching functions. In M. C. Wittrock (Ed.), *Handbook of research on teaching* (pp. 376-391). New York: MacMillan.

Shepard, L. A. (1989). Why we need better assessment. *Educational Leadership, 46*(2), 4-8.

Slee, R., & Weiner, G. (2001). Education reform and reconstructions as a challenge to research genres: Reconsidering school effectiveness research and inclusive schooling. *School Effectiveness and School Improvement, 12*(1), 83-97.

Slee, R., & Weiner, G., with Tomlinson, S. (Eds.). (1998). *School effectiveness for whom? Challenges to the school effectiveness and school improvement movements.* London: Falmer Press.

Smith, L., & Sanders, K. (1981). The effects on student achievement and student perception of varying structure in social studies content. *Journal of Educational Research, 74,* 333-336.

Stenmark, J. K. (1992). *Mathematics assessment: Myths, models, good questions and practical suggestions.* Reston, VA: NCTM.

Sternberg, R. J. (1988). Mental self-government: A theory of intellectual styles and their development. *Human Development, 31,* 197-224.

Teddlie, C., & Reynolds, D. (2000). *The International Handbook of School Effectiveness Research.* London: Falmer Press.

Teddlie, C., & Stringfield, S. (1993). *Schools make a difference: Lessons learned from a ten year study of school effects.* New York: Teachers College Press.

Thrupp, M. (2001a). Sociological and political concerns about school effectiveness research: Times for a new research agenda. *School Effectiveness and School Improvement, 12*(1), 7-40.

Thrupp, M. (2001b). Recent School effectiveness counter-critiques: Problems and possibilities. *British Educational Research Journal, 27*(1), 443-458.

Tomlinson, C. (1999). *The differentiated classroom: Responding to the needs of all learners.* Alexandria, VA: Association for Supervision and Curriculum Development.

Walberg, H. J. (1986). Syntheses of research on teaching. In M. C. Wittrock (Ed.), *Handbook of research on teaching* (pp. 214-229). New York: Macmillan.

Wubbels, T., Brekelmans, M., & Hooymayers, H. (1991). Interpersonal teacher behaviour in the classroom. In B. J. Fraser & H. J. Walberg (Eds), *Educational environments: Evaluation, antecedents and consequences* (pp. 141-161). Oxford: Pergamon.

Yair, G. (1997). When classrooms matter: Implications of between-classroom variability for educational policy in Israel. *Assessment in Education, 4*(2), 225-248.

CHAPTER 3

NEW DIRECTIONS FOR SCHOOL EFFECTIVENESS RESEARCH

Toward School Effectiveness Without Schools

Daniel Muijs

In this chapter I discuss the impact of important contextual changes impacting research into educational effectiveness. These changes render highly problematic the traditional emphasis of researchers in the field of educational effectiveness on state-funded, self-contained public schools. Specifically, the socio/political context of marketization, public sector reform, and globalization is leading to new forms of school organization, with expanded functions, increased connectivity and increased competition between schools characterizing the education systems of many developed countries. So far, however, effectiveness research has largely ignored these changes, and researchers in the field have tended to act as if the traditional school can be examined in isolation from these trends.

Effective Schools, 43–58
Copyright © 2006 by Information Age Publishing
All rights of reproduction in any form reserved.

THE ORIGINS AND IMPACT OF SCHOOL
EFFECTIVENESS RESEARCH

School effectiveness research started in the early 1970s as a radical movement aiming to transcend the prevailing pessimism about the impact of schools and education on students' educational performance (e.g., Jencks et al., 1972). A group of researchers attempted instead to move towards studying those within-school factors that may lead to better performance for students, regardless of their social background (Reynolds et al., 1994). This was a key move, resulting in methodological advances (such as the advent of multilevel modeling to study hierarchical systems), the identification of a reasonably consistent set of organizational characteristics of schools that contribute to enhanced educational outcomes (Teddlie & Reynolds, 2000), and added impetus to school improvement policies and procedures (Reynolds, Sammons, Stoll, Barber, & Hillman, 1996).

The school effectiveness movement has been highly successful on a number of levels. First, the prevailing pessimism of the 1960s has well and truly been swept away, with the current view that schools can make a difference even to students in socioeconomically disadvantaged circumstances now being almost universally accepted (Mortimore, 1991; Thrupp, 2001), even prompting some school effectiveness researchers warn against overinflating the influence that schools can have (which, typically, accounts for 10%-20% of the variance in students' achievement (e.g., Mortimore & Whitty, 1997).

School effectiveness research does, however, suffer from a number of well-understood weaknesses, such as undertheorization, its susceptibility to misappropriation of findings for political purposes, the creation of oversimplified lists of effectiveness factors, insufficient empirical research on certain findings and a somewhat myopic focus on test results as the measure of outcomes (Slee & Weiner, 1998; Teddlie & Reynolds, 2000; Thrupp, 2001). Critics of school effectiveness have pointed to the lack of attention to the social context of schools, and the way in which pupils' socioeconomic, ethnic, and gender status may constrain their performance. They have also pointed to specific methodological flaws characterizing some school effectiveness studies.

Weaknesses in school effectiveness research have been widely discussed in different fora (see, among others, the special issue of *School Effectiveness and School Improvement, Vol. 12, No. 1* concerning debate on the validity of school effectiveness research), so I will not repeat them in detail again here. A key weakness I do wish to address, however, is one that I believe will become increasingly important in future. This weakness is central to the origins of school effectiveness research, but may also provide great opportunities for school effectiveness researchers in the future. As mentioned above school effectiveness research originated in part to help show that *schools* can make a difference to the educational performance of students. This predisposition has meant that researchers in the area have concerned themselves primarily with schools as organizations. Moreover, because school effectiveness research originated in contexts (particularly the United States and the United Kingdom) in which the traditional public school, providing free education to all students financed by the state, was the only form of provision for students from disadvantaged backgrounds (always a prime target of interest for school effectiveness researchers), the overwhelming focus of interest has been this type of school. In previous decades this focus was defensible, as the traditional public school was, and largely still is, the very heart and focus of Western educational systems. However, I argue that this focus will become increasingly problematic for a number of reasons discussed below, which result from far-reaching changes in both the social and political contexts in which education operates.

THE TRADITIONAL PUBLIC SCHOOL, THE MODEL OF THE FUTURE?

The traditional model of the school, which is the one school effectiveness research has primarily studied, is one of an organization which is publicly funded and can be described as a concrete physical and organizational structure within which all of formal education occurs. For children from nonwealthy areas in Anglo-Saxon countries, the state has traditionally been the monopoly provider of formal education (Wolf, Macedo, Ferrero, & Venegoni, 2004). The traditional public school, of course, provides researchers with a convenient arena for research, thanks to the self-contained nature and strong focus of schools as organizations. However, the question must be asked to what extent to this model will future retain this unique position in the educational landscape. A number of evolutionary changes ongoing at present suggest that this might not be the case. As well as potentially altering the education system in more or less radical ways, these changes will require a fundamental rethink of school effectiveness research. These changes include the move towards more flexible forms of organizing schools, extending schools with a wider remit than has traditionally been the case, the emergence of new providers of schooling into the "market," the increasing internationalization of education, the increasing multiculturalism of our societies and schools, and the move towards distributing education outside the school.

Flexible Organization

Since the 1970s Western politics and media have been characterized by a heightened emphasis on education, driven in part by decreasing political influence on economic policy as a result of globalization, and in part by an increased awareness of the importance of education to societal development in the information age. Increased accountability, state, and international comparative testing, and the open publication of school data have led to a dramatic increase in expectations of educational quality. Moreover, increased expectations have led, since the early 1980s, to sustained attempts to improve schools and education systems (Teddlie & Reynolds, 2000). Initially, these attempts were focused on changes within or to individual schools, while retaining organizational structures across schools. The lack of sustained system-wide improvement resulting from individual-school efforts has, however, led many educators to rethink the organization of schools in ways which are seen as more likely to deliver genuine change.

This rethinking is increasingly leading towards a partial dissolution of the traditional single school model in favour of more flexible modes of organization. Two main organizational reforms are emerging: the disaggregation of large schools into smaller entities (the so-called small schools movement) and the development of stronger linkages between schools.

The small schools movement is based on the premise that smaller organizational units allow for the development of a stronger community culture and shared values, as well as closer and more personal connections between staff and students, both of which are said to lead to enhanced student outcomes in the cognitive and affective domains (Lee & Smith, 1995; Raywid, 2001). Acceptance of this premise has led to calls to dissolve the large schools that had grown up in many countries, for example by creating subunits within existing schools (such as the "house system" employed in many U.K. and U.S. schools), or even through the actual dissolution of large schools into smaller units. In some cases the resulting smaller schools exist on the same shared site as the old school, but in some cases entirely new small schools have been established. There is some support for a link between smaller school size and higher academic performance of students (Lee & Smith, 1997; Raywid), though questions remain concerning the cost effectiveness of the strategy, the relative importance of school size compared to other school effectiveness characteristics, and possible intake effects in many studies. One recent systematic review of the evidence, for example, found ambiguous results concerning the relationship between school size and pupil outcomes for secondary schools (Garrett et al., 2004). What is clear, however, is that the small-schools movement, if sustained, presents some challenges to the school as the traditional unit of analysis in school effectiveness research. The more schools are dissolved into smaller organizations on one site, the more the question of the relative effectiveness of these smaller units with respect to one another will arise, which is likely to raise some interesting questions regarding organizational culture and composition effects.

The second important change to the organization of schools as autonomous but unified single units takes the form of increased networking between schools. Increased networking is premised on the principle of improving capacity by sharing best practices and increasing levels of creativity through confrontation with other practices and views. Creating "communities of practice" in which all school staff work together for school improvement is therefore a key aim of networking (Day & Hadfield, 2004).

Networks themselves take on different forms and levels of complexity. In their simplest form they consist of groups of, usually geographically proximal, schools coming together for specific school improvement purposes, often under the auspices or encouragement of a local education authority. A step up from this first form are more permanent consortium arrangements, where schools work together over time across a range of issues. Arrangements in which geographically nonproximal schools link-up are increasingly possible with the aid of evolutions in communication technology, and it is thus likely that groupings of schools with shared philosophies or pedagogical approaches may increasingly work closely together in this way. Such nonproximal collaborations are already happening in a number of instances (e.g., the Basic Schools Network), albeit more often at present under the auspices of an external body than through school-initiated action. An interesting further step is the formation of so-called Federations of schools in the United Kingdom. In their so-called "hard" form, schools set up joint governing bodies, management structures or principalships in order to establish Federations (Department for Education and Skills, 2005). In some cases schools offering different types of educational provision (such as mainstream and special schools) form a Federation to offer a more integrated approach to education. In other examples, successful schools may link federally with failing schools in order to improve provision in the latter schools.

Again, for researchers in school effectiveness the key questions revolve around the unit of research (is this the individual school or a network or Federation?) and the benefit to students of the emerging models of school organization. There is currently, however, still a surfeit of advocacy over empiricism in this area.

Extended Schools

As well as schools being restructured, in many countries the role of schools is being redefined. Traditionally, schools have been largely single purpose institutions, devoted to educating children of a particular age and stage of learning. Depending on the educational culture of the particular country additional pastoral goals may be more or less developed and important, and in different contexts factors such as well-being, attitudes to learning and self-esteem have been deemed important outcomes of education (e.g., Van Landeghem, Van Damme, Opdenakker, De Frairie, & Onghena, 2002). However, essentially schools have been occupied with the cognitive and to a lesser extent social development of youngsters up to age 18. Recently, though, an increased emphasis on schools as centers for their communities has started to emerge, both in the rhetoric of education reformers and in practical policy initiatives in a number of countries such as the United Kingdom and parts of the United States. Community engagement is seen as especially beneficial where schools are serving disadvantaged areas (Department for Education and Skills, 2003). Again, the redefinition of schools is linked to an increased concern for school quality, and the perceived failure of traditional school effectiveness approaches to lead to sustained improvement, especially to the performance of students from socioeconomically disadvantaged backgrounds. Redefinition is also influenced by the perceived dissolution of traditional family and community structures. Increasingly, schools and education in general are seen as alternative vehicles for socialization that are needed to replace declining traditional structures.

Two key premises underlie the extended schools movement: the potential power of schools as organizations to reach out to their community, and the importance of stronger linkages with the community to improving parental involvement and, as a result of this, student performance (Hiatt-Michael, 2003). The vehicle through which this will happen is increasingly seen to be the creation of "extended schools," offering child care, social services, adult education, and other forms of provision to the community.

However, while the vehicle is the same, the two underlying premises are based on essentially contrasting views of the role and esteem of schools in the community. "Outreach" proponents assume that schools are well-embedded organizations, which will enhance attitudes of community members to services held within schools. The "improving parental involvement" view supposes that parents may have negative views or experiences of school, and that facilitating their interaction with schools in a new context these problems may be overcome. This latter view has received some support from research evidence in school improvement, where schools in disadvantaged communities have been found to be quite successful in increasing parental involvement through adult education and service provision initiatives (Muijs, Harris, Chapman, Stoll, & Russ, 2004). Whether incorporating social services (as opposed to say, adult education classes) into schools is likely to have this effect is a moot point as these services are not always themselves popular with recipients, and can be seen as alienating in their own right. However, this movement has received considerable support in some "futures scenarios" (e.g., Organization for Economic Cooperation and Development, [OECD], 2001) and therefore more experiments in this area are likely.

This extended schools movement raises a few key questions for school effectiveness research: is the concentration on educational outcomes as the main or, in most studies, only goal of schooling still suitable in view of the many goals that integrated schools may have? If that *is* still the case, the question will have to asked as to whether and to what extent extending schools in this way leads to a dissipation of energies possibly impacting on the "academic focus" found to be important in school effectiveness studies (Teddlie & Reynolds, 2000)? Other key questions include: do extended schools require different forms of management, different cultures or structures, and how does this impact on staff relationships, workload and professional development needs?

Different Providers

The search for improved outcomes for education has also influenced the next change taking place in education, the growing presence of non-state providers. Public sector reform, and education reform more specifically, has been characterized by a rise in the use of market based methods and borrowing from the private sector. These trends, in turn, have led to the development of quasi-markets revolving around school choice, and the encouragement of competition between schools through the publication of school performance data and "league tables" of schools. School based management, designed to free schools from the centralization evident in most education systems in the developed world, and the borrowing and dissemination of private sector leadership and management methods are also evident. Increasingly, however, governments are starting to allow genuine markets in education, where private organizations are providing education in contexts where they would not traditionally have featured.

Marketization and privatization represent potentially major changes for educational effectiveness research, especially in contexts where the state school has been the monopoly, or at least primary, provider of education. (The chief exceptions to the state monopoly in many contexts have been faith-based schools, for example, the large Catholic education sector in many countries. However, these schools too have operated largely within the constraints of the state system, and have in most countries been funded through state subsidy mechanisms in similar ways to nonfaith schools (Wolf et al., 2004)). This picture is changing, however, and in some cases quite rapidly. In the United Kingdom, for example, the new Academies program is designed to introduce private sector involvement to state schooling, through combined private-public funding (although the extra government and private sector funding for these schools compared to other state schools does not seem to have led to the expected improvements in performance (PriceWaterhouseCoopers, 2005). Furthermore, while private schooling has traditionally aimed at a very wealthy market, with fees far out of reach of many ordinary parents, tentative moves towards for-profit schools aimed at a less affluent market are afoot, such as evidenced by the Edison project in the United States and the GEMS and Cognita projects in the United Kingdom.

Supporters of more involvement of the private sector in schooling claim that privatization will improve school effectiveness for three main reasons:

- Increased competition between providers is likely to compel schools to improve the effectiveness of their practices, or go out of business, as in the private sector;
- The introduction of private sector management practices is supposed to lead to decreased inefficiencies than are common, according to privatization proponents, in the public sector; and
- The introduction of a profit motive may lead to higher investment and better incentivization of staff than is currently present in the state-funded system (Tooley, 2002a).

Opponents doubt these advantages, questioning the extent of inefficiency currently in state systems, and pointing to the likelihood of inequalities arising from differential access to information depending on the social class of parents (Hatcher, 2001).

For school effectiveness researchers the increased involvement of private sector providers has a number of consequences. First, it is necessary for us to go beyond an exclusive concentration on state schools, and attempt to study the effectiveness of these new providers. This will inevitably be challenging where commercial interests are at stake. However, this is imperative as what research now exists, is marred by the partisan nature of most of the writing in this area (Tooley, 2002a and Hatcher, 2001 are good examples of this).

Outside the Western context, that has so dominated educational research, there is the interesting phenomenon of private school provision in some the poorest areas of a number of countries (as diverse as India, China, and Nigeria). These are profit-making organizations, that cater for families that have limited means to pay tuition fees. While state and non-governmental organizations have often criticized these schools, some evidence is starting to emerge from work by Tooley (2002b) that these schools may in fact be more effective than most State schools in these countries, and certainly that they are often chosen by parents over state schools.

Internationalization and Multiculturalism

Another challenge for school effectiveness research and practice, which has actually existed for quite some time without being fully addressed, is the need to deal with issues of internationalization and evermore multicultural classrooms and schools. These are related but distinct issues.

Like other sectors of societies, globalization has increased the international flow of ideas in education. As a result, dissemination of school effectiveness research internationally is quite well advanced, through amongst others the work of the World Bank and OECD (e.g., Heneveld & Craig, 1996; Scheerens, 1999), and clearly there is a strong interest in the principles and philosophy of school effectiveness research worldwide. This interest does, however, lead us to the question of the extent to which findings in Western contexts (within which the vast majority of school effectiveness research has been conducted) translate to non-Western contexts. Our limited experience within non-Western contexts would certainly suggest that translation will only be partial in most cases (Scheerens). We know that, while many school effectiveness findings do appear to hold across countries in general terms, there are clear differences even between relatively similar Western contexts—let alone between Western and non-Western contexts. For example, the size of school-level effects on achievement vary from almost 50% in some countries, such as Flanders, to less than 10% in others, such as Singapore (Teddlie & Reynolds, 2000). There is therefore a need for more specific research in cross-national contexts, which attempts to specify particular contextual features affecting school effectiveness.

The increasingly multicultural nature of schools resulting from increased international mobility of people, in particular relating to migration from developing to developed countries, is another issue that urgently deserves more attention from school effectiveness research. Most school effectiveness research is still largely conducted in relatively homogeneous ethnic contexts, that is, in schools dominated by one ethnic group, be it the majority group in the country or a minority group concentrated in a particular (usually urban) area served by the school. However, this condition is rapidly changing. In the large cities, such as London, and even in more provincial settings, demographic and social trends are now creating very different school contexts, where monocultural assumptions may not apply (Lindsay & Muijs, 2004). This change has heightened the need to take account of multicultural diversity in school organization, teaching, and learning (Lumby, Harris, Morrison, Muijs, & Sood, 2005), and poses some awkward questions for school effectiveness researchers who have traditionally attempted to find universal recipes and generalize these across contexts. As Lumby and Muijs point out, this may be particularly problematic in multicultural contexts, where values such as a shared culture, found to be so important to effectiveness and improvement research, may conflict with the need to value and support diversity both among students and staff.

Distributed Schooling?

So far, the challenges we have discussed are relatively limited in the sense that they leave the basic organizational foundation of school effectiveness untouched. The school, whatever form it may take, is the basic arena for education. Some other evolutions, however, bought about in large part by the rapid technological changes taking place in our societies, are pointing in a different direction. Will, in future, "school" education still predominantly take place in detached physical settings? Or will the school become a networked entity, where education may in part take place online, in a variety of buildings specialized to accommodate different subjects, and in the home? It is not possible to accurately predict the future direction of schooling. What is clear, though, is that the technical possibilities for distributed schooling are rapidly increasing. There is also some evidence that dissatisfaction with the school system is leading to an increased search for alternatives to school based education.

The homeschooling movement has grown rapidly in countries where the legal framework allows this (Stevens, 2001). The extent to which homeschooling challenges established school systems is provocative. On the one hand, homeschooling does challenge the perceived effectiveness of traditional schooling, and the extent to which traditional schooling caters for the diverse needs of different constituencies. On the other hand, it is hard to see homeschooling ever becoming more than a minority pursuit, in the light of the demands it makes on families. It is hard to imagine homeschooling being sustainable in two parent families where both parents work, or in single parent families where the need to provide financially is pressing. As, in most cases, it is the mother who provides the bulk of schooling, homeschooling could also be seen as a potentially unwelcome setback to the cause of gender equality in society (Stevens). Strong claims have been made as to the effectiveness (or otherwise) of homeschooling compared to regular schooling by both proponents and opponents. Proponents point to evidence that homeschooled students are as likely to perform well in state examinations and to continue on to further education as regularly schooled children (Meehan & Stephenson, 1994; Rudner, 1999). As effectiveness researchers, however, we would have to point to the overwhelmingly middle class composition of the home-schooled cohort as one explanation for this finding (Rudner; Stevens). Opponents claim homeschooled students are missing out on key social development, but again evidence for this is limited (Meehan & Stephenson). While the discussion on homeschooling may seem somewhat divorced from mainstream concerns, it gains more importance when looked as at one of the avenues that future forms of schooling may take (OECD, 2001). It would certainly appear imperative that effectiveness research informs and becomes part of futures thinking in education, and an overly conservative concentration on the traditional school may hinder this involvement.

Similarly, there is a need to get to grips better with the emerging issues of distance and online learning. While still much more limited than some overenthusiastic proponents predicted several years ago (e.g., Clark, 1989), this is undoubtedly a growing area in education as a result of the evolution of information technology which has facilitated the development of cheaper and more flexible modes of delivery. Discussion of these trends has so far, however, mainly taken place in the Educational Technology community, with little contact being made with the world of effectiveness research. There is therefore a deficit of research studying the relative effectiveness of different modes of delivery, with what research exists on modal effectiveness being mainly concerned with higher education. Again, while modal impacts are still limited at the school age level, the lack of interest in these issues from effectiveness researchers is problematic if effectiveness researcher want to help steer an informed debate on the future of education.

At a broader level, if the education system does move towards distributed schooling, the whole basis of "school effectiveness" is called into question. What, in distributed circumstances, would be a "school?" What is the entity we would be researching? Once again the question arises as to whether the school will remain the proper unit of analysis in terms of gaining the best understanding of how we can maximize the effectiveness of learning for our students.

IMPLICATIONS FOR SCHOOL EFFECTIVENESS RESEARCH

School effectiveness research has strongly enriched our understanding of schools and education, and in many cases has led to genuine improvements in the way schools are run and organized. However, as mentioned above, the focus of effectiveness research and development has been very much on the state run public school charged with providing education for all. As we have seen above, sociopolitical and sociocultural changes affecting education policy and practice are eroding the centrality of this type of school, even though at present it remains central in most education systems. Thus sociopolitical-sociocultural change poses a serious challenge to school effectiveness research. If these changes continue, as is likely in the case of at least some of them, traditional school effectiveness research may find itself becoming increasingly sidelined. So does this mean that effectiveness researchers need to gracefully retire, leaving the field of educational research to others? On the contrary. These changes require the attention of school effectiveness researchers more than ever. However, a reconceptualization of the field will be needed.

What is needed is both a reclaiming of the basic methodology of effectiveness research and a broadening of its areas of interest. The basic methodology we need to reclaim focuses on looking at "what works," using an input-process-output research model, which is basically value free in terms of its willingness to take an empirical stance towards a range of possible educational outcomes and the means to achieve them (Scheerens & Bosker, 1997). This methodology and its underlying epistemology is a major strength of the effectiveness approach. Moreover, this approach becomes even more important to educational policy and practice in times of change, during which many solutions are touted as the way forward, or equally strongly opposed by actors influenced by ideology and self-interest rather than empirical fact.

Ideology and self-interest are not in themselves necessarily bad things, as innovation and change often originates among "true believers," and innovations tend to have little chance of success if they are not espoused strongly and passionately (Kotter, 2002). However, there is an obvious danger of allowing education policy and practice to be determined on the basis of enthusiasms which have not been empirically tested. Especially where new models are being created, there is an overriding need to test the educational effectiveness of competing models in delivering the goals they are claiming to deliver. Furthermore, there is a need to compare the effectiveness of these models to traditional alternatives, and to ascertain that new models do not lead to a surfeit of negative unintended consequences, such as extended schooling leading to a loss of focus on teaching and learning, or private schooling increasing inequity. Where new models are created, we also need to find out what are the optimal circumstances, policies, cultures, and structures in which these models can be effective. Are small schools better? Do Federations benefit performance? Does an extended school require a different style of leadership? Does online learning require a specific pedagogy? Effectiveness research can provide a crucial perspective on these and related questions, and therein lies its importance whichever way the education system evolves over the next decades.

Obviously, in reaffirming the importance of the effectiveness perspective, we do need to reorient ourselves to some extent. An exclusive focus on the traditional school as an organization may no longer be tenable in the light of the societal changes that are impacting on education. We need to look at the effectiveness of *education*, rather than schools per se, and education needs to be defined in the broadest possible terms.

International involvement in effectiveness research needs to be strengthened. We need to develop our international networks, and where possible, work with research institutions in the developing world to build research capacity where it is currently weak. This cooperation will benefit the international knowledge base of school effectiveness, and may make a valuable contribution to strengthening the potential of education as a tool for development, especially in those countries where basic levels of education are being reached, and the next steps towards more effective education need to be taken.

Finally, it is of key importance that effectiveness research does not fall into the trap of so much educational research, in allowing ideology and rhetoric to come before empirical research and findings. An open-minded focus on empirical results is necessary, even where they may conflict with previously held views and challenge previously held findings, such as may be the case where diversity in schools challenges views on culture that are strongly held and supported in the school effectiveness community. School effectiveness research is challenged by diversity, but again the need for effectiveness research is strengthened rather than weakened by this challenge. We may need to explore different models of effectiveness, and different outcomes that take more account of diversity, but the need to ascertain what does make for effective education is as strong as ever. Are there models where diversity and shared cultures do not conflict, and what do they look like? How do we create educational environments that effectively address the needs of students and parents with very different values, religious or otherwise? These factors lead us to question some current findings, but they certainly do not lessen the need for effectiveness research.

An open-minded approach is needed, in particular where innovations or changes are highly controversial. In these cases, such as that of the involvement of the private sector in schooling, the force of argument and rhetoric is in danger of overwhelming evidential scholarship more than ever, and it is imperative that the various arguments are tested empirically within an effectiveness framework, even if this may challenge our own beliefs and values. At the end of the day, our approach should be to determine what leads to the best outcomes for students, regardless of whether this fits into any prior belief, or fits into the interests of governments, business, teachers, administrators, religious groups, or unions. Similarly, an affection for the schools we have grown up with, must not blind us to the possible effectiveness of other models.

Overall then, changes are afoot that challenge traditional school effectiveness research. Rather than weakening the need for us as school effectiveness researchers, I have argued that these changes, by contrast, strengthen that need. However, to ensure the ongoing contribution of school effectiveness research, effectiveness researchers need to conceptualize themselves as researchers into "educational effectiveness" in its broadest sense, looking at what works in an empirical way, using a variety of research methods both quantitative and qualitative, but always with the bottom line of improving education for all in mind.

REFERENCES

Clark, G. (1989). Distance learning: A spectrum of opportunities. *Media and Methods, 26*(1), 22-27.

Day, C., & Hadfield, M. (2004, April). *From networking to school networks to "networked" learning: The challenge for the Networked Learning Communities Programme.* Paper presentation (with Mark Hadfield) at the annual meeting of the American Educational Research Association, San Diego, CA.

Department for Education and Skills (2003). *Every child matters.* London: Her Majesty's Stationery Office.

Department for Education and Skills (2005). *What Are federations?* http://www .standards.dfes.gov.uk/federations/what_are_federations/?version=1

Garrett, Z., Newman, M., Elbourne, D., Taylor, B., Taylor, J., West, A., et al. (2004). *Secondary school size: A systematic review.* London: EPPI-Centre.

Hatcher, R. (2001). Privatisation and schooling. In C. Chitty & B. Simon (Eds.), *Promoting comprehensive education in the 21st century.* Stoke-on-Trent, England: Trentham Books.

Hiatt-Michael, D. (2003). *Promising practices to connect schools with the community: Family, school, community partnership.* Greenwich, CT: Information Age.

Heneveld, W., & Craig, H. (1996). *Schools count: World Bank project designs and the quality of primary education in Sub-Saharan Africa.* World Bank Technical Article, No. 303.

Jencks, C. S., Smith, M., Ackland, H, Bane, M, Cohen, D., Ginter, H., et al. (1972). *Inequality: A reassessment of the effect of the family and schooling in America.* New York: Basic Books.

Kotter, J. (2002). *Leading change.* Cambridge, MA: Harvard Business School Press.

Lee, V. E., & Smith, J. B. (1995). Effects of high school restructuring and size on early gains in achievement and engagement. *Sociology of Education, 68*(4), 241-270.

Lee, V. E., & Smith, J. B. (1997). High school size: Which works best, and for whom? *Educational Evaluation and Policy Analysis, 19*(3), 205-227.

Lindsay, G., & Muijs, D. (2004, April). *Raising the educational achievement of Black Caribbean, Black African and White UK-Born Boys.* Paper Presented at the Annual Meeting of the American Educational Research Association, San Diego, CA.

Lumby, J., Harris, A., Morrison, M., Muijs, D., & Sood, K. (2005). *Leadership, development and diversity in the learning and skills sector.* London: Learning and Skills Research Centre.

Lumby, J., & Muijs, D. (2004, April). *Leadership development and diversity: Towards transformational leadership? Early soundings from the field.* Paper presented at the annual conference of the Centre for Excellence in Leadership, Wisham, Warks, England.

Meehan, N., & Stephenson, S. (1994). *Homeschooling in the United States: A review of recent literature.* (ERIC Document Reproduction Service No. ED 424 922)

Mortimore, P. (1991). School effectiveness research: Which way is the crossroads? *School Effectiveness and School Improvement, 2*(3), 213-229.

Mortimore, P., & Whitty, G. (1997). *Can school improvement overcome the effects of disadvantage?* London: Institute of Education.

Muijs, D., Harris, A., Chapman, C., Stoll, L., & Russ, J. (2004). Improving schools in socio-economically disadvantaged areas: An overview of research. *School Effectiveness and School Improvement, 15*(2), 149-176.

Organization for Economic Cooperation and Development (2001). *What schools for the future?* Paris: Author.

PriceWaterhouseCoopers. (2005). *Academies evaluation: Second annual report.* London: Department for Education and Skills.

Raywid, M. (2001). What to do with students who are not succeeding. *Phi Delta Kappan, 82*(8), 589-584

Reynolds, D., Creemers, B. P. M., Nesselrodt, P. S., Schaffer, E. C., Stringfield, S., & Teddlie, C. (Eds.). (1994). *Advances in school effectiveness research and practice.* Oxford, England: Pergamom Press

Reynolds, D., Sammons, P., Stoll, L., Barber, M., & Hillman, J. (1996). School effectiveness and school improvement in the United Kingdom. *School Effectiveness and School Improvement, 7*(2), 133-158.

Rudner, L. (1999). Scholastic achievement and demographic characteristics of home school students in 1998. *Education Policy Analysis Archives, 7*(8), 36-45.

Scheerens, J. (1999). *School effectiveness in developed and developing countries: A Review of the research evidence.* Washington DC: The World Bank.

Scheerens, J., & Bosker, R. (1997). *The foundations of educational effectiveness.* London: Pergamon.

Slee, R., & Weiner, G. (1998). *School effectiveness for whom?* London: Falmer Press.

Stevens, M. (2001). *Kingdom of children: Culture and controversy in the homeschooling movement*. Princeton NJ: Princeton University Press.

Teddlie, C., & Reynolds, D. (Eds.). (2000). *The International Handbook of School Effectiveness Research*. London: Falmer Press

Thrupp, M. (2001). Sociological and political concerns about school effectiveness research: Time for a new research agenda. *School Effectiveness and School Improvement, 12*(2), 7-40.

Tooley, J. (2002a). *Market approaches to education. Examples and evidence*. London: Reform.

Tooley, J. (2002b). Serving the needs of the poor: The private education sector in developing countries. In J. Tooley (Ed.), *Can the market save our schools* (pp. 23-38). Vancouver, British Colombia, Canada: Fraser Institute

Van Landeghem, G., Van Damme, J., Opdenakker, M-C., De Frairie, B., & Onghena, P. (2002). The effect of schools and classes on noncognitive outcomes. *School Effectiveness and School Improvement, 13*(4), 429-451.

Wolf, P., Macedo, S., Ferrero, D., & Venegoni, C. (2004). *Educating citizens. Intenational perspectives on civic values and school choice*. Washington, DC: The Brookings Institution Press.

Part II

ON PEDAGOGY

CHAPTER 4

IDENTIFYING THE CONNECTION BETWEEN CULTURALLY RELEVANT PEDAGOGY, MOTIVATION, AND ACADEMIC PERFORMANCE AMONG ETHNIC MINORITY YOUTH

Kenneth M. Tyler, R. Trent Haines, and Eric M. Anderman

In this chapter, the authors seek to better understand the role that motivation plays in the association between culturally relevant pedagogy and school performance. Whereas culturally relevant pedagogy is championed as one way to effectively address achievement difficulties faced by many ethnic minority students, the empirical link between it, the psychological capacities of such instruction and students' academic outcomes, has not been made clear, at least from an empirical standpoint. Towards this end, a conceptual model of school performance for ethnic minority

Effective Schools, 61–103

students exposed to culturally relevant instruction and related learning activities is proposed.

ETHNIC MINORITY STUDENT REPRESENTATION AND ACHIEVEMENT

Recent data has shown that the United States is rapidly approaching its most ethnically diverse population in history (United States Bureau of the Census, 2001). The U.S. Census Bureau recently reported that by 2050, the primary ethnic minority groups, including Latino, African, and Native Americans, will make up roughly 50% of the U.S. population. Whereas the population of Native Americans is expected to remain at approximately 1% of the total population, by 2050, the African American population is expected to increase from 13 to 15% of the population and Latino American from 11 to 24% (Cartledge & Loe, 2001). While European Americans will maintain status as the largest ethnic group in the United States, projections reveal that Latino Americans will be the second largest ethnic group, followed by African, Asian, and Native Americans (Bernal, Trimble, Burlew, & Leong, 2001). It has also been reported that, by 2050, African, Latino, and Native Americans will constitute nearly 60% of all U.S. public school students (Bernal et al.).

Yet, in spite of increased representation among ethnically diverse populations in public school classrooms, poor academic performance outcomes continue to permeate the schooling experiences of African, Latino and, Native American students, particularly when compared to their European American school-age counterparts. For example, some evidence suggests that over 60% of African American students perform below basic levels on eighth grade standardized math tests, whereas only 21% of European American school-aged students experience such poor performance. From the opposite end of the spectrum, roughly 7% of African American students achieve at either proficient or advanced academic levels, while nearly 40% of their European American counterparts achieve such status (Hall, Weiner, & Carey, 2003). Findings from the National Center for Education Statistics (2000) also report that the average standardized test scores of the average 17-year old African American student were commensurate to those of a 13-year old European American student.

For Latino Americans, the picture is even more dismal. Though projected to have the largest population increase in 2050 (from 11 to 24% of the U.S. population), Latino Americans are twice as likely to drop out of high school than their African American counterparts and are more than 3 times as likely to do so than European American secondary students

(Tapia, 2004). According to Conchas (2001), the high school dropout rate for Latino Americans is at 31%; for Latina Americans, 26%. African Americans students have the second highest dropout rates, with 13 and 12% for male and female students, respectively. Finally, the rates for European American male students are 8% and 7% for female students. In addition, reading performance for Latino Americans is substantially lower than that of their European American counterparts, with Latinos lagging behind well over 2 years.

Though Native American population statistics and projections may pale in comparison to those of other ethnic minority populations, it cannot be overlooked that Native Americans have the highest level of within-group diversity (Hodgkinson, 1990). In particular, Garrett, Bellon-Harn, Torres-Rivera, Garrett, and Roberts (2003) cite that within the Native American population, there are 558 federally acknowledged Native nations, 365 state-recognized tribal communities spread across 304 federal reservations in 31 states and well over 250 distinct languages. In spite of such heterogeneous representation in reservation-based public schools and those in more urbanized areas, some reports have shown that most Native American school-aged children, regardless of tribal membership, experience academic difficulties that often result in the decision to drop out of school (Pavel, Thomas, & Whitener, 1998). At one point, Native American students had the highest dropout rate recorded among ethnic minority groups, at 35% (Allison & Vining, 1999).

COUNTERING ACHIEVEMENT DIFFICULTIES AMONG ETHNIC MINORITY STUDENTS

Whereas the present chapter focuses on students in the United States, the pattern of one majority group demonstrating higher academic achievement than several other minority groups is evident throughout the world. Given the population projections and performance statistics for school-aged students in each of these ethnic minority groups, education researchers and practitioners are in dire need to develop and disseminate strategies that can enhance these students' schooling experiences.

Indeed, as the United States becomes increasingly and rapidly dependent on technologically sophisticated advances in communication, commerce, education, and even agriculture, society can ill-afford to have a substantial number of citizens unable to demonstrate mastery of basic educational requirements. In a similar vein, the increasing numbers of ethnically diverse persons in the United States and throughout the world who can effectively contribute to economic and social affairs in this country will require that U.S. citizens—regardless of ethnic background—demonstrate competence in their ability to fully appreciate the integrity-based cultural values, dialects, and activities such persons possess and utilize.

To address these issues, education researchers and practitioners have become even more proactive in their quest to determine the factors linked to the academic difficulties. They have also sought to configure those factors which promote academic success among ethnically diverse public school students whose school performance and educational attainment indices have historically trailed European American students. One factor identified and heavily referenced in the literature on school performance of ethnically diverse students, especially African, Latino, and Native American students, is culture.

Linking Culture to School Performance

Culture—defined as a core set of values, beliefs, and orientations that permeate the behaviors, activities, and customs of a given population—has been linked to the academic successes of ethnic minority students in the United States and abroad (Strickland, 2000). It has also been viewed as a central source of schooling difficulties faced by these populations. Specifically, the research linking culture to cognitive development and academic performance has fashioned two areas of inquiry. The first, cultural discontinuity, views the perceived disconnect between the in-school and out-of-school cultural values and resulting behavioral preferences as a source of academic complexity for ethnic minority students (Delgado-Gaitan, 1994; Delpit & White-Bradley, 2003; Deyhle & LeCompte, 1994; Hilberg & Tharp, 2002; Hollins, 1996; Inglebret & Pavel, 2000; Neal, McCray, Webb-Johnson, & Bridgest, 2003; Rieckmann, Wadsworth, & Deyhle, 2004; St. Germaine, 1995; Valencia & Black, 2002; Webb-Johnson, 2002). The second area, often viewed as an empirical response to the former, examines the role and effects of what has been coined culturally relevant pedagogy on the development of cognitive skills and overall academic performance. This line of research, coined culturally relevant pedagogy, has shown that African, Latino, Native American, and Pacific Islander students thrive in experimental and classroom learning contexts where aspects of their cultural worldviews and corresponding preferences and behaviors are intricate components of learning and instructional activities (Bell & Clark, 1998; Boykin & Bailey, 2000; Boykin & Cunningham, 2001; Dill & Boykin, 2000; Gay, 2000; Howard, 2001; Ladson-Billings, 2001; Lee, 1991; Teel, Debruin-Parecki, & Covington, 1998; Tharp & Gallimore, 1989; Wortham & Contreras, 2002).

Given that the majority of this research has employed experimental designs wherein performance on an academic task is often viewed as dependent on various levels of an experimental intervention, it is clear that many education researchers have tested the link between culturally relevant pedagogy and academic performance from a cause-effect perspective. In several experimentally designed studies, when students do well in the experimental condition, which often affords learning opportunities consistent with the students' home culture, their performance is typically attributed to the contrived condition. Thus, culturally relevant instruction is viewed as causing or allowing or, more directionally speaking, facilitating the academic performance of ethnic minority student participants. Indeed, careful reads of the experimentally designed studies on culturally relevant pedagogy have revealed discussions illustrating a direct effect between culturally relevant instruction and school performance (Boykin & Allen, 1998).

New Directions in Researching the Effects of Culturally Relevant Pedagogy

Yet, while it is important to examine those tangible factors that aid ethnic minority students' efforts towards becoming and remaining strong academic achievers, to better understand the causal link between culturally relevant pedagogy and school performance, it is equally important to investigate factors that may not be as ostensible, but are, nonetheless, linked to ethnic minority students' school performance. Though several articles and research studies have corroborated the link between culturally relevant pedagogy and school performance (Boykin, 2001, 2002; Lee, 2001; Teel, Debruin-Parecki, & Covington, 1998), we are not sure that the link between culturally relevant pedagogy and academic performance is as straightforward as the research literature proclaims. We suspect that many psychologists would agree that the link between culturally relevant pedagogy and school performance is mediated by a variety of psychological and emotional factors within the individual.

Our focus on the need to examine the mediating factors of the culturally relevant instruction-academic performance association duly acknowledges and builds upon the paradigmatic shift—particularly in educational psychology—from a behaviorist perspective to that of cognitivist perspective. A major impetus for the shift was the recognized role of the individual's psychological faculties. In particular, the early works of Clark Hull and other neo-behaviorists helped the study of behavior in education settings (e.g., learning) move beyond prevailing S—R psychologies which permeated the first quarter of the twentieth century. An overarching theme guiding this shift was the contention that S—R explanations of human behavior were too simplistic as they systematically refuted the existence of psychological faculties not only present in the organism (primarily humans), but also serving as mediators of environmental stimulus-behavioral response connections.

Despite this recognized movement away from a behaviorist position in the study of learning and behavior (Robins, Gosling, & Craik, 1999), the literature linking culture to academic performance appears to operate in somewhat similar fashion. That is, much of the empirical research on culturally relevant instruction and academic performance has omitted any data-driven discussion of the latent, person-centered factors mediating such a relationship. Further, there is a paucity of research examining the effects of culturally relevant instruction on psychological variables linked to cognitive development and school performance. What can be currently gleaned from the research literature on culturally relevant pedagogy and achievement is when classroom instruction and activities do not incorporate or reflect the value-laden, culture-based behavioral preferences and tendencies of ethnic minority students, school difficulties emerge. Conversely, when classroom instruction and activities, do, in fact, incorporate or reflect the value-laden, culture-based behavioral preferences and tendencies of many ethnic minority students, favorable schooling performance outcomes typically occur.

PURPOSE AND STRUCTURE OF THE CHAPTER

In writing this chapter, we are interested in determining why and how these schooling outcomes tend to surface as a result of the presence or absence of culturally relevant instruction. Stated differently, why does culturally relevant pedagogy help to enhance academic performance outcomes for many ethnic minority students? How does culturally relevant instruction facilitate the school performance of many economically and socially marginalized ethnic minority students? Similarly, why do many ethnic minority students not exposed to culturally relevant instruction tend to have unfavorable school experiences? How does the absence of culturally relevant pedagogy affect academic performance?

Each response to the above queries requires some understanding of the role of the individual, particularly his or her psychological faculties, in the link between culturally relevant instruction and academic performance. It is important to identify which psychological factors are activated when culturally relevant instruction is either present or absent from formal school contexts and their proxies. It is equally important to identify the effect that these activated, albeit latent factors have on more observable variables such as academic performance. One latent psychological factor identified to have a significant influence on the academic performance of all students is achievement motivation. It is certainly plausible that culturally relevant instruction facilitates ethnic minority students' academic performance by increasing their motivation to achieve in school contexts. As stated elsewhere, culture provides the motivation for students, particularly ethnic minority students, to achieve or fail (Trueba, 1993). It is equally plausible to consider the moderating effects of academic motivation and culturally relevant learning experiences on students' school performance.

This chapter seeks to offer some redress to the current empirical literature which does not fully consider or assess the role of latent, person-centered variables such as academic motivation on students' performance in culturally relevant learning and instructional conditions. To do so, we will offer some discussion on the link between culture and cognitive development. Following this, we will turn to a discussion of the specific cultural values and themes found in mainstream institutions such as public elementary schools serving low-income ethnic minority students. Next, we shall discuss the salience and significance of the culture-based values found in the out-of-school socialization experiences of African, Latino, and Native American elementary level students. This discussion will help compose a review on research on the widely cited cultural discontinuity hypothesis which argues that many academic performance difficulties faced by these populations are, at least partially due, to perceived mismatch between those value-laden behaviors and activities socialized outside the classroom and those sanctioned within it. The published research on cultural discontinuity, its perceived effects and their remedy, vis-à-vis culturally relevant instructional and classroom practices, will also be offered. Finally, an assessment of whether these works have appropriately tied enhanced school outcomes to internal, psychological factors such as achievement motivation will be made. That is, in those published studies linking some variant of culturally relevant instruction to improved scholastic performance, we will argue the existence of motivation as a mediating factor of the relationship between the independent variable (culturally relevant instruction) and the dependent variable (school/task performance). Suggestions for statistical examination of these associations will also be offered. While we fully recognize the importance of culture in the academic lives of all elementary age students, we limit our discussion on culture, cultural values and schooling outcomes to those ethnic minority students that have historically been underserved by U.S. public schools, namely African, Latino, and Native American (Gutierrez & Rogoff, 2003).

CULTURE IN THE STUDY OF PSYCHOLOGY

The term culture first came into social science jargon back in 1871 when Tylor used it to explain various social phenomena. Betancourt and Lopez (1993) have noted, however, that culture and its role in human cognition and behavior has been recognized for centuries, dating back to its early theoretical development by Hippocrates. Discussions of culture can also be traced back to Plato and Herodotus, both of whom provided earlier speculations on how culture should be utilized in the quest for knowledge (Cole, 1995). Further evidence of the role of culture in psychology's development is found in the early twentieth century teachings of Wilhelm Wundt, who argued that specific genetic (historical, developmental) research methods are necessary to deal with "culturally mediated, historically contingent, higher psychological processes" (Cole).

There have been many conceptualizations of culture. Culture has been defined as the values, traditions, and beliefs mediating the behaviors of a particular social group (Parsons, 2003). It is considered the lens through which all learning experiences are filtered and produced, a medium of learning for all (Hollins, 1996). It is the "how and why we behave in certain ways, how we perceive reality, what we believe to be true, what we build and create, and what we accept as good and desirable" (Westby, 1993, p. 9). Gordon and Armour-Thomas (1991) argued that culture is a multidimensional construct consisting of at least five dimensions (a) the judgmental or normative, (b) the cognitive, (c) the affective, (d) the skill and (e) the technological. The judgmental or normative dimension of culture refers to social standards and values and behavior patterns that people regard as right, proper, natural, and otherwise, informed by mores and traditions. The cognitive dimension relates to social perceptions, conceptions, attributions, and connotations, all of which are categories of human cognition that may be expressed through language. It involves the communicative functions and structures of a social unit and includes not only what one thinks about, but how one thinks. The affective dimension refers to the emotional structure of a social unit, inclusive of its common feelings, its sources of motivation, joy and sorrow, and its sense of value. The skill dimension signifies those special capabilities that members of a culture develop in order to meet the demands of their social environment. Here, the authors note that the skills necessary for survival and success within each culture tend to vary and children are trained from an early age to acquire these skills. Finally, the technological dimension refers to the portion of culture which encompasses accumulated artifacts, instrumentation, and techniques and the manner in which these are used.

While a focus on the role of culture in human sociocognitive functioning has been traced over several past decades, psychology's focus on the influence of culture in cognitive and human interpersonal functioning was not fully appreciated or even recognized in these areas until mid-twentieth century (Cole, 1995; Rogoff, 2003; Shweder, 1995). Bernal et al. (2001) forwarded that many early psychological studies examining human performance in academically related areas such as memory and recall rarely used culture as an explanatory variable in observed human behaviors. The worry has been and continues to be that attending to cultural variation in what is to be valued, esteemed, or performed complicates social scientists' abilities to make generalizations about human thought and activity (Betancourt & Lopez, 1993; Rogoff; Rogoff & Chavajay, 1995; Strickland, 2000). In particular, Gergen, Gulerce, Lock, and Mistra (1996) suggested that in earlier times, and in some current instances, culture has factored in the study of psychology in general and human learning and performance in two ways. The first views culture as a moderating, categorical variable that combines with initial independent variables of interest to affect some dependent variable of interest. The variance in the dependent variable of interest accounted for by the role of culture is typically de-emphasized in order to offer empirical support for universally applicable, theoretical assertions regarding human behavior. This view of culture in psychology has often been carried out in research characterized as cross-cultural (Cole).

Rather than de-emphasize observed cultural influences in behavior, Gergen et al. (1996) suggest that the second way culture factors into psychology is by not becoming a phenomenon of interest at all. For several decades, the forging of psychology as a methodologically sound, theoretically derived social science was premised on psychologists' ability to formulate and empirically test hypotheses that, more often than not, did not duly consider culture in the study of human phenomenon. In fact, variation in performance as a function of cultural distinctiveness was perceived as an impediment to the achievement of psychology's broader goal, which was to establish universal, data-driven theories of human behavior (Rogoff, 2003).

The declining significance of behavioristic explanations of human phenomenon during the second and third quarters of the twentieth century sprouted the emergence of several theoretical propositions calling for an examination of human mental processes and their role in behavior. With this paradigm shift, psychology witnessed a renewed focus on culture. During these times, particularly in educational psychology, culture began to be recognized as a major shaper of human thought, value, knowledge, and behavior. Culture became viewed as a major influence in cognitive development and was shown to be linked to tasks and activities carried out in formal contexts such as public school classrooms and informal learning contexts like home environments (Luria, 1976; Vygotsky, 1962;

Wertsch, 1985). Specifically, the newly translated research stemming from the Russian troika (Alexander Luria, Alexander Leontiev, and Lev Vygotsky) during the second quarter of the twentieth century (Cole, 1995) was instrumental in helping educators better understand that the manner in which individuals approached specific tasks was a function of the historically situated, cultural values such tasks and their corresponding artifacts contained (Leontiev, 1932; Luria, 1976; Vygotsky, 1962, 1978; Van der Veer & Valsiner, 1994). The later research of Michael Cole, Sylvia Scribner, Patricia Greenfield, Jean Lave, and Barbara Rogoff was equally instrumental in detailing the mediating role of culture in human activity and thought processes among Russian, Asian, Mayan and still others whose cultural backgrounds were dissimilar to those which major theories of cognitive development in the United States were predicated.

Emerging from this new focus on culture during the third and into the fourth quarter of the twentieth century was the identification of specific culture-based values and belief systems for both mainstream and many ethnic minority groups, including African, Latino, and Native Americans. A focus on how these values informed cognitive skill development and academic task performance among African, Latino, and Native American ethnic populations also emerged. Much of this work responded to the then current cultural deficiency or deprivation hypothesis (Bereiter & Engelmann, 1966), which claimed that discrepancies in academic performance between mainstream (i.e., European American) students and their ethnic minority counterparts resulted from the perceived differences in the culture-based socialization experiences between these two populations. That is, European American students were argued to be socialized towards values and behaviors typically endorsed in mainstream institutions such as the public school. Some of these values and activities found among upper-middle class European American families include attending live theater and classical music performances, reading and possessing large numbers of classical and nonfiction books and visiting museums (Monkman, Ronald, & Theramene, 2005). Conversely, ethnic minority students were believed to be socialized towards values and behaviors that were not aligned with those reinforced in school (Moynihan, 1967). Such socialization experiences and resulting value orientations were not viewed as part of a preferred cultural-historical worldview among ethnic minorities, but rather a function of economic poverty and sociopolitical disenfranchisement. This perspective led to the development of several federally funded programs designed to enhance the social and academic lives of ethnic minority children, primarily by allowing them to have experiences similar to those of their mainstream counterparts.

To tackle the rather unsettling assumptions of the cultural deficiency hypothesis, many researchers turned to Vygotsky's theoretical framework and existing methodologies to critically discern the culture-based values and belief systems operating in the lives of ethnic minority students Au & Jordan, 1981; (Boykin, 1983, 1986; Cole, 1995; Gallimore & Goldenberg, 2001; Howard & Scott, 1981; Morgan, 1980; Rogoff & Chavajay, 1995). Like the work of the Russian troika, several psychologists began to gather evidence to illustrate how ethnic minority students engaged in preferred social practice, particularly that which fostered cognitive skill development. Such practices were linked to the specific cultural values passed on from generation to generation. Rather than the values and practices found among ethnic minorities being deficient, it became clear to some that the cultural deficit hypothesis was, itself, lacking. Resulting from the efforts of several educators and psychologists was a pragmatic understanding of how such values and beliefs shaped the preferred and salient thought and behavioral patterns manifested among many ethnic minority populations.

With budding empirical research to support the belief that the values and corresponding behaviors of ethnic minority populations in the United States were different from mainstream yet integral to their lived experiences, more and more psychologists began to pay more attention to the link between culture, cognitive development, and school performance. This line of research, which identified mainstream cultural values found in children's schooling experiences and those promoted outside of the school by many ethnic minority groups, not only forged a deeper understanding of how cultural belief systems and values permeate how people think and behave in particular contexts, but also set the tone for current efforts in psychology and education to increase efforts to understanding diversity of thought, value and behavior resulting from cultural variation (Tracey, 2005). We turn now to a discussion of the results stemming from these theoretical and empirical efforts to identify the cultural values permeating mainstream institutions such as the public and also those salient in the lives of African, Latino and Native American students.

CULTURE AND AMERICAN SCHOOLING

Mainstream Cultural Values

Individualism

Individualism refers to one's disposition toward fundamental autonomy, independence, individual recognition, solitude, and the exclusion of others (Spence, 1985). Several aspects of this mainstream cultural theme are presented in the literature and tend to inform additional mainstream cultural themes. For instance, taken from earlier research (Sampson,

1977), the description of self-contained individualism lies in the ideal that one is to strive for intramental self-sufficiency. That is, to be successful, there is a need to achieve without depending on others for assistance. Sampson claimed that the socialization goals present throughout several mainstream institutions, including the pubic school, "try to facilitate persons' emergence from their embeddedness in the family, in school, and in other collective settings to take their place on their own two feet, as autonomous (self-contained) individuals." Here, efforts to obtain help from others without utilizing one's abilities to their fullest extent are frowned upon. Another type of individualism is possessive individualism. Possessive individualism has to do with one's identity and status being bound to what one owns or possesses (Boykin, 1983). This type of individualism allows for one's mundane and/or material possession to define who he or she is within a given social context (Safran & Safran, 1994). It dictates one's position in life and secures one's identity as an individual. An additional form of individualism includes rugged individualism (Boykin), a feeling that one's ultimate responsibility is to oneself. In this type, the individual is the primary unit and therefore, strives to be the best at all costs.

Competition

Competition refers to one's preoccupation with doing better than others. In order for a participant to succeed, others must fail in some fashion (Boykin, 1983). Competition between and within groups appears to be reinforced by the self-contained individualism notion. It not only refers to one being all he or she can be, but also focuses on one striving to be better than others. Competition manifests itself as individual competition, where one is trying to be the best among others (i.e., "me against the world"); interpersonal competition, where one is attempting to beat out another in direct head to head rivalry; and group competition, where one "team" is attempting to surpass others (Boykin, Tyler, & Miller, 2005). Among U.S. citizens, competition is viewed as a central component of life (Safran & Safran, 1994).

Earlier work lends credence to the existence of the mainstream cultural values typically found across several institutions in the United States, particularly public schools. For example, Gay (1975) asserts that students are taught to be individualistic and competitive. Gordon (1982) forwarded that public schools promote docility, minimize social interaction, and expect individualized, competitive effort which is characteristic of the norms of the dominant society. Earlier work by Johnson (1982) concluded that the classroom infrastructures within the public schools are structured to reinforce individualism and competition mainstream cultural themes. In particular, Johnson's work exemplifies the fact that, in just 6 years of schooling (from kindergarten through sixth grade), the public school—through its classroom infrastructure and curriculum—accomplishes the goal of advancing and reinforcing mainstream cultural ways of operation.

Learning and instruction in U.S. public schools serving predominantly ethnic minority students, according to Paradise (1998), contain European-based sociocultural practices believed to best promote academic excellence. Some empirical evidence to support this claim has been provided in the literature (Raeff, 1997; Greenfield, Quiroz, & Raeff, 2000; Rothstein-Fisch, Greenfield, & Trumbell, 1999). In a study by Sheets (1996), elementary school teachers serving predominately African American students reported feeling pressure to maintain controlled, quiet classrooms where students worked by themselves. Similar findings were reported by Stokes, Kibour, Martin, Miller, and Wilson (1997). More recently, Boykin, Tyler, & Miller (2005) reported in a qualitative study of over 20 public school classrooms serving African American elementary students, 341 of 513 observations were in reference to the individualism and competition.

ETHNIC MINORITY GROUP CULTURAL VALUES

Before we turn to a discussion of the cultural values found in the lives and activities of African, Latino, and Native American groups, we acknowledge a major shortcoming in the research literature pertaining to this topic. Upon our review, it has been uncovered that much of the literature does not duly consider within-group variation when describing the culturally grounded practices and orientations of African, Latino, and Native American groups. We noted earlier, for example, that Native Americans, there are over 500 tribal nations, each potential with an existing, distinct set of cultural values and customary practices. Yet, some research fails to specify which Native American groups are being investigated or whether there are variations in cultural values among the diverse groups (Garrett, Bellon-Harn, Torres-Rivera, Garrett, & Roberts, 2003). In categorizing African American in the literature on cultural values, the articles and chapters unpacking the term African to include persons of African descent born in the United States and abroad (born on the African continent and neighboring isles) were scarce. Furthermore, Latino Americans are also considered one of the more diversified ethnic groups in this country. While many have used the term Latino or Latino American or Hispanic to describe persons of Mexican ancestry, Latino Americans in the U.S. represent at least nine different countries, including Mexico, Peru, Guatemala, Bolivia, Puerto Rico, Cuba, Dominican, and Panama (Canning, Salazar-Guenther, & Polanco-Noboa, 2002).

Despite recorded knowledge of such ethnic group heterogeneity, much of the literature on the cultural values of African, Latino, and Native Americans has not focused on the cultural values of each ethnic group represented within the overarching ethnic African, Latino, and Native categories. The danger of this omission, with respect to cultural values and behaviors, is the assumption that there is little or no variation among ethnic groups represented by these terms. In light of this shortcoming, we will use the existing literature carefully to build our stance on the interface of culture, motivation and school performance.

African American Cultural Values

Wade Boykin, a leading researcher on the role of culture and achievement for African American school-age population, has advanced the argument that a set of authentic culture-based values and orientations does, in fact, govern the behaviors of many African Americans.

Communalism

Communalism is defined as the perceived fundamental interdependence of people. Under communalism, one acts in accordance with the notion that duty to one's social group is more important than individual rights and privileges. Hence, among biological and fictive kinship families, social identity is intricately tied to group membership rather than individual status and possessions. Sharing is promoted because it affirms the importance of social interconnectedness, while self-centeredness and individual greed are frowned upon.

Movement

Movement indicates a premium placed on the amalgamation of movement, polyrhythm, dance, percussiveness, and syncopation embodied in the musical beat (Boykin & Allen, 1998). The movement cultural theme is divided into three dimensions.

1. Movement expressiveness—where movement, music, and a rhythmic orientation toward life is manifested in speech patterns, movements, and patterns of activity.
2. Psychological health—movement and music conceived either independently or joined in coordination are ways of engaging life and are vital to one's psychological health.
3. Movement repertoire—refers to the manifestation and receptiveness to a rich, expansive movement, and gestural repertoire.

Verve

Boykin (1983) defined verve as the propensity for high levels of physical or sensate stimulation. The physical stimulation has been coined in terms of qualities of intensity or liveliness, variability, and density of stimulation. Boykin, along with other researchers (Bailey, 1994; Walton, 1994) have expanded the verve paradigm. Different facets include:

(a) Intensity or liveliness—distinctions having to do with volume of stimulation and behavioral vigor.

(b) Variability—connotes levels of changeability or alternation among activities or stimuli in one's environment or induced by the individual.

(c) Density—refers to the number of stimulus elements or activities simultaneously present. It can convey: (1) the number or distinct events occurring at the same time; (2) the simultaneous engagement in more than one activity or simultaneous focus on several distinct stimulation sources by an individual, and; (3) the focus on one or more tasks while there is discernible background activity or stimulation present.

Despite the reported salience of and preference for activities and structures that afford many African American students the opportunity to express such cultural values (Boykin, Albury, Tyler, Hurley, Bailey, & Miller, in press; Boykin & Bailey, 2000; Tyler, Boykin, Boelter, & Dillihunt, 2005; Tyler, Boykin, & Miller, 2005), public schools are often viewed as discounting these values and related practices (Boykin, Tyler, & Miller, 2005; Boykin, Tyler, Watkins-Lewis, Hurley, & Kizzie, in press; Rogoff, 2003; St. Germaine, 1995; Tyler, Boykin, & Walton, in press). This often is seen as the catalyst for problematic transactions between students and teachers and problematic attitudes toward the schooling experience, which result in poor academic performance. Boykin and his colleagues have examined the presence of and preference for three Afrocultural themes, namely communalism, movement, and verve.

To test this assumption, Boykin and associates have initiated a research program examining the presence of cultural discontinuity in the African American children's schooling experiences (Boykin, Tyler, & Miller, 2005; Boykin, Albury, Tyler, Hurley, Bailey, & Miller, in press; Boykin, Tyler, Watkins-Lewis, Hurley, & Kizzie, in press; Tyler, Boykin, & Walton, 2005; Tyler, Boykin, & Miller, 2005; Tyler, 1999; Bell, 2001). In these studies, it was shown that African American parents and their school-age children report that communalism, verve, and movement are not endorsed or largely present in their children's classrooms, despite their prevalence in the reported preferred learning activities carried out at home. Similarly, in these studies, teachers also reported or were perceived as endorsing classroom learning behavior which reflected mainstream cultural themes such as individualism and competition significantly more than the Afrocultural themes of communalism, movement, and verve.

Throughout their research, Boykin and his colleagues have also examined the effects of incorporating aspects of such children's out-of-school cultural experiences in formal learning settings such as the public school classroom. A consistent finding throughout each of their experimentally designed research studies is that low-income African American elementary and middle grade level students perform at optimal achievement levels when their experimental and actual classroom tasks build upon the said cultural themes and values brought to school from home (Bailey & Boykin, 2001; Boykin, 1983, 1986; Boykin, Coleman, Lilja, & Tyler, 2004; Boykin & Cunningham, 2001; Boykin, Lilja, & Tyler, 2004). The favorable achievement outcomes resulting from students' exposure to such culturally relevant contexts and materials have been found across language arts (i.e., reading comprehension and recall, metacognition, analogical reasoning), mathematics (multiplication, product estimation, addition, subtraction, and multiplication with fractions), and in the social sciences (i.e., geography) tasks. Similar findings have been garnered in other studies with low-income African American elementary students with the communal, movement expressive and vervistic learning conditions (Allen & Butler, 1996; Bell & Clark, 1998; Hale, 2001; Ladson-Billings, 2001; Lee, 1991, 2001; Neal, McCray, & Webb-Johnson, 2001; Neal, McCray, Webb-Johnson, Bridgest, 2003; Teel, DeBruin, & Parecki, 1998; Webb-Johnson, 2002).

Latino American Cultural Values

The research illuminating the cultural values salient among Latino American populations has been carried out by several researchers, each of whom has examined both Latino Americans in their native and the U.S. context. A well-know example of the cultural values that can enhance school performance was brought about in the motion picture, *Stand and Deliver*, a story about Jaime Escalante, a high school math teacher who used the cultural strengths of low-achieving Latino adolescents to prepare them for advanced mathematics examinations. In educational psychology, leading researchers on Latino American culture include Barbara Rogoff and her colleagues, whose research has uncovered several underlying cultural themes and beliefs in the daily activities of Mayan populations. Patricia Greenfield, Ronald Gallimore, and Claude Goldenberg have also investigated longitudinally esteemed cultural values and practices several generations of Latino Americans. Much of their work, along with several others, has helped to improve instructional practices among this population (Delgado-Gaitan, 1994; Tapia, 2004; Wortham & Contreras, 2002).

Similar to African American populations, the literature on cultural values among Latino American populations frequently cites collectivism as a major cultural theme (Greenfield, Quiroz, & Raeff, 2000; Oyserman, Coon, & Kemmelmeier, 2002; Hui & Triandis, 1989). Some qualitative work has found that a fundamental sense of interconnectedness is found not only among families within the same household, but also among family members in different households, thereby making it a customary cultural theme in Latino American households, particularly among U.S. Mexican and Puerto Rican families (Tapia, 2004). Greenfield, Quiroz, and Raeff describe the collectivistic ideal as one where an individual is interdependent and he or she strives to make personal contributions and achievements that benefit the family. Like communalism found in African American cultures, social responsibility is centered around the good of the whole group/family and one's responsibilities are geared towards advancing or maintaining the group. As families are viewed as the primary source of social support among Latino American families, isolating the family to focus on one individual within it often results in conflict (Cavanagh & Lopez, 2004).

Notions of collectivism have been found across several activities and orientations found in the lives of many Latino American families. Collectivistic tendencies, for example, have been found in the sleeping arrangements of Mayan families (Morelli, Rogoff, Oppenheim, & Goldsmith, 1992). Research by Patricia Greenfield, Claude Goldenerg, Ronald Gallimore and colleagues has shown that the moral development of Latino children strongly emphasizes collectivistic or familial tendencies. For example, among Mexican and Central American citizens, the term education focuses squarely on the child's ability to behave and address elders and social others with respect. Additionally, Latino parents who endorse education expect their children to be obedient, quiet and cordial.

Education is conceptually linked to collectivism as many Latino American families believe that what the child does both in and out of the home is a reflection of the type of rearing and socialization experienced at home. Therefore, children whose activities and behavioral preferences do not reflect education are believed to be reared incorrectly and can project an image of inadequate socialization, which could, from a collectivistic perspective, be detrimental. A study by Greenfield, Quiroz, and Raeff (2000) corroborated this claim. In particular, they found that among parent-teachers conferences with Latino parents and European American teachers, the parents were more often concerned with their child's social behavior (i.e., is the child respectful towards the teacher) in the classroom, while teachers placed more emphasis on the child's academic and self-expressive capabilities. Research by Reese, Balzano, Gallimore, and Goldenberg (1995) also found that, of 12 activities Latino American parents reported as important to do with their children, teaching the children right from wrong along with good manners, particularly in social situations, were among the top two activities.

Another cultural theme infused in the behaviors of Latino Americans is what Wortham and Contreras (2002) call spatiotemporal fluidity. Similar to Velez-Ibanez's (1996) simultaneity description of Latin American homes and Boykin's (1986) verve description of African American households, Wortham and Contreras characterized spatiotemporal fluidity as a variety of multiple activities occurring at the same time. It is also viewed as the active engagement in such activities simultaneously. Based on their qualitative research on an English as a second language classroom teacher, Wortham and Contreras noted that most of the teacher's Latino students were highly engaged in classroom activities. This notion of spatiotemporal fluidity or simultaneity has also been found in the work of Barbara Rogoff and her colleagues. In one study, Rogoff, Mistry, Göncü, and Mosier (1993) found that among the rural families (Native American and Mayan), there was much more simultaneity observed than in the more affluent U.S. families. Though their study questions the role of social class in the socialization and child-rearing activities families maintain in their households, the authors concluded that culture was responsible for the differentiated household activities observed. In a similar study, Chavajay and Rogoff (1999) found that Mayan parents were more likely to attend to multiple and often competing events than were European American parents, who often alternated their attention to one event at a time. This finding of attention variation also surfaced for Mayan children.

Native American Cultural Values

The qualitative work of Michael Garrett and Donna Deyhle has sought to uncover the specific cultural value differences among Native American students and their families. Though not as scientifically rigorous as the experimentally-derived research conducted with African American and Latino student populations, much of Garrett's and Deyhle's research has not only revealed several distinct cultural values and practices among various Native American families and tribes, but has also provided rather unsettling evidence to support the cultural discontinuity hypothesis claiming mismatch between culturally laden behaviors brought to school by Native American children and those sanctioned in school (Deyhle, 1986a, 1986b, 1995; Deyhle & LeCompte, 1994; Rieckmann, Wadsworth,

& Deyhle, 2004; LaFromboise & Dixon, 1981; LaFromboise, Trimble, & Mohatt, 1990; Bee-Gates, Howard-Pitney, LaFromboise, & Rowe, 1996; Bryant & LaFromboise, 2005; Garrett, 1995; Garrett, Bellon-Harn, Torres-Rivera, Garrett, & Roberts, 2003).

In unpacking Native American cultural values, it is important to acknowledge that variation in what is valued and practices is present among the 550 federally recognized tribes situated across hundreds of sovereign land reservations in the United States. It has been suggested that because of their unique cultures and languages, Native American tribes have very different perceptions of what child-rearing, medicine and learning are (Allison & Vining, 1995). Garrett and his colleagues (1995, 2003), however, have led a research program that seeking to unveil the cultural values that span across the majority of Native American tribes. These cultural values, which are conceptually similar those listed among African and Latino American populations, include:

- Sharing and cooperation; importance of the tribe and extended family
- Noninterference;
- Harmony with nature
- A present-time orientation
- A deep respect for elders (Garrett, Bellon-Harn, Torres-Rivera, Garrett, & Roberts, 2003).

Under cooperation, the belief that whatever is possessed by the individual also belongs to the group is held. Survival of the individual is synonymous with survival of the family and larger community (Garrett et. al., 2003). Such interconnectedness and its perceived absence from mainstream culture is evidenced when mainstream modes of introduction upon initial meeting entail questions such as "What do you do for a living" as opposed to "Where do you come from" or "Who is your family." The former is perceivably aligned with mainstream notions of individualism, where the individual inquires about whom one is in relation to his or her self ("What do you do"). In Native American culture, the latter inquires as to whom one is in relation to his or her family and background ("Where do you come from or who is your family"). Moreover, competition and individualism are often not valued or encouraged in Native American communities. Competition results in a losing individual feeling shamed, typically by not being able to acquire what the winning individual has (Garrett, 1995). This notion of individualism, by way of competition, is typically frowned upon in Native American families and tribes.

Under the noninterference value, it is believed that because everything was created to fulfill a specific purpose, interference in fulfillment of that purpose is discouraged. As a result, many Native American parents, adults, and even children are allowed to withdraw and be left alone during an emotional or even academic disturbance. What is more, the individual is welcomed back into the larger group without any explanation needed. This notion of noninterference complies with the harmony with nature cultural value found among many African Americans. Here, allowing situations to occur uninterrupted promote a sense of harmony not only between a troubled individual and an intervening one, but also within the troubled individual. What ever is the matter with he or she, it is purposeful and something that he or she is supposed to go through. Therefore, the situation should remain free of outside intervention.

Similar to social time perspective among African Americans (Boykin, 1983), present-time orientation focuses on Native American beliefs in the "here and now." Unlike the future-time orientation present in mainstream culture (Sue & Sue, 1987), where a timepiece (i.e., clock, watch) indicates when activities are to occur (e.g., begin and end workday), present-time orientation among Native American and still other ethnic minority populations suggests that things begin when everyone arrives and end when they are socially completed (i.e., when everyone agrees that the end has been reached). Along with present-time orientation, there is a strong reverence for elders within the family and community of Native Americans. Believed to possess wisdom acquired throughout their decades of lived experience, elders in the Native American community often play important roles such as parent, teacher and spiritual leader (Garrett et al., 2003). This reverence for elders is taught to Native American children at young ages and is often manifested by avoidance of eye contact between the elder and the younger individual and an absence of critical analysis of an elder's knowledge (Garrett, 1995). In addition, there is little interjection and oftentimes, immediate responses are signs of absence of thought and are typically not present.

Researchers underscoring the salience of the specific cultural values that inform the observed practices of Native Americans have also sought to confirm that these values and practices are not duly acknowledged or reinforced in Native American students' school experiences. Safran and Safran (1994) note that in public schools serving predominantly Native American populations, cultural discontinuity often results in some misunderstanding of the Native children's behaviors. For example, they cite that the downward glance or lack of eye contact exhibited by Native children is often viewed by their teachers as unassertive or uncertain, each of which are expectations of students served in mainstream public schools. In Lake's (1990) story of Wind-Wolf, a young

Native American male student, he describes the student's difficulties in school as a result of avoiding eye contact with the teacher and lack of immediate responses to the teacher's queries. In his attempt to uphold Native American cultural values of being respectful towards elders and taking time to reflect on what has been said, Wind-Wolf's teacher inter- prets his actions as characterizing as lack of interest or lack of intelli- gence, or even both. Similarly, a Native American student that does not participate in competitive classroom activities is likely to be viewed by his or her teacher as unmotivated or antisocial. Also, those students raised to not question or verbally analyze situations or statements, but rather learn through careful observation and listening will most often be viewed by teachers as inattentive, slow, withdrawn, or lazy (Garrett, 1995). Also, mainstream public school-based performance evaluations, which are almost always timed, do not accommodate the culturally situ- ated performance characteristics of Native American youth, which are typically premised on a present-time orientation, patience and reflec- tion (Garrett; Hilberg & Tharp, 2002). Additional instances where Native American cultural values, traditions, and customs have been mis- represented and/or de-emphasized in public school classrooms exist (Adams, 1988; Charleston & King, 1991; Deyhle, 1986b; Pewewardy, 2004; Sparks, 2000; Stokes, 1997).

To counter the effects of cultural discontinuity in the academic lives of Native American youth, some research has called for the incorporation of Native culture in classroom learning experiences (Allen, Christal, Perrot, Wilson, Grote, & Earley, 1999). The results of these efforts have had a sig- nificant effect on Native American student performance. For example, Hilberg and Tharp (2002) reviewed several empirical studies where Native American students outperform students from other ethnic groups when testing activities are aligned with the modal form of learning and behavior occurring outside of the schooling context. A study by Cardell, Cross, and Lutz (1978) found that students who were exposed to an experimental condition characterized by group activities across multiple learning stations outperformed their peers in mathematical assessments. One reason provided for the superior performance yielded by the stu- dents in the experimental condition is the fact that they were allowed to be self-directed, that is, no intervention on behalf of the experimenters, parents or classroom instructor. Here, the notion of noninterference was utilized and to some degree, facilitated Native students' academic perfor- mance. Similar findings were garnered in a study by Hopkins and Bean (1999) in language arts and Hilberg, Tharp, and DeGeest (2000) in math classrooms.

Linking Culture to Pedagogy and School Performance

Much of the literature recording cultural discontinuity in the academic lives of African, Latino, and Native American school-aged youth has noted a discrepancy between the values that such students bring to school and those already present in school. Specifically, several educators and researchers mentioned throughout this chapter have determined both anecdotally and scientifically, the presence of specific mainstream cultural themes permeating ethnic minority children's schooling experiences. They have also found that most of the cultural themes brought to school by these children are not wholly accepted, recognized, or utilized in their classrooms. This discontinuity between cultural values and corresponding behavioral and performance modalities has been linked to the academic difficulties experienced by a majority of ethnic minority children. Most education researchers addressing this dilemma have sought to advocate inclusion of culturally relevant activities and behaviors of ethnic minority children into their formal classroom learning experiences. Much of the research stemming from this position has demonstrated that favored academic outcomes emerge when aspects of school learning reflect the cultural themes, values, behavioral tendencies, and preferences of African, Latino, and Native American students.

Still, an explanation for why many ethnic minority children prosper in either experimental or actual academic learning contexts containing structures and activities that mirror their out-of-school socialization experiences has not been fully developed in many of the research studies reviewed here. In the research carried out by Boykin and colleagues, why did many of the low-income African American school aged subjects outperform other students when operating in and working with culturally aligned learning contexts? Why are these students performing significantly better on several academic subjects when exposed to communal, movement expressive, and vervistic learning conditions than when exposed to competitive and/or individualistic learning conditions?

Turning to the findings for Latino American students, how did modifying the traditional classroom environment into what mirrored their out-of school cultural experiences lead to increased academic engagement and a decrease in behaviors that often obstruct one's path towards academic excellence (i.e., school drop-out, truancy, absenteeism)? What happened in the classrooms of Jaime Escalante, Margaret Contreras, and Henry Trueba where students who were given up on, were able to successfully matriculate advanced placement mathematics and scholarly writing courses? More importantly, what happened to or within these students during the classroom exposure that sparked the shift from being placed at risk for academic failure to becoming solid academic achievers?

Among Native American students, beyond the presence of and expo-sure to a culturally aligned curriculum, how can researchers account for the significant change in academic performance produced by these stu-dents? Was there a change in students' psychological factors that were not only linked to performance ability, but also to the favored performance outcome produced? If so, what were these factors and is there a need for research on culturally relevant pedagogy to begin to empirically examine this relationship between culturally relevant instruction, student psycho-logical factors and achievement outcomes? In following the early cognitiv-ists like Hull and Vygotsky and more importantly, to better assess and articulate the outcomes yielded by ethnic minority students learning and working in culturally aligned contexts, a logical first step in addressing these queries requires a reintroduction of the psychological factors within the individual students that equally contribute to their success under such learning conditions.

In this next section, we will delve further into the psychological factors related to achievement in an effort to speak to the past findings on cultur-ally relevant pedagogy, where ethnic minority students were reported to perform at high levels when exposed to culturally consistent learning con-ditions. While we will seek to cover a variety of psychological factors, our discussion will be limited to achievement motivation.

ACADEMIC MOTIVATION AND CULTURALLY RELEVANT PEDAGOGY

The field of achievement motivation provides several frameworks for expansion and understanding of the relations between culture and learn-ing. Although some work has examined motivational variables in minority populations (e.g., Graham, 1994), much of the motivation research has not specifically examined minority student populations. Thus, this is an area that merits additional empirical and theoretical attention. More importantly, this work is only just now starting to be applied to actual changes in classroom practice and discourse, in order to facilitate the learning of minority youth.

Several theoretical perspectives have dominated the achievement moti-vation literature. These perspectives provide a framework for understand-ing the ways in which motivation may mediate the relations between culture and learning. Indeed, culture does not operate in a vacuum; the effects of cultural variables on student outcomes are related to students' motivational beliefs. In particular, we will provide several exemplars of motivational theories and research that frame the larger issues of the rela-tions of culture to learning. We begin with an examination of stage-environment fit theory, which serves as a metatheoretical perspective; we then provide more detailed examples using two specific motivation theories: expectancy-value theory and goal orientation theory. We argue that these theories are related to the specific types of instructional practices that teacher use, and therefore, these theories can assist educators in adapting instructional techniques to meet the unique needs of minority youth.

Person-Environment Fit

Eccles, Midgley, and their colleagues adapted developmental work on person-environment fit (e.g., Hunt, 1975) to examine the negative effects of the transition from elementary school to middle or junior high school on early adolescent motivation (Eccles & Midgley, 1989; Eccles et al., 1993). This theoretical perspective guided much of Eccles and her colleagues' work examining declines in adolescent motivation. Person-environment fit theory maintains that individuals will be optimally motivated when contexts (environments) match the needs of the individual.

Specifically, Eccles and her colleagues have argued and demonstrated that the environments associated with many middle grades schools are antithetical to the developmental needs of adolescents. More specifically, middle schools often are characterized by low-level (rote) cognitive tasks, few opportunities for autonomy and choice, disharmonious relationships with adults, and few opportunities to interact in meaningful ways with peers; these contextual shifts in environment occur at a time when from a developmental perspective, adolescents need cognitively engaging tasks, positive relationships with adults and peers, and opportunities for autonomy and choice (Anderman & Maehr, 1994; Eccles & Midgley, 1989). In addition, negative changes in other contextual variables across the middle school transition (e.g., the decline in teacher efficacy) also contribute to downward shifts in adolescent motivation (e.g., Midgley, Feldlaufer, & Eccles, 1989).

Applying Person-Environment fit Theory to the Relations Between Culture and Learning

As we have described, there is often a disconnect between the mainstream values espoused in schools and the cultural values that ethnic minority students bring to educational settings. Whereas this has not been examined via person-environment fit theory, there is good reason to support the application of this theoretical perspective to the study of culture and learning.

As the numbers of ethnic minority students in schools increase both in the United States and elsewhere, it becomes imperative to examine the mismatch between school environments and students' home cultures. Although the relation between culture and learning has been acknowledged historically (e.g., Betancourt & Lopez, 1993; Brice-Heath, 1983; Jones, 1997), specific examinations of discontinuities between the environments provided by contemporary schools and the cultures of these schools' clients are lacking.

Person-environment fit theory calls for detailed examinations of the expectations and needs of minority students and their families, and the types of responses to those needs that are provided by schools. If the goal of education is to truly educate youth, then the values supported by schools may need to change; if schools only espouse mainstream cultural values, some minority students may not excel to their potentials. In particular, an endorsement of this perspective calls for a critical examination of the appropriateness of the use of instructional practices developed for white majority youth, with minority youth.

Boykin's work examining the cultural values that regulate the behaviors of many African Americans serves as a good example of the mismatch between the needs of individual students and the types of environments provided by typical schools in the United States. As we previously reviewed, some of the ways in which African Americans express their cultural values include movement, verve, affect, orality, and communalism. These types of behaviors often are not supported or valued in American schools (e.g., Rogoff, 2003). Indeed, rather than supporting communalism and interactive conversation, American public schools often foster environments that are controlled, quiet, and somewhat unexciting (e.g., Gay, 2000; Sarason, 1997). Thus, the environments provided by schools do not often meet the cultural needs of African American youth (Boykin, Tyler, & Miller, 2005; Boykin, Albury, Tyler, Hurley, Bailey, & Miller, in press; Boykin, Tyler, Watkins-Lewis, & Kizzie, in press). Nevertheless, as suggested by person-environment fit theory, when the environment provided by the educational setting (and the specific instructional practices used by teachers) do match the needs of African American youth, learning is likely to be facilitated (e.g., Krater, Zeni, & Cason, 1994).

Expectancy-Value Theory

Expectancy-value theory has a broad history in the field of achievement motivation. Atkinson's seminal work in this area guided much current research (e.g., Atkinson, 1957, 1964). However, recent work by Eccles and her colleagues has established the importance of this perspective in current research on academic motivation.

Briefly summarized, an individual's motivation to engage with a particular task is purported to be a function of the individual's expectations of succeeding at the task, and the individual's valuing of the task (Eccles, 1983; Wigfield & Eccles, 1992). The value component is actually comprised of four distinct aspects of value: attainment value (the perceived importance of the task), interest value (how intrinsically interesting the task is perceived to be), utility value (the perceived extrinsic utility of the task), and cost (the perceived negative aspects of engaging with a particular task). Although Atkinson originally proposed an inverse relation between expectancies and values (Atkinson, 1957, 1964), current research suggests that these variables are related positively (Wigfield & Eccles).

Expectancies and values are important because in longitudinal studies, they have been determined to be important predictors of valued educational outcomes. For example, expectancy beliefs tend to predict achievement in courses, whereas values predict behavioral outcomes such as future enrollment in courses (Eccles, 1983; Meece, Wigfield, & Eccles, 1990; Wigfield & Eccles, 1992).

Applying Expectancy-Value Theory to
the Relations Between Culture and Learning

Although expectancy-value theory is a prominent framework in the field of motivation, little work has specifically examined the roles of expectancies, and more specifically values, in explaining the relations between cultural values and learning. The work completed in this area has primarily focused on African American youth.

As noted by Graham in her comprehensive review of motivation in African Americans, there is little evidence to support the hypothesis that African American youth have lower expectancies for success than do nonminority youth (Graham, 1994). As noted by Graham, "Both expectancy for future success and self-concept of ability among African Americans remain relatively high even when achievement outcomes indicate otherwise" (Graham, p. 103).

In a study directly applying expectancy-value theory to the study of achievement values in minority adolescents, Graham, Taylor, and Hudley (1998) found that minority male adolescents placed little value on high-achieving male students. Male minority students were perceived as being poor students by a variety of adolescents. Interestingly, minority females did not espouse the same negative views of high achievers as did minority males. Indeed, adolescent males in particular may turn away from schooling as a means of managing the negative stereotypes associated with their academic abilities (e.g., Steele, 1997). Also, it is perceivable that the African American male adolescents may have dissociated with school achievement because the culture-laden preferences and activities that are central to their achievement identities may not be fully appreciated by either classroom teachers or their female counterparts.

Minority Students' Achievement Values

Some minority students, at times, may value different educational outcomes than do majority students. As noted previously, a number of researchers have documented the unique values of various Latino American youth (e.g., Gallimore & Goldenberg, 2001; Rogoff, 2003; Wortham & Contreras, 2002).

Nevertheless, most schools do not necessarily adapt their environments to match the values of their constituents, especially students. As noted previously, there are some notable examples (e.g., the example of Jaime Escalante, see Hilliard, 1991) that demonstrate that students' achievement values can be used to guide curriculum and instruction; however, such cases are the exception and not the norm. Nevertheless, those cases can be interpreted in terms of expectancy-value theory, wherein instructors carefully math their pedagogical practices to the core values of their students.

Because the valuing of academic subjects in particular is predictive of future engagement with those same content areas, it is particularly important to develop positive achievement values in minority youth. Indeed, if an ethnic minority adolescent has no reason to value mathematics, it is unlikely that the student will pursue additional math-related courses, and subsequently consider a career involving math-related skills. This is compounded by the fact that expectancies are positively correlated with values—this may lead to self-fulfilling prophecies, where low achievement in certain courses is related to lesser valuing of those same courses. Since students' values often are reflections of their broader community and familial values, and the cultural worldviews that inform each, educational environments need to foster those values through culturally relevant pedagogical practices, in order to facilitate the academic engagement of minority adolescents. In some cases, this may not be difficult; for example, research indicates that the parents of many immigrant Latino children greatly value formal schooling (Goldenberg, Gallimore, Reese, & Garnier, 2001).

However, the support of other minority student cultural values may be less easy to facilitate. For example, as noted previously, many Latino and Native American cultures value communalism and can benefit from socially-oriented learning environments (Gay, 2000); nevertheless, the history of the use of groups for learning is sporadic; the use of collaborative and cooperative techniques has risen and fallen throughout the past century (Webb & Palinscar, 1996). Whereas group learning can and often does facilitate student learning (Slavin, 1992), the consistent use of proven group-based techniques that build upon the cultural values of minority youth is scarce.

Goal Orientation Theory

In recent years, goal orientation theory has become a prominent framework in the study of academic motivation. Briefly summarized, goal orientation researchers argue that students characterize their goals for engagement with academic tasks in several ways. Students display mastery-oriented goal orientations when their goal when engaging with a particular academic task is to truly master the task at hand; such students compare their current performance to their own previous performance, and value effort, improvement, and challenges. Students also at times display performance-oriented goals. The literature identifies two types of performance goals: *performance-approach* and *performance-avoid* goals. Students display performance-approach goals when they are interested in demonstrating their ability relative to others (i.e., showing how "smart" they are); in contrast, students display performance-avoid goals when they are interested in hiding their lack of ability relative to others (for reviews, see Anderman, Austin, & Johnson, 2002; Anderman & Wolters, in press; Dweck & Leggett, 1988; Elliot & Harackiewicz, 1996; Harackiewicz, Barron, & Elliot, 1998; Meece, Blumenfeld, & Hoyle, 1988; Pintrich, 2000; Urdan, 1997).

Research indicates that goal orientations are related to valued educational outcomes in predictable ways. In general, mastery goals are related to beneficial educational outcomes, such as effort, the use of effective cognitive strategies, and academic engagement; performance-avoidance goals are, for the most part, related negatively to adaptive educational outcomes; results for performance-approach goals are mixed, with some studies finding positive relations and others finding negative relations to desirable outcomes such as achievement (for a comprehensive review, see Anderman & Wolters, in press).

Research also indicates that the types of goals that students adopt are largely determined by the contexts of classrooms, and by the instructional practices of teachers. More specifically, various instructional practices lead students to perceive mastery or performance-oriented classroom goal structures; it is the perceptions of these goal structures that leads to the adoption of individual personal goals within classrooms. Thus a student who perceives a performance goal structure in her English classroom is likely to adopt personal performance goals in that classroom (Kaplan, Middleton, Urdan, & Midgley, 2002; Meece, Anderman, & Anderman, in press; Roeser, Midgley, & Urdan, 1996).

Applying Goal Orientation Theory to
the Relations Between Culture and Learning

Few studies have examined ethnicity and goal orientation. Of these, one has shown that African American students may be slightly more mastery-oriented at times than are nonethnic minority students (Middleton & Midgley, 1997). Other theoretical work suggests that mastery-oriented classrooms may enhance the motivation of African American students (e.g., Kaplan & Maehr, 1999). The types of instructional practices used in classrooms are predictive of the types of goals that students will adopt in their classrooms. If the instructional practices used by teachers reflect values that are familiar and meaningful to the student, then those practices are likely to facilitate that adoption of congruent goals which should lead to enhanced learning (Gay, 2000).

It is clear that some types of classroom practices will be more aligned with minority students' cultural values than will others. As previously noted, the cultural values of African American, Latino American, and Native American youth stress sharing and cooperation; nevertheless, American classrooms often stress individualism and competition. Indeed, current federal legislation in the United States clearly stresses individual success, and competition among schools and the students within them as a fundamental principle of operation (e.g., No Child Left Behind Act of 2001). Thus, if teachers clearly stress individual accountability to students, then students are likely to adopt individualistic goals. This can be problematic, because if the students' goals are performance oriented, and most specifically, if they are performance-avoidance oriented (wherein students' goals are to not appear incompetent or unable in comparison with others), research suggests that negative outcomes will accrue (e.g, Elliot & Church, 1997; Pintrich, 2000). Nevertheless, because quasi-experimental research indicates that changes in teachers' instructional practices lead to changes in students' goals (e.g., Anderman, Maehr, & Midgley, 1999), the application of goal orientation theory to the study of culturally relevant pedagogy for minority youth offers much promise.

Culturally Relevant Instruction, Motivation, and Academic Performance: A Path Model

Whereas the literature on motivation is vast and that concerning the effects of culturally relevant pedagogy is still growing, little empirical research addresses the link between these two schooling factors and their relations to academic outcomes. Some have, however, implied such an association between these factors exists. For example, in each study carried out by Boykin and colleagues, there is a direct causal association made between culturally aligned instruction and activities and academic performance. Throughout these works, a heightened sense of student academic motivation is implied in their discussion. Yet, none of them actually measured the impact of motivation on the association between culturally aligned instruction and achievement outcomes. This is also the case in several additional studies with other ethnic minority students (Pinkard, 1999; Wortham & Contreras, 2001; Lee, 2001; Rubie, Townsend, & Moore, 2004).

How, then, can we effectively model this phenomenon empirically for minority students in America? Granted, there is a literature that suggests that the presence of culturally aligned instructional strategies facilitates academic performance of ethnic minority students. Particularly, the research of Boykin and associates has, for over 20 years, demonstrated the positive effects of experimental and actual classroom based instruction and activities—which incorporated aspects of African American students' home culture—on academic performance. Equally, there are several dozen empirical studies linking motivation to ethnic minority students' academic achievement. Yet, for ethnic minority students placed at-risk for academic failure, there are virtually no empirical works that have sought to investigate how the link between culturally relevant pedagogy and achievement is mediated by students' recorded level of motivation after being exposed to such instruction.

Without a unique analysis of the role motivation plays in students' achievement outcomes in particular contexts (culturally relevant or traditional learning contexts), psychologists and educators alike become situated in a study of learning and school performance that mirrors the stimulus (culturally relevant pedagogy)/response (achievement outcome) theme rampant throughout psychology's stint with behaviorism. Such techniques could provide a more constructive way of empirically accounting for change in achievement outcomes resulting from exposure to or utilization of culturally relevant instructional or educative materials. Path modeling and related analyses (i.e., structural equation modeling) would allow researchers to address queries such as why does culturally relevant pedagogy enhance performance outcomes for ethnic minority students, and what does such instruction do for the actual student? What psychological variables are triggered and facilitate academic engagement and achievement when students are exposed to culturally relevant instruction and materials?

We argue that the relations between pedagogy, motivation, and academic performance should be analyzed through the use of path models. Based on the past review of relevant literature, our proposed basic model suggests that culturally relevant pedagogy sways student motivation in achievement-based contexts, which in turn enhances academic performance.

Given the variety of instruments that can assess these variables, the next logical step in promoting culturally aligned instruction and curriculum in public schools serving ethnically diverse populations is to determine the predictive relations among culturally relevant instruction, motivation and academic performance. From an experimental standpoint, those studies that measure the academic performance of students exposed to either culturally relevant or more traditional learning contexts could add measures of academic motivation to establish the presence of relations among the three factors.

For example, in its simplest form, a score could be provided to students exposed and not exposed to culturally relevant instruction and/or curriculum. In each condition, a measure of academic motivation and achievement is administered and completed by students. Following the criteria for mediation model analysis (Baron & Kenny, 1986), should relations exist between culturally relevant pedagogy and motivation, motivation and academic performance, and culturally relevant pedagogy and academic performance, then, the above path model can be tested for tests of goodness of fit. Whereas goodness of fit indices would indicate the degree of fit the data have to the proposed model, testing the model would provide a set of standardized path coefficients that would estimate the size of the effects of exogenous or predictor variables (culturally relevant pedagogy and motivation) on the dependent variable (academic per-

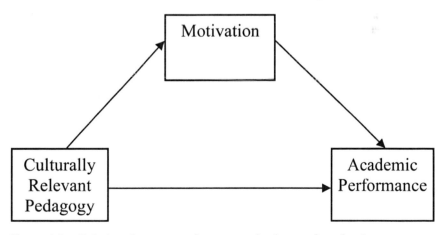

Figure 4.1.   Relations between pedagogy, motivation, and academic performance.

formance) (Klem, 1995). Our expectation, given our review of the literature, is that the strongest effect would be between culturally relevant pedagogy and achievement. However, we would hold an expectation for this relationship to be mediated by the presence and degree of academic motivation experienced and reported by students exposed to either experimental condition (culturally relevant pedagogy or traditional classroom operation). That is, the indirect relations between culturally relevant pedagogy and performance would be mediated by achievement motivation. Thus standardized path coefficients would indicate whether motivational variables mediate the relation between culturally relevant pedagogy and academic performance.

CONCLUSION

Reform efforts have and continue to seek the best and most innovative schooling practices to improve the academic realities of the nation's at-risk student populations, namely African, Latino, and Native American children and adolescents. While the current model of school reform typically examines the effects of a reform-based intervention on reported student performance outcomes, it is rare for researchers to examine why the yielded outcome was produced or what exposure to this reform intervention "did" to or for the student and thus, to his or her recorded performance. With most of the experimental research literature suggesting culturally relevant pedagogy enhances academic performance reported by students and recorded in several research reports, a common theme emergent throughout these works is the assumption that there is a direct association between reform-based context such as culturally relevant pedagogy and students outcomes. Given current analysis of psychological factors and their link to student academic success, researchers must begin to more fully incorporate—from a measurement perspective—the role of various psychological factors that account for the variance in student performance outcomes along with exposure to culturally responsive instruction. That is, culturally relevant pedagogy, just like traditional classroom environments that do not necessarily build on the cultural strengths and preferences of ethnic minority students, actually *do* something to and/or for the student exposed to it.

It will greatly benefit educational stakeholders—from teachers to students and parents to educational psychologists, anthropologists and the like—to know, empirically, how culturally relevant pedagogy or lack thereof, actually impacts student achievement motivation and related psychological variables. For example, teachers will, then, know that the types of culturally aligned activities and curriculum modules established for their students have psychological benefit that goes beyond feelings of academic self-efficacy, particularly when a student exposed to culturally relevant instruction succeeds. They, like the students, will understand that, even in the absence of high academic success outcomes for students under culturally relevant pedagogy, there is some element of instruction that is keeping students motivated and therefore, engaged in the culturally aligned academic task, two demonstrated components of academic success. Education researchers, therefore, should begin to examine the intersection of culturally relevant instruction, motivation and academic performance. The proposed model allows for at least one psychological variable possessed by the student to be assessed and therefore, we do not make the mistake of attributing student outcomes to "what the culturally relevant context did," but rather, "what the culturally relevant context did for the student producing such outcomes."

REFERENCES

Adams, D. W. (1988). Fundamental considerations: The deep meaning of Native American schooling, 1880-1900. *Harvard Educational Review, 58*, 1-28.

Allen, B. A., & Butler, L. (1996). The effects of music and movement opportunity on the analogical reasoning performance of African American and White school children: A preliminary study. *Journal of Black Psychology, 22*, 316-328.

Allen, N., Christal, M., Perrot, D., Wilson, C., Grote, B., & Earley, M. A. (1999). Native American schools move into the new millennium. *Educational Leadership, 56*(7), 71-74

Allison, S., & Vining, C. B. (1999). Native American culture and language. *Bilingual Review, 24*(1/2), 193-207.

Anderman, E. M., Austin, C. C., & Johnson, D. M. (2002). The development of goal orientation. In A. Wigfield & J. S. Eccles (Eds.), *Development of achievement motivation. A volume in the educational psychology series* (pp. 197-220). San Diego, CA: Academic Press.

Anderman, E. M., & Maehr, M. L. (1994). Motivation and schooling in the middle grades. *Review of Educational Research, 64*(2), 287-309.

Anderman, E. M., Maehr, M. L., & Midgley, C. (1999). Declining motivation after the transition to middle school: Schools can make a difference. *Journal of Research and Development in Education, 32*, 131-147.

Anderman, E. M., & Wolters, C. (in press). Goals, values, and affect. In P. Alexander & P. Winne (Eds.), *Handbook of educational psychology* (2nd ed.). Mahwah, NJ: Erlbaum.

Atkinson, J. W. (1957). Motivational determinants of risk taking behavior. *Psychological Review, 64*, 359-372.

Atkinson, J. W. (1964). *An introduction to motivation*. Princeton, NJ: Van Nostrand.

Au, K., & Jordan, C. (1981). Teaching reading to Hawaiian children: Finding a culturally appropriate solution. In H. Trueba, G. Guthrie, & K. Au (Eds.), *Cul-

ture and the bilingual classroom: Studies in classroom ethnography (pp. 139-152). Rowley, MA: Newbury House.

Bailey, C. (1994). *The influence of cultural attributes and stimulus variability on the academically relevant task performance of African-American schoolchildren.* Unpublished master's dissertation, Howard University, Washington, DC.

Bailey, C. T., & Boykin, A. W. (2001). The role of task variability and home contextual factors in the academic performance and task motivation of African American elementary school children. *Journal of Negro Education, 70,* 84-95.

Baron, R. M., & Kenny, D. A. (1986). The moderator-mediator variable distinction in social psychological research: Conceptual, strategic, and statistical considerations. *Journal of Personality and Social Psychology, 51*(6), 1173-1182.

Bee-Gates, D, Howard-Pitney, B., & LaFromboise, T. (1996). Help-seeking behavior of Native American Indian high school students. *Professional Psychology: Research & Practice, 27*(5), 495-499.

Bell, S. R. (2001). *An examination of learning experiences within the socialization practices of African-American parents: An Afrographic analysis.* Unpublished manuscript, Howard University, Washington, DC.

Bell, Y. R., & Clark, T. R. (1998). Culturally relevant reading material as related to a comprehension and recall in African-American children. *Journal of Black Psychology, 24*(4), 455-476.

Bereiter, C., & Engelmann, S. (1966). *Teaching disadvantaged children in the preschool.* Englewood Cliffs, NJ: PrenticeHall.

Bernal, G., Trimble, J. E., Burlew, A. K., & Leong, F. T. L (2001). Introduction: The psychological study of racial and ethnic minority psychology. In *Handbook of racial and ethnic minority psychology.* Thousand Oaks, CA: Sage.

Betancourt, H., & Lopez, S. R. (1993). The study of culture, ethnicity and race in American psychology. *American Psychologist, 48*(6), 629-637.

Boykin, A. W. (1983). The academic performance of Afro-American children. In J. Spence (Ed.), *Achievement and achievement motives: Psychological and sociological perspectives.* San Francisco. Freeman.

Boykin, A. W. (1986). The triple quandary and the schooling of Afro-American children: In U. Neisser (Ed.), *The school achievement of minority children* (pp. 57-92). Hillsdale, NJ: Erlbaum.

Boykin, A. W. (2001). The challenges of cultural socialization in the schooling of African American elementary school children: Exposing the hidden curriculum. In W. Watkins, J. Lewis, & V. Chou (Eds.), *Race and education: The roles of history and society in educating African American students* (pp. 190-199). Boston: Allyn and Bacon.

Boykin, A. W. (2002). Integrity-based approaches to the literacy development of African American children: The quest for talent development. In B. Bowman (Ed.), *Love to read: Essays in developing and enhancing early literacy skills of African American children* (pp. 47-61). Washington, DC: National Black Child Development Institute.

Boykin, A. W., Albury, A. Tyler, K. M., Hurley, E. A., Bailey, C. T., & Miller, O. A. (in press). The influence of culture on the perceptions of academic achievement among low-income African and Anglo American elementary students. *Cultural Diversity and Ethnic Minority Psychology.*

Boykin, A. W., & Allen, B. A. (1998). Enhancing African American children's learning and motivation: Evolution of the verve and movement expressiveness paradigms. In R. Jones (Ed.), *African American youth* (pp. 115-152). Hampton, VA: Cobb & Henry.

Boykin, A. W., & Bailey, C. T. (2000). *The role of cultural factors in school relevant cognitive functioning: Synthesis of findings on cultural contexts, cultural orientations, and individual differences* (Technical Report No. 42). Washington, DC: Center for Research on the Education of Students Placed At Risk (CRESPAR)/ Howard University.

Boykin, A. W., & Cunningham, R. T. (2001). The effects of movement expressiveness in story content and learning context on the analogical reasoning performance of African American children. *Journal of Negro Education, 70*(1/2), 72-83.

Boykin, A. W., Coleman, S. T., Lilja, A. J., & Tyler, K. M. (2004). *Building on children's cultural assets in simulated classroom performance environment.* (Research Vistas in the Communal Learning Paradigm, Report No. 68). Washington, DC: Howard University, Center for Research on Evaluation Standards and Student Testing.

Boykin, A. W., Lilja, A. J., & Tyler, K. M. (2004). The influence of communal versus individual learning context on the academic performance of African-American elementary school students. *Learning Environments Journal, 7,* 227-244.

Boykin, A. W., Tyler, K. M., & Miller, O. A. (2005). In search of cultural themes and their expressions in the dynamics of classroom life. *Urban Education, 40*(5), 521-549.

Boykin, A. W., Tyler, K. M., Watkins-Lewis, K. M., Tyler, K. M., & Kizzie, K. (in press). Culture in the sanctioned classroom practices of elementary school teachers serving low-income African American students. *Journal of Education of Students Placed At-Risk.*

Brice-Heath, S. (1983). *Ways with words: Language, life, and work in communities and classrooms.* New York: McGraw-Hill.

Brown, E. L. (2004). What precipitates change in cultural diversity awareness during a multicultural course? *Journal of Teacher Education, 55*(4), 325-340.

Bryant, A., & LaFromboise, T. D. (2005). The racial identity and cultural orientation of Lumbee American Indian high school students. *Cultural Diversity & Ethnic Minority Psychology, 11*(1), 82-89.

Canning, C., Salazar-Guenther, M., & Polanco-Noboa, J. (2002, February). *Reflecting Latino culture in our classrooms: A quick start for teachers.* Paper presented at the Annual Meeting of the Association of Teacher Educators, Denver, CO.

Cardell, G. W., Cross, W. C., & Lutz, W. J. (1978). Peer learning among Indian students: Extending counselor influence into the classroom. *Journal of American Indian Education, 17*(2), 7-12.

Cartledge, G., & Loe, S. (2001). Cultural diversity and social skill instruction. *Exceptionality, 9*(1/2), 33-46.

Cavanagh, M., & López, M. A. (2004). Understanding the Latino experience. *Independent School, 63*(2), 96-104.

Charleston, G. M., & King, G. L. (1991). *Indian nations at risk task force: Listen to the people*. Washington, DC: Department of Education, Indian Nations At Risk Task Force. (ERIC Document Reproduction Service No. ED343754)

Chavajay, P., & Rogoff, B. (1999). Cultural variation in management of attention by children and their caregivers. *Developmental Psychology, 35*(4), 1079-1092.

Cole, M. (1995). From cross-cultural to cultural psychology. *Swiss Journal of Psychology, 54*(4), 262-276.

Conchas, G. Q. (2001). Structuring failure and success: Understanding the variability in Latino school engagement. *Harvard Educational Review, 71*(3), 475-504.

Delgado-Gaitan, C. (1994). Socializing young children in Mexican-American families: An inter-generational perspective. In P. M. Greenfield & R. R. Cocking (Eds.), *Cross cultural roots of minority child development* (pp. 55-86). Hillsdale, NJ: Erlbaum.

Delpit, L., & White-Bradley, P. (2003). Educating or imprisoning the spirit: Lessons from ancient Egypt. *Theory Into Practice, 42*(4), 283-288.

Deyhle, D. (1986a). Success and failure: A micro-ethnographic comparison of Navajo and Anglo students' perceptions of testing. *Curriculum Inquiry, 16*(4), 365-89.

Deyhle, D. (1986b). Break dancing and breaking out; Anglos, Utes, and Navajos in a border reservation high school. *Anthropology and Education Quarterly, 17*(2), 111-27.

Deyhle, D., & LeCompte, M. (1994). Cultural differences in child development: Navajo adolescents in middle schools. *Theory Into Practice, 33*(3), 156-167.

Deyhle, D. (1995). Navajo youth and Anglo racism: Cultural integrity and resistance *Harvard Educational Review, 65*(3), 403-445.

Dill, E., & Boykin, A. W. (2000). The comparative influence of individual, peer tutoring and communal learning contexts on the text recall of African American students. *Journal of Black Psychology, 26*(1), 65-78.

Dweck, C. S., & Leggett, E. L. (1988). A social-cognitive approach to motivation and personality. *Psychological Review, 95*(2), 256-273.

Eccles, J. S. (1983). Expectancies, values and academic behaviors. In J. T. Spence (Ed.), *Achievement and achievement motives* (pp. 75-146). San Francisco: Freeman.

Eccles, J. S., & Midgley, C. (1989). Stage/environment fit: Developmentally appropriate classrooms for early adolescents. In R. E. Ames & C. Ames (Eds.), *Research on motivation in education* (Vol. 3, pp. 139-186). New York: Academic Press.

Eccles, J. S., Midgley, C., Wigfield, A., Miller-Buchanan, C. M., Reuman, D., Flanagan, C., et al. (1993). Development during adolescence: The impact of stage-environment fit on young adolescents' experiences in schools and in families. *American Psychologist, 48*(2), 90-101.

Elliot, A. J., & Church, M. A. (1997). A hierarchical model of approach and avoidance achievement motivation. *Journal of Personality and Social Psychology, 72*, 218-232.

Elliot, A. J., & Harackiewicz, J. M. (1996). Approach and avoidance achievement goals and intrinsic motivation: A mediational analysis. *Journal of Personality and Social Psychology, 70*, 461-475.

Gallimore, R., & Goldenberg, C. (2001). Analyzing cultural models and settings to connect minority achievement and school improvement research. *Educational Psychologist, 36*(1), 45-56.

Garrett, M. W. (1995). Between two worlds: Cultural discontinuity in the dropout of Native American youth. *School Counselor, 42*(3), 186-196.

Garrett, M. T., Bellon-Harn, M. L., Torres-Rivera, E, Garrett, J. T., Roberts, L. C. (2003). Open hands, open hearts: Working with Native Youth in the schools. *Intervention in School & Clinic, 38*(4), 225-235.

Gay, G. (1975). Cultural differences important in education of black children. *Momentum, 3*, 30-33.

Gay, G. (2000). *Culturally responsive teaching*. New York: Teachers College Press.

Gergen, K. J., Gulerce, A., Lock, A., & Misra, G. (1996). Psychological science in cultural context. *American Psychologist, 51*, 496-503.

Goldenberg, C., Gallimore, R., Reese, L., & Garnier, H. (2001). Cause or effect? A longitudinal study of immigrant Latino parents' aspirations and expectations, and their children's school performance. *American Educational Research Journal, 38*(3), 547-582.

Gordon, B. M. (1982). *Towards a theory of knowledge acquisition for black children. Journal of Education, 40*, 90-108.

Gordon, E. W., & Armour-Thomas, E. (1991). Culture and cognitive development. In L. Okagaki & R. Sternberg (Ed.), *Directors of development: Influences on the development of children's thinking* (pp. 101-120). Hillsdale, NJ: Erlbaum.

Graham, S. (1994). Motivation in African Americans. *Review of Educational Research, 64*(55-117).

Graham, S., Taylor, A. Z., & Hudley, C. (1998). Exploring achievement values among ethnic minority early adolescents. *Journal of Educational Psychology, 90*(4), 606-620.

Greenfield, P. M., Quiroz, B., &. Raeff, C. (2000). Cross-cultural conflict and harmony in the social construction of the child. In S. Harkness, C. Raeff, & C. R. Super (Eds.), *The social construction of the child: The nature of variability* (pp. 93-108). San Francisco: Jossey-Bass.

Gutierrez, K. D., & Rogoff, B. (2003). Cultural ways of learning: Individual traits or repertoires of practices. *Educational Researcher, 32*(5), 19-25.

Hale, J. (2001). Culturally appropriate pedagogy. In W. Watkins, J. Lewis, & V. Chou (Eds.), *Race and education: The roles of history and society in educating African American students*. Boston: Allyn and Bacon.

Hall, D., Weiner, R., & Carey, K. (2003). What new "AYP" information tells us about schools, states and public education. *Education Trust*, 1-12. (ERIC Document Reproduction Service No. ED481814)

Harackiewicz, J. M., Barron, K. E., & Elliot, A. J. (1998). Rethinking achievement goals: When are they adaptive for college students and why? *Educational Psychologist, 33*, 1-21.

Hilberg, R. S., & Tharp, R. G. (2002). *Theoretical perspectives, research findings, and classroom implications of the learning styles of American Indian and Alaska Native students*. Charleston, WV: ERIC Clearinghouse on rural education and small schools. (ERIC Accession No. 468000)

Hilliard, A., III. (1991). Do we have the will to educate all children? *Educational Leadership, 49,* 31-36.

Hodgkinson, H. (1990). *The demographics of American Indians: One percent of the people: Fifty percent of the diversity.* Washington, DC: Institute for Educational Leadership, ERIC Accession Number 330509.

Hollins, E. R. (1996). *Culture in school learning: Revealing the deep meaning.* Mahwah, NJ: Erlbaum.

Hopkins, G., & Bean, T. (1999). Vocabulary learning with the verbal-visual word association strategy in a Native American community. *Journal of Adolescent & Adult Literacy, 42*(4), 274-282.

Howard, T. C. (2001). Telling their side of the story: African-American students' perceptions of culturally relevant teaching. *The Urban Review, 33,* 131-149.

Howard, A., & Scott, R. (1981). The study of minority groups in complex societies. In R. Munroe, R. Munroe, & B. Whiting (Eds.), *Handbook of cross-cultural human development.* New York: Garland.

Hui, C. H., & Triandis, H. C. (1989). Effects of culture and response format on extreme response style. *Journal of Cross-Cultural Psychology, 20,* 296-309.

Hunt, D. E. (1975). Person-environment interaction: A challenge found wanting before it was tried. *Review of Educational Research, 45,* 209-230.

Inglebret, E., & Pavel, M. D. (2000). Curriculum planning and development for Native American and Alaska Natives in higher education. In F. W. Parkay & G. Hass (Eds.), *Curriculum planning: A contemporary approach* (pp. 493-502). Boston: Allyn & Bacon.

Johnson, B. N. (1982). Education as environmental socialization: Classroom spatial patterns and the transmission of sociocultural norms. *Anthropological Quarterly, 55*(1), 31-43.

Jones, J. M. (1997). *Prejudice and racism* (2nd ed.) New York: McGraw-Hill.

Kaplan, A., & Maehr, M. L. (1999). Enhancing the motivation of African American students: An achievement goal theory perspective. *Journal of Negro Education, 68*(1), 23-41.

Kaplan, A., Middleton, M. J., Urdan, T., & Midgley, C. (2002). Achievement goals and goal structures. In C. Midgley (Ed.), *Goals, goal structures, and patterns of adaptive learning* (pp. 21-53). Mahwah, NJ: Erlbaum.

Klem, L. (1995). Path analysis. In L. Grimm & P. R. Yarnold (Ed.), *Reading and understanding multivariate statistics* (pp. 65-98). Washington, DC: American Psychological Association.

Krater, J., Zeni, J., & Cason, N. D. (1994). *Mirror images: Teaching writing in black and white.* Portsmouth, England: Heinemann.

Lake, R. (1990). An Indian father's plea. *Education Digest, 56*(3), 20-23.

Ladson-Billings, G. (2001). Unpacking culture, teaching and learning: The power of pedagogy. In W. Watkins, J. Lewis, & V. Chou (Eds.), *Race and education: The roles of history and society in educating African American students* (pp. 73-88). Boston: Allyn and Bacon.

Ladson-Billings, G. (2005). Is the team all right? *Journal of Teacher Education, 56*(3), 229-234.

LaFromboise, T. D., & Dixon, D. N. (1981). American Indian perception of trust-worthiness in a counseling interview. *Journal of Counseling Psychology, 28*(2) 135-39.

LaFromboise, T. D., Trimble, J. E., & Mohatt, G.V. (1990). Counseling intervention and American Indian tradition: An integrative approach. *Counseling Psychologist, 18*(4), 628-654.

Lee, C. (1991). Big picture talkers/words waling without masters: the instructional implications of ethnic voices for an expanded literacy. *Journal of Negro Education, 60*, 291-304.

Lee, C. (2001). Is October Brown Chinese? A cultural modeling activity system for underachieving students. *American Educational Research Journal, 38*, 97-143.

Leontiev, A. N. (1932). Studies of cultural development of the child: The development of voluntary attention in the child. *Journal of Genetic Psychology, 37*, 52-81.

Luria, A. R. (1976). Cognitive development: Its cultural and social foundations. Cambridge, MA: Harvard University Press.

Meece, J. L., Anderman E. M., & Anderman, L. H. (in press). Educational psychology: Structures and goals of educational settings. *Annual Review of Psychology, 56*.

Meece, J. L., Blumenfeld, P. C., & Hoyle, R. H. (1988). Students' goal orientations and cognitive engagement in classroom activities. *Journal of Educational Psychology, 80*(4), 514-523.

Meece, J. L., Wigfield, A., & Eccles, J. S. (1990). Predictors of math anxiety and its influence on young adolescents' course enrollment intentions and performance in mathematics. *Journal of Educational Psychology, 82*(1), 60-70.

Middleton, M. J., & Midgley, C. (1997). Avoiding the demonstration of lack of ability: An underexplored aspect of goal theory. *Journal of Educational Psychology, 89*, 710-718.

Midgley, C., Feldlaufer, H., & Eccles, J. S. (1989). Change in teacher efficacy and student self- and task-related beliefs in mathematics during the transition to junior high school. *Journal of Educational Psychology, 81*(2), 247-258.

Monkman, K., Ronald, M., & Theramene, F. D. (2005). Social and cultural capital in an urban Latino school community. *Urban Education, 40*(1), 4-33.

Morelli, G. A., Rogoff, B., Oppenheim, D., & Goldsmith, D. (1992). Cultural variation in infants' sleeping arrangements: Questions of independence. *Developmental Psychology, 28*(4), 604-614.

Morgan, H. (1980). How schools fail Black children. *Social Policy, 11*, 49-54.

Moynihan, D. P. (1967). *The Moynihan Report and the politics of controversy*. Cambridge, MA: MIT Press.

Neal, L. I., McCray, A. D., & Webb-Johnson, G. (2001). Teachers' reactions to African American students' movement styles. *Intervention in School and Clinic, 36*, 168-174.

Neal, L. I., McCray, A. D., Webb-Johnson, G., & Bridgest, S. T. (2003). The effects of African American movement styles on teachers' perceptions and reactions. *The Journal of Special Education, 37*(1), 49-57.

Oyserman, D, Coon, H. M., & Kemmelmeier, M. (2002). Rethinking individualism and collectivism: Evaluation of theoretical assumptions and meta-analyses. *Psychological Bulletin*, *128*(1), 3-73.

Paradise, R. (1998). What's different about learning in schools as compared to family and community settings? *Human Development*, *41*(4), 270-278.

Parsons, E. C. (2003). Culturalizing instruction: Creating a more inclusive context for learning for African American students. *The High School Journal*, *86*(4), 23-30.

Pavel, M. D., Curtin, T. R., & Whitener, S. D. (1998). Characteristics of American Indian and Alaska Native Education: Results from the 1990-91 and 1993-94 schools and staffing survey. *Equity & Excellence in Education*, *31*(1) 48-54.

Pewewardy, C. (2004). Playing Indian at halftime: The controversy over American Indian mascots, logos, and nicknames in school-related events. *Clearing House, 77*(5), 180-185.

Piaget, J., & Inhelder, B. (1969). *The psychology of the child* (H. Weaver, Trans.). New York: Basic Books.

Pinkard, N. D. (1999). Lyric reader: An architecture for creating intrinsically motivating and culturally responsive reading environments. *Interactive Learning Environments, 7*(1), 1-30.

Pintrich, P. R. (2000). Multiple goals, multiple pathways: The role of goal orientation in learning and achievement. *Journal of Educational Psychology, 92*(3), 544-555.

Raeff, C (1997). Maintaining cultural coherence in the midst of cultural diversity. *Developmental Review, 17*(3), 250-261.

Reese, L., Balzano, S., Gallimore, R., & Goldenberg, C. (1995). The concept of educación: Latino family values and American schooling. *International Journal of Educational Research, 23*(1), 57-81.

Reese, L., Garnier, H., Gallimore, R., & Goldenberg, C. (2000). Longitudinal analysis of the antecedents of emergent Spanish literacy and middle-school English reading achievement of Spanish-speaking students. *American Educational Research Journal, 37*(3), 633-662.

Rieckmann, T. R., Wadsworth, M. E., & Deyhle, D. (2004). Cultural identity, explanatory style, and depression in Navajo adolescents. *Cultural Diversity & Ethnic Minority Psychology, 10*(4), 365-382.

Robins, R. W., Gosling, S. D., & Craik, K. H. (1999). An empirical analysis of trends in psychology. *American Psychologist, 54*(2), 117-128.

Roeser, R. W., Midgley, C., & Urdan, T. (1996). Perceptions of the school psychological environment and early adolescents' psychological and behavioral functioning in school: The mediating role of goals and belonging. *Journal of Educational Psychology, 88*, 408-422.

Rogoff, B. (2003). *The cultural nature of cognitive development*. New York: Oxford University Press.

Rogoff, B., & Chavajay, P. (1995). What's become of research on the cultural basis of cognitive development? *American Psychologist, 50*(10), 859-877.

Rogoff, B., Mistry, J., Göncü, A, Mosier, C. (1993). Guided participation in cultural activity by toddlers and caregivers. *Monographs of the Society for Research in Child Development, 58*(8), 1-174.

Rothstein-Fisch, C., Greenfield, P. M., & Trumbull, E. (1999). Bridging cultures with classroom strategies. *Educational Leadership, 56,* 64-67.

Rubie, C. M., Townsend, M. A. R., & Moore, D. W. (2004). Motivational and academic effects of cultural experiences for indigenous minority students in New Zealand. *Educational Psychology, 24*(2), 143 - 160.

Safran, S., & Safran, J (1994). Native American youth: Meeting their needs in a multicultural society. *Journal of Humanistic Education & Development, 33*(2), 50-58.

Sampson, E. E. (1977). Psychology and the American ideal. *Personality and Social Psychology, 35*(11), 767-782.

Sarason, S. B. (1997). The public schools: America's achilles hell. *American Journal of Community Psychology, 25,* 771-786.

Sheets, R. H. (1996). Urban classroom conflict: Student-teacher perception: Ethnic integrity, solidarity, and resistance. *The Urban Review, 28*(2), 165-183.

Shweder, R. (1995). Cultural psychology: What is it? In N. R. Goldberger & J. B. Veroff (Eds.), *The culture and psychology reader* (pp. 41-86). New York: University Press.

Slavin, R. E. (1992). When and why does cooperative learning increase achievement? Theoretical and empirical perspectives. In R. Hertz-Lazarowitz & N. Miller (Eds.), *Interaction in cooperative groups: The theoretical anatomy of group learning* (pp. 145-173). Cambridge, England: Cambridge University Press.

Sparks, S. (2000). Classroom and curriculum accommodations for Native American students. *Intervention in School and Clinic, 35,* 259-263.

Spence, J. T. (1985). Achievement American style: The rewards and costs of individualism. *American Psychologist, 40*(12), 1285-1295.

St. Germaine, R. (1995). *Drop-out rates among American Indian and Alaska Native students: Beyond cultural discontinuity.* Charleston, WV: ERIC Clearinghouse on rural education and small schools. (ERIC Accession No. 388492)

Steele, C. (1997). A threat in the air: How stereotypes shape intellectual identity and performance. *American Psychologist, 52,* 613-629.

Stokes, A., Kibour, Y., Martin, S., Miller, O., & Wilson, B. K. (1997). *A focus group insight into African-American students' attitudes and perceptions of classroom life.* Paper presented at the annual meeting of the American Educational Research Association, Chicago.

Stokes, S. M. (1997). Curriculum for Native American students: Using Native American values. *Reading Teacher, 50,* 576-584.

Strickland, B. R. (2000). Misassumptions, misadventures, and the misuse of psychology. *American Psychologist, 55*(3), 331-339.

Sue, D., & Sue, S. (1987). Cultural factors in the clinical assessment of Asian Americans. *Journal of Consulting and Clinical Psychology, 55*(4), 479-487.

Tapia, J. (2004). Latino households and schooling: economic and sociocultural factors affecting students' learning and academic performance. *International Journal of Qualitative Studies in Education, 17*(3), 415-436.

Teel, K. M., Debruin-Parecki, A., & Covington, M. V. (1998). Teaching strategies that honor and motivate inner-city African American students: A school-university collaboration. *Teaching and Teacher Education, 14*(5), 479-495.

Tharp, R., & Gallimore, R. (1989). Rousing minds to life: Teaching learning and schooling in *social context*. New York: Cambridge University Press.

Tracey, M. D. (2005). Enhancing diversity in APA. *APA Monitor, 36*(10), 66-67.

Trueba, H. T. (1993). *From failure to success: The roles of culture an cultural conflict in the academic achievement of Chicano students*. (ERIC Document Reproduction Service No. ED387285)

Tylor, E. (1871). *Primitive culture*. London: Murray.

Tyler, K. M. (1999). *Black parents' preferences toward and practices of six distinct cultural learning orientations*. Unpublished master's dissertation, Howard University, Washington, DC.

Tyler, K. M., Boykin, A. W., Boelter, C. M., & Dillihunt, M. L. (2005). Examining mainstream and Afrocultural value socialization in African American households. Journal of Black Psychology, 31(3), 291-311.

Tyler, K. M., Boykin, A. W., & Miller, O. A. (2005). Investigating cultural discontinuity in the classroom experiences of low-income African American school children. Submitted to *Social Psychology Of Education*.

Tyler, K. M., Boykin, A. W. & Walton, T. R. (in press). Cultural considerations in teachers' perceptions of student classroom behavior and achievement. *Teaching and Teacher Education*.

Urdan, T. (1997). Achievement goal theory: Past results, future directions. In M. L. Maehr & P. R. Pintrich (Eds.), *Advances in motivation and achievement* (Vol. 10, pp. 99-141). Greenwich, CT: JAI Press.

U.S. Bureau of the Census. (2001). *Overview of race and Hispanic origin*. Washington, DC: U.S. Deparment of Commerce, Economics, and Statistical Administration.

Valencia, R. R., & Black, M. S. (2002). Mexican-Americans don't value education!—-on the basis of the myth, mythmaking, and debunking. *Journal of Latinos and Education, 1*(2), 81-103.

Van der Veer, R., & Valsiner, J. (1994). *Understanding Vygotsky*. Oxford, England: Blackwells.

Velez-Ibanez, C. (1996). *Border visions: The cultures of Mexicans of the southwest United States*. Tucson: University of Arizona Press.

Vygotsky, L. S. (1962). *Thought and language*. Cambridge, MA: MIT Press.

Walton, S. (1994). *The influence of task variability and background stimulation on the task performance of low-income African-American and Euro-American children*. Unpublished master's dissertation, Howard University, Washington, DC.

Webb-Johnson, G. (2002). Are schools ready for Joshua? African American culture among students identified as having behavioral/emotional disorders. *Qualitative Studies in Education, 15*(6), 653-671.

Webb, N., & Palinscar, A. S. (1996). Group processes in the classroom. In D. Berliner & R. Calfee (Eds.), *Handbook of educational psychology* (pp. 841-873). New York: Simon and Macmillan.

Wertsch, J. V. (1985). *Vygotsky and the social formation of mind*. Cambridge, MA: Harvard University Press.

Westby, C. (1995). Developing cultural competence: Working with culturally/linguistically diverse families. In *Teams in early intervention introductory module*.

Albuquerque, NM: Training and Technical Assistance Unit. New Mexico University Affiliated Program University of New Mexico School of Medicine.

Wigfield, A., & Eccles, J. S. (1992). The development of achievement task values: A theoretical analysis. *Developmental Review, 12*(3), 265-310.

Wortham, S., & Contreras, M. (2002). Struggling toward culturally relevant pedagogy in the Latino diaspora. *Journal of Latinos and Education, 1*(2), 133-144.

CHAPTER 5

TEXTBOOK PEDAGOGY

A Sociocultural Analysis of Effective Teaching and Learning

Richard Walker and Mike Horsley

VIGNETTE

My name is Julie Delrayne and I am currently Head Teacher of Science at Greendale High School. I have taught Senior Science for 10 years at six different government comprehensive high schools in New South Wales, Australia. I have been a Higher School Certificate Examination Science marker for more than 3 years and have also worked as a consultant on a senior Science textbook. As an executive teacher in my school, I am also involved in implementing the Quality Teaching Program in my major subject of physics. I also have been involved in an international educational project, working with science teachers from junior secondary schools and villages from Samoa. Together we look at ways of incorporating more practical science experiences into teaching and helping the Samoan teachers to try to instigate these changes themselves without relying on the education authority.

I guess that my teaching styles have changed since I first began teaching. I depend less heavily on existing learning materials and feel that some teach-

Effective Schools, 105–133

ing strategies are more effective at helping students search out the meaning of information. I use textbooks and photocopied pages to provide opportunities for skill development in areas like literacy and comprehension, technology skills (for example, the use of the internet), numeracy skills, scientific skills involving scientific equipment, and to provide opportunities for independent skills (for example reading, summarizing, and analysing).

I am always modifying and adapting published learning materials to suit my classes by photocopying, cutting and pasting, and making class sets of notes from other books. At one of the schools I taught at the school had very few sets of texts, they were very old and we had to make our own copied notes all the time. I also construct worksheets, including diagrams, on the computer to help the students understand critical concepts.

The reason for modifying and adapting learning materials for my Science classes is to adjust materials to suit the ability levels of my students and to leave out information not in the course or to leave out outdated or inaccurate material. This allows me to scaffold student learning, something that is important for all students but most important for students who are less self-directed, such as middle school students Another important reason is to allow me to add to the textual material in various ways such as to include processing questions to accompany diagrams, to add definitions or explanations (or to provide spaces for students to add their own definitions), or to make the material more interesting.

Last year I was asked to speak to a group of beginning teachers about to teach Year 12 Physics for the first time, about their choice of textbook (there are four Physics texts on the market) for their class. I told them that one of the texts was most difficult for students and two were easier for students to understand. I told the beginning teachers to choose the most difficult, because the students will search out the other easier ones anyway to help them learn and thus will use a range of texts and information sources in the course—whereas if they have the easier less complex text they will never look for the more difficult one and as a result will tend to use only one text and information source for their learning.

Effective schooling (Reynolds, Bollen, Creemers, Hopkins, Stoll, & Laagerweij, 1996) and teaching (Berliner, 1994) have been studied extensively. Research into effective schooling has been concerned with showing that schools do make a difference to student academic performance and other educational outcomes. The effective schooling literature has shown that factors like professional leadership, high expectations, purposeful teaching, a learning organization and homeschool partnerships are important in effecting change in valued student outcomes. While much research into effective schooling has been conducted independently of effective teaching research (Ayres, Sawyer, & Dinham, 2004), this latter research literature has been concerned to show that student outcomes are influenced in important ways by teacher activities. The effective schooling literature has shown that effective teachers take a very active role in the classroom, maximize student instructional time, ensure that students achieve mastery in new content areas, emphasize review of prior learning, and are adept at responding to student answers and questions. Australian research into effective teaching in the context of high stakes external examinations (Ayres, Sawyer, & Dinham) shows that effective teachers of high achieving final year high school students have well managed classrooms, deploy a range of learning and teaching strategies from whole class learning to independent student study, and develop an engaging classroom learning climate which involves good relationships with students.

Research into effective teaching and schooling, however, has tended to ignore the textbook pedagogy, or use made of textbooks and other learning resources, of good teachers. This chapter explains the notion of textbook pedagogy and analyses its complementarity with an important aspect of effective teaching, that of pedagogical content knowledge. The chapter then presents a sociocultural analysis of the teacher use of textbooks and other learning resources in the classroom. Subsequently, a series of research studies of textbook and learning resource use in classrooms are presented and interpreted in terms of this sociocultural analysis. Two empirical studies, conducted by members of the Teaching Resources and Textbook Research Unit (TREAT) at the University of Sydney, examine how teachers adapt and use textbooks and other resources in their classrooms. A further Australian national study conducted by TREAT members explores the use of photocopied materials in primary and secondary classrooms using Copyright Australia Limited data (Horsley & Walker, 2003) and investigates the way that teachers utilized these materials in their classrooms.

TEXTBOOK PEDAGOGY AND TEXTBOOK RESEARCH

The term *textbook pedagogy* was initially used by Lambert (2002) in his discussion of research on the classroom use of textbooks and teaching and learning materials. The term refers (Horsley & Walker, 2003; Lambert) to the ways that teachers use texts in the classroom, how they access and adapt texts, and how they create a context for their use. As such the term refers to the teacher mediated use of textbook, worksheet, and learning resource artifacts. The term has also been used to refer to text features and characteristics that may improve or constrain learning through their impact on teacher use of the text in the classroom.

The necessity for this term emerged from recent developments in the area of textbook research (Horsley & Lambert, 2001; Lambert, 1999, 2000, 2002). There have been three main foci in research about textbooks, the first has been conducted from the perspective of the economics of education and has involved surveys of textbook supply and expenditure. Watson (2000), for instance, examined the relationship between textbook spending and student performance data and showed that schools with higher spending patterns on school texts had statistically higher levels of student achievement. In the United States, as a result of the equity and finance legal reform movement a number of studies were undertaken comparing state spending and school finance systems on textbook spending (Indiana State Department of Education, 1999). This movement, and the research associated with it established adequacy formulas for the funding of educational resources, including textbooks. The second focus has been concerned with content and/or style analyses of textbooks and teaching materials (Horsley, 2001; Horsley & Lambert). In this latter approach textbooks and text resources have commonly been studied as if they were inert artifacts. The major focus in this research orientation has been content analysis of texts, with the analyses of the content being used as the basis for inferences about possible social effects of textbooks. Sleeter and Grant (1991), for instance, analyzed the representation of race, gender, disability, and social class in American social studies, language arts, reading, science, and mathematics textbooks used in first grade through to eight grade. The third focus has involved research into the design and features of school textbooks considered optimal for student learning and understanding (Altbach, Kelly Petrie, & Weiss, 1991; Chambliss & Calfee, 1998; Elliott & Woodward, 1990). This research has considered such issues as text difficulty and readability (Chall & Conrad, 1991), text organization and structure (Anderson & Armbruster, 1984; Chambliss & Calfee), and questions (Armbruster & Ostertag, 1993) and illustrations in text (Levin & Mayer, 1993). This type of research has culminated in publications (e.g., Ciborowski, 1992; Singer & Donlan, 1989) which provide teachers with an understanding of text features and ways of using these text features to improve student understanding and learning of textbook content. Although this research focus has involved examination of student comprehension and learning from textbooks in classrooms, it has not involved investigation of the ways that textbooks are used by teachers in their teaching.

While several studies (Alverman, 1987, 1990; Zahorik, 1990, 1991) have investigated teacher use of textbooks in classrooms, the focus of these studies has been on teacher decision making and teacher style. Alvermann found that the textbook is an important influence in interactive decision making by the teacher and that teachers use textbooks to

mediate teacher and student discussion in different ways. Zahorik found
that teachers had a dominant style in their teaching with textbooks and
that this style was related to their beliefs and ideology. These studies, however, as with textbook research from the three foci identified above, have
provided little understanding of the specific ways teachers use textbooks
and teaching resources in their teaching, or how they modify textbook
and teaching resources for classroom use. This weakness of the textbook
research literature has led textbook researchers to call for greater research
into the classroom *use* of textbooks and other teaching and learning materials (Horsley & Lambert, 2001; Pingel, 1999). Horsley and Lambert have
noted that very little research into the use of textbooks has been based on
actual observation of teachers selecting textbooks and teaching materials
and using them with their students in their classrooms. Nor has research
taken the next step and, after examining teacher mediated use of texts,
explored how students use teaching and learning materials, together or
independently, to learn. Furthermore, despite the fact that much teaching
and learning material used in classrooms is photocopied (Horsley, 2002)
little research has been undertaken to analyze how teachers select, copy
and use these materials in their teaching, nor has research considered the
role teacher pedagogical knowledge plays in the selection and adaptation
of teaching and learning materials.

PEDAGOGICAL CONTENT KNOWLEDGE

Pedagogical content knowledge (Shulman, 1987) refers to the specialized
professional knowledge that teachers have concerning the concepts that
students will find difficult, the most appropriate strategies for teaching
these concepts, and the most useful resources for teaching them. It consists of three main components: knowledge of the subject matter, knowledge about students and their characteristics, and third, knowledge of the
school, community, and classroom contexts in which the learning takes
place. Pedagogical content knowledge inevitably embodies, invokes, and
focuses on "those aspects of the subject that are most germane to its
teachability" (Shulman). This knowledge includes the most regularly
taught topics, the most useful forms of representation of the concepts,
most successful analogies, demonstrations, examples, and illustrations,
and the ways of making the subject discipline familiar and understandable to others. As such pedagogical content knowledge is related to and
complements textbook pedagogy.

It is now widely accepted that teachers develop pedagogical content
knowledge (Shulman, 1987) through their teaching experiences and
interactions with students, and that this knowledge is an important aspect

of their teaching expertise. Thus, pedagogical content knowledge can be learned and is often passed on within a professional community such as that which exists in a school or subject department. Though teaching can appear to be highly individualized, the strength of the school or departmental culture, and associated resources, can be so powerful that professional knowledge is often shaped significantly by received wisdom and observed practice (Lambert, 2002). Professional knowledge is also powerfully shaped by textbooks as they provide an important representation of disciplinary knowledge. The professional and disciplinary knowledge presented in textbooks is important for many teachers but is particularly influential for novice teachers who are often most comfortable teaching what has been taught before, using "authorised" methods and teaching resources (Horsley & Laws, 1993).

Pedagogical Content Knowledge and Textbook Pedagogy

As noted in the preceding section, pedagogical content knowledge and textbook pedagogy are related and complementary; a significant component of pedagogical content knowledge is teacher knowledge of concepts students find difficult to learn, and a significant component of textbook pedagogy is teacher use of resources to assist student learning of these concepts, as well as teacher knowledge of how these resources can be located, and adapted for use in lessons.

This complementarity, although little researched, has been the subject of some investigation. In their book *Missing the Meaning* Peacock and Cleghorn (2004) have advanced the notion of the Teacher—Learner—Text (TLT) interface to frame studies exploring the use of print and non-print text materials in science classrooms. They argue that interactions between teachers, texts, and learners are central to effective learning environments, and that choice and use of texts is explained by the interactions between;

- teachers' education, experiences, views of learners and science, and preferred teaching approaches
- learners' characteristics such as language, preconceptions, gender and culture and
- features of text materials such as quality, demands on learners, embedded assumptions in various school, social and cultural settings.

Although they do not refer explicitly to pedagogical content knowledge or textbook pedagogy, many of the studies reported in *Missing the*

Meaning explore textbook pedagogy and some examine the interaction of textbook pedagogy and pedagogical knowledge. In an observational study of Kenyan science teachers, for instance, Murilla (2004) identified lack of subject content knowledge as influencing ways teachers used texts and other resources in class.

The complementarity has also been investigated in studies by Sikorova (2003) and Sartor (2004); Sikorova and Sartor explored the way that teachers customize, modify, and change published textbooks and other associated learning materials to make them more suitable for use in specific learning situations. In Sikorova's study of the transformation of curriculum materials by teachers of mathematics and the Czech language, it was found that the most popular reason for modifying maths learning materials was to fit in with curriculum requirements, whereas the most popular reason for modifying Czech language learning materials was to make the texts more interesting. After conducting interviews with teachers of maths and the Czech language in primary and lower secondary schools, Sikorova identified the following ways the teachers modified textbook subject matter:

- making the subject matter more comprehensible for students (e.g., more examples, other ways of presenting, illustrations)
- making the subject matter better organized, more transparent (e.g., networking, mapping)
- making the subject matter more interesting (attractive to students)
- selecting the core subject matter
- simplifying the subject matter, making it easier
- reducing the subject matter
- leaving out complicated matters and tasks
- producing teacher prepared text

The investigation of teachers' modification of texts revealed that pedagogical content knowledge and textbook pedagogy practices were complementary in that teachers used their pedagogical content knowledge to adapt, change, select, and procure and then use texts based on the perceived needs of the students in their classrooms. Sartor (2004), in an unpublished study on secondary science teachers resourcing of their teaching, also found that teachers used their pedagogical content knowledge and textbook pedagogy to select, procure, and then use teaching and learning resources that matched their approach to teaching, curriculum, assessment and reporting requirements, and met the learning needs of their students.

SOCIOCULTURAL THEORIES AND TEXTBOOK PEDAGOGY

Sociocultural theory and research provides an important body of knowledge for textbook researchers to use in their analysis of classroom based observations of teachers and of the teacher mediated use of teaching and learning resources and artifacts. Sociocultural theories in education have their origins in the work of the Russian psychologist Lev Vygotsky and his colleagues. They emphasize the social nature of learning and thinking, the embeddedness of learning and thinking in social, cultural, and historical contexts, as well as the distribution of learning and thinking across other persons, resources, and artifacts. Sociocultural researchers concerned with school learning have explored student learning in collaborative contexts (Rogoff, 1998) and in classroom communities of learners (for instance, Brown, 1997).

While there are many sociocultural theories which derive from the initial work of Vygotsky (for instance Greeno & The Middle-School Mathematics Through Applications Project Group, 1998; Engestrom, 1987; Rogoff, 1998), all share the following assumptions (John-Steiner & Mann, 1996): learning and cognitive development are considered to be fundamentally social and to have their origins in social processes; language and other symbol systems are considered to play a central role in learning and cognitive development; learning and cognitive development need to be considered in the historical context of the individual's own activities, as well as those of the community and culture more generally. Although sharing these common assumptions, some sociocultural researchers have emphasized the view that learning and cognitive development involve participation in, and enculturation into, the cultural practices of various communities (Rogoff), while others have focussed their attention on the aspects of the environment (Greeno & The Middle-School Mathematics Through Applications Project Group) that can facilitate or support learning and cognitive development, or alternatively constrain or limit these processes. Yet other researchers have developed sociocultural understanding of the activity systems (Engestrom) within which human beings learn, work, and otherwise conduct their affairs.

A central notion in the sociocultural approach which links learning and cognitive development, and which has therefore been of significance to educators, is that of the Zone of Proximal Development (ZPD). This notion is also important in that it provides a sociocultural explanation of the way in which processes which exist at a social level are transformed so that they become individual processes and attributes. The zone of proximal development has been defined (Vygotsky, 1978) as "the distance between the actual developmental level as determined through problem solving under adult guidance or in collaboration with more capable peers" (p. 86). Vygotsky and subsequent sociocultural theorists consider that it is through the creation of zones of proximal development that learners become able to successfully engage in activities, with the assistance of more capable others, that they are unable to complete successfully by themselves. The cognitive scaffolding provided by more capable others when zones of proximal development are created allows learners to internalize or appropriate higher order thinking skills, such as problem solving and self-regulation.

The internalizing of thinking in the zone of proximal development is assisted by the mediating role played by cultural artifacts and tools. These tools may range in scope from symbol systems such as reading, writing, and mathematics to computer programs, textbooks and other learning resources. Textbooks, worksheets and teaching, and learning materials arc cultural artifacts and tools which can provide scaffolding and cognitive structuring for learners as they engage in activities for which they are developing cognitive competence and skill. In effective teaching and learning, such tools and artifacts are mediated in their use in the zone of proximal development by more capable others, such as teachers and other students, who scaffold the appropriate use of the materials in learning. For this reason, the sociocultural analysis of textbook use in classrooms emphasizes the extent to which teachers use texts in ways which create zones of proximal development.

It is in the Zone of Proximal Development that learning occurs, according to Vygotsky (1978), and it is in this zone that learning contributes to, and leads development. This is in contrast to what Vygotsky referred to as the Zone of Actual Development (ZAD). The Zone of Actual Development refers to what students can do alone and unassisted. When skills learned in the Zone of Proximal Development have been fully mastered they become part of the Zone of Actual Development and no longer contribute to development. Therefore, when teachers assign tasks and students are able to complete them without assistance, the tasks are within the students' Zone of Actual Development and the skills required have already been mastered. Similarly, from the perspective of textbook research, when students use textbooks in the absence of mediation by the teacher, or other students, and are able to successfully complete assigned tasks they are operating in the Zone of Actual Development.

Two major sociocultural theories are used in this chapter to further develop the notion of textbook pedagogy and the mediated use of textbooks by teachers: the cultural practice approach of Rogoff (1998, 1994) and colleagues (Rogoff, Matusov, & White, 1996) and the extension to the zone of proximal development by Valsiner (1987, 1997). Although these two theoretical approaches are quite distinct, key notions from both theories can profitably be applied to the understanding of the mediated use of textbooks by teachers

The cultural practice approach (Rogoff, 1994, 1998), has extended upon Vygotsky's initial ideas concerning the zone of proximal development by emphasizing the way in which individuals become established members of a community of practice. The term "community of practice" refers to a sociocultural group that collaborates to achieve shared goals through particular practices and activities. Although these practices might vary considerably between different communities, such as the practices of various professional communities and those of lifestyle communities like surfers and motorcyclists, they are highly valued by their members and they provide the context (Miller & Goodnow, 1995) in which learning and development takes place. The members of such communities vary greatly in their mastery of community practices, however the community provides the context in which the more established members assist the less established in their mastery of community practices through joint involvement and collaboration. As individuals are enculturated into the practices of a community their identity undergoes change (Rogoff) and they may likewise contribute to change in community practices.

Schools and the classrooms within them constitute a particular kind of community of practice, sometimes called a community of learners (Brown & Campione, 1994). In these school communities of practice students are enculturated into academic practices in general, as well as the practices of specific academic disciplines. Textbooks and other learning materials play an important role in these enculturation processes. Textbooks, as the main representations of knowledge within particular academic domains, also enculturate students into both general academic practices and the practices of specific academic disciplines. As students progress from elementary school to high school the kinds of textbooks used changes so that the relative emphasis on general academic practices becomes less important while the emphasis on disciplinary knowledge and practices becomes paramount. In senior high school textbooks are explicitly concerned with enculturating students into the central assumptions and foundational knowledge of disciplines, as well as disciplinary ways of thinking and creating knowledge. Thus textbooks are important cultural tools which enculturate learners into academic and disciplinary knowledge and which assist teachers in the scaffolding of student learning.

Valsiner's (1987, 1997) theoretical reconstruction and extension of the zone of proximal development, which has been applied to other sociocultural issues (for example, Pressick-Kilborn & Walker, 2002), is also valuable in extending the sociocultural analysis of textbook use in the classroom. While Valsiner (1997) retains the notion of the Zone of

Proximal Development, the concept is reconstructed with the aim of relating it to two new zones of learning and development: the Zone of Free Movement (ZFM) and the Zone of Promoted Action (ZPA). Essentially these two new zones are concerned with the constraints and affordances for learning and development which operate in the present moment. The Zone of Free Movement (ZFM) notion explains the impact of constraints or limitations on learning and development while the Zone of Promoted Action explains the promotion of learning and development. All three zones are considered by Valsiner to be socially constructed and all are interlinked, however, the two new zones are concerned with the present moment while the zone of proximal development is concerned with near future possibilities. Thus, the promotion of learning in the Zone of Promoted Action (ZPA) and the constraints on learning posed in the Zone of Free Movement (ZFM), provide the possibilities for learning and action which become actualized in the zone of proximal development.

From the perspective of textbooks and their use by teachers, Valsiner's system of zones provides a way of considering the affordances or benefits of texts as well as their limitations or constraints. Textbooks can therefore be considered as tools which both promote and constrain learning and which provide important possibilities for learning in the zone of proximal development. Teachers can use texts in ways which promote or constrain learning, and there are aspects of textbook design and presentation which impact on the mediated use of texts by teachers. The use of the textbook by the teacher determines the extent to which learning from text is promoted or constrained.

Changing conceptions of the nature and role of textbooks are very much in accord with sociocultural analyses of textbooks and their use by teachers. The changing conception of textbooks, as indicated in Table 5.1, is very much related to changing views and theories concerning the nature of student learning. When, under the influence of behaviorist theories, learning was considered to involve the acquisition of knowledge textbooks were primarily vehicles for transmitting knowledge and therefore focussed on the provision of information and congruent activities. Teachers and textbooks were the knowledge authorities and textbooks structured programs of learning for both teachers and students. As learning came to be conceptualized as knowledge construction in constructivist theories, textbooks were increasingly conceptualized as providing opportunities for students to construct understanding through the provision of multiple knowledge sources; multiple sources provided parallel narratives involving written text and illustrations and allowed students to develop their own understandings. Textbooks also increasingly provided students

Table 5.1.   Changing Conceptions of Textbooks

Roles	Transmission	Constructivist	Sociocultural
Teaching and learning materials e.g., textbooks	Source of information Basis of transmission Knowledge authority Structure of a teaching and learning program	Activity and inquiry source Provision of multiple sources within text for student knowledge construction Multiple sources for teacher selection	Scaffolds learning Enculturates students into disciplinary knowledge and practices Source of inquiry activities Basis of explicit teaching
Student	Passive recipient of information provided in teaching and learning materials and by teacher	Active agent in text inquiry activities	Uses text in collaboration with other students, Engages in authentic activities of disciplinary communities
Teacher	Authority in knowledge domain, Dissemination of appropriate knowledge	Creator of environments for active learning and inquiry.	Collaborative participant in enculturation process. Uses text to establish common student goals, Identifies and utilizes texts to create ZPD for students Uses materials to enculturate students into key disciplinary understandings

with activities for learning, reflecting constructivist views of the active nature of learning.

As sociocultural theories increasingly come to dominate understandings of the nature of learning, and as sociocultural analyses of textbooks become more prominent conceptions of textbooks are likely to change in ways suggested in this chapter. Textbooks are likely to increasingly be seen as enculturating students into disciplinary knowledge and practices, as the basis of scaffolded learning experiences and explicit teaching, and as the basis for collaborative student activity. As Table 5.1 indicates, the roles of teachers and students have also changed as theories of learning have changed.

Empirical Studies of Textbook and Learning Material Use

We turn now to a consideration of the mediated use of textbooks and learning materials in three empirical studies: two analyses of expert and novice teacher textbook and learning resource use respectively, and an analysis of Copyright Agency Limited (CAL) school photocopying records. In the two studies of expert and novice teachers an observational schedule, the TEXTOR (textbook observational record) was used as the basis of data gathering and analysis; the TEXTOR was first developed by Horsley and Laws (1993) for use in classroom observational studies of textbook and resource use. The value of this observational instrument in classroom based textbook research has been acknowledged by Pingel (1999).

In the two empirical studies of teachers the TEXTOR schedule sought to identify the following aspects of textbook and learning material use:

- how students read the text
- whether prereading or activation and assessment of prior learning took place
- what tasks were set by the teacher
- the teacher's purpose for using the texts in class
- how students used the text in the classroom
- the length of time texts were used in teaching and learning
- the use of texts for homework
- how the student gained access to texts
- the details and condition of the materials being used
- the length of time taken to issue and collect texts

Although this observational instrument was not developed according to a sociocultural theoretical framework, it does lend itself to such an analysis and interpretation. Observational schedule items such as student reading and prereading activities provide insights into teacher scaffolding of textbook activities, while items concerning teacher set tasks and student learning activities provide an understanding of the mediated use of textbooks in the classroom. Other schedule items provide information on the availability, utility and appropriateness of texts used in the classroom. Finally, it needs to be noted that while information on all of the schedule items was collected in the two empirical studies, research data are reported selectively in the endeavor of demonstrating the importance of textbook pedagogy, and of analyzing textbook pedagogy in terms of sociocultural theories.

STUDY 1 EXPERT TEACHER USE OF TEXTBOOKS AND LEARNING RESOURCES

Background to the Study

This study provided an in-depth examination of an expert teacher's use of textbooks and other learning resources. The teacher observed in this study, a teacher of secondary English and history, met expert teacher criteria in a number of ways. She had a strong academic background with an honors degree in one of her teaching subjects, and teaching credentials corresponding to accomplished teaching standards. She was an experienced teacher with 5 years experience in two different schools and had developed a considerable body of pedagogical knowledge. The principal of her school identified her as one of the "strongest teachers in the school"; she was active in school curriculum development, extracurricular activities, and at the time of the study she was contributing to the professional development of other teachers through presentations at conferences organized by her professional subject associations. As well, she had started studying in a master's degree program in education.

She taught in a private catholic girls school, with approximately 800 students, in the western suburbs of Sydney. The school's textbook policy required that students purchase their books from subject booklists provided to them. In both English and history students purchased their own texts, either second hand or from the school hire scheme.

The teacher was observed teaching selected lessons in Grades 7, 8, 9 and 11 over the period of a week; in all, 12 lessons were observed. In general, this teacher's use of textbooks was consistent across such factors as the subject taught and the grade level of students. While the teacher adjusted her teaching according to student ability and subject area taught, she nevertheless showed considerable consistency in the ways she used textbooks to assist student learning and understanding. For this reason, the findings discussed below are not differentiated according to subject area or student level or ability.

Findings of the Study

Access to Resources

Students brought their own texts and used them in class for 7 out of the 12 lessons observed in the study. Where students did not have access to relevant text material, the teacher provided these materials by:

- distributing handouts especially designed by the teacher for the lesson (six lessons)
- reading from or making overheads from a text that only she had a copy of (two lessons)
- handing out cards on which photocopied documentary material had been pasted on (one lesson)
- using books from the library (one lesson)
- using primary sources (1950s women's weeklies) (one lesson)

Text materials derived from textbooks and kits were used in 10 of the 12 lessons observed. Textbooks were used in seven lessons, though not for the entirety of the lesson, and in ways that reflected the teacher's goals and not the underlying structure of the text. Additionally, for the 10 lessons where text materials were used they were used for approximately forty minutes or 75% of the instructional time available while over the twelve lessons observed text materials were used for 58% of the instructional time available.

Student and Teacher Reading

The teacher used a wide variety of techniques to engage students with the texts used in her classroom. These included the teacher reading in class, students reading silently, and students reading aloud individually or in groups. However, it was not uncommon for all of these activities to occur in the one lesson. It was also not uncommon for the teacher to organize different groups of students who were assigned to read portions of texts in different ways. For instance, in a lesson on a drama script the teacher read the text and then students read aloud in groups and then some students were chosen to read parts from the script. Generally, the teacher followed best practice in asking students to read silently but often modelled good reading practice by reading initial passages or passages that were seen as particularly important.

Photocopying of Resources

The photocopied handouts used by the teacher fell into two categories:

1. Text material that was designed as the knowledge and activity basis of the lesson. This material consisted mostly of extracts photocopied from a range of textbooks and kits that the students did not have access to.

2.   Major assignments and project tasks for students which required significant documentation.

The teacher gave students photocopied handouts in 9 out of the 12 lessons and in total distributed 575 pages. This represented a total of 48 pages per lesson for the 12 lessons observed, or approximately several pages per student per lesson. Approximately 6 minutes of each lesson were taken up with organizing the distribution of handouts to students, a process which required effective management routines on the part of the teacher.

Teaching and Learning Strategies Observed

A feature of the lessons observed was the quantity and quality of the prereading strategies that the teacher employed. Prereading activities were employed in 10 (83%) of the lessons observed. The teacher used a number of different prereading techniques to assist students in the development of reading schemas and to focus and direct their reading for specific purposes. Preview of vocabulary occurred in three lessons (25%), questions posed prior to reading featured in five lessons, written questions were explained prior to reading in four lessons (25%).

Examples of other prereading activities included: explanations; circling and discussing words in primary sources; recapping stories before reading on; discussion of vocabulary in the reading; reading through handouts and then explaining activities; setting the scene before individuals read; discussing stimulus material (graphs and illustrations in a textbook) and explaining how to complete activities; and questions posed during reading.

Teacher Purpose in use of Text Materials

The teacher's purpose in using text materials was inferred from the TEXTOR observation schedule by analyzing how the teacher used the materials. She used the texts for the following wide variety of purposes:

- source of knowledge for student activity (eight lessons)
- source of stimulus material for activity (six lessons)
- aid to organizing cooperative and collaborative learning (five lessons)
- basis of class discussion (five lessons)
- independent student work (five lessons)
- source of problems and exercises for student problem solving (two lessons)
- support for individual progression (one lesson)

The tasks that students were assigned in relation to textual material were extremely varied and included: small group discussion, whole class discussion, answering teacher/worksheet questions, summarizing, comparison of text sources, and student research work.

Homework

The teacher used textbooks and text materials for homework activities in 8 of the 12 lessons (66%). This was made easier by the fact that students had their own copies of the texts and so could use them at home. In most cases the homework developed from classroom lessons and involved a variety of activities; in only one lesson did the homework consist of finishing off questions started in class. Homework activities over the period of the study consisted of: tables constructed from text to answer teacher set questions; writing monologues for a character using the text as an information source; summarizing work done in class; developing role plays based on role cards from a kit; subtexting activities started in class to be finished for homework.

ANALYSIS OF THE FINDINGS

Perhaps the most important finding from this study was the considerable use made by the teacher of textbook and other text-based learning resource materials. This is notable in itself as Australian teachers, unlike teachers in some states in the United States for instance, are not required to use specific textbooks and are not encouraged in their training or by their professional associations to use textbooks. This finding, therefore, highlights the importance of the use of such resources by highly experienced teachers and suggests that this area of teaching should be given greater attention in studies of effective teaching.

Although the study did not specifically address the teacher's pedagogical knowledge, the variability in the teacher's use of textual material suggests that this usage was dependent upon her extensive pedagogical experience. She clearly used texts and other learning materials in very adaptive and flexible ways to meet the needs of her students. The proportion of instructional time in lessons devoted to the use of textual materials, as well as the large numbers of photocopied pages used in lessons, indicates the very considerable lengths the teacher went to in assisting her students in their learning and understanding. While texts were mostly used as a basis for constructive student learning activities and cooperative learning they were also used to a considerable extent as a way of providing students with critical disciplinary content, and thus were used by the teacher to enculturate students into the disciplines of history and English.

The study showed that the expert teacher's main use of textbooks was to represent and provide subject matter content for her students. She did not photocopy exercises or activities as she was confident of designing these activities for herself, instead she chose to compile resources from sources that reflected her view of the discipline.

The study also showed that the expert teacher used texts in the classroom in many different ways, thus demonstrating the importance of the notion of textbook pedagogy. She made use of texts in varied ways in general in her lessons as well as in the course of a single lesson; for instance, she read from the text, had students read aloud from the text individually and in groups, and had students read silently from the text. She used textual materials as the basis of both individual student learning activity and collaborative student learning and discussion. In all instances, however, the teacher scaffolded student learning to a very considerable extent; this scaffolding included a variety of prereading activities such as explanation and previewing. There were no instances where the teacher did not provide such scaffolding prior to or during the use of textual material. From the perspective of sociocultural theories, this finding leads to two important and related inferences. First, as the students were always working with assistance, they spent little or no time in the zone of actual development. Second, the teacher, through this scaffolding, was creating zones of proximal development for her students and contributing to their learning and development. The very considerable adaptations that the teacher made to textbook and textual material suggest that she was attempting to create affordances for student learning, and was creating zones of promoted action. It is also clear, from the sociocultural perspective, that textbooks and other learning resources are important learning artifacts for both teachers and students.

STUDY 2 NOVICE TEACHER USE OF TEXTBOOKS AND LEARNING RESOURCES

Background to the Study

This study investigated the textbook and learning resource use of a group of novice teachers. Ten lessons of seven newly qualified teachers were observed within the first 3 months of the teachers commencing their teaching careers. Seven of the novice teachers were observed once and three of them were observed on two occasions. The teachers were all members of teacher professional subject associations and became involved in the study through attendance at a conference for beginning teachers.

Findings of the Study

Access to Resources

Of the 10 lessons observed, 5 were resourced through teacher notes and handouts, 3 involved the use of photocopied chapters from textbooks, 1 lesson was resourced through textbooks from a book room, and 1 lesson did not involve textbook resources. In the 10 lessons the seven teachers handed out photocopied sheets in eight (80%) of the lessons. The use of photocopied textbooks in three lessons occurred because textbooks were not available due to school funding constraints. In one of these lessons an old text was updated through the addition of photocopied material while in another lesson the teacher photocopied two chapters on the same topic from different textbooks so that students had access to multiple sources of information. In these three lessons the teachers and students used the materials as both sources of knowledge and as sources for class activities.

Photocopying of Resources

The seven teachers handed out 532 photocopied pages in the 10 lessons observed. Since the lessons contained 207 students, the teachers handed out approximately two and a half pages per student per lesson. When asked why they selected and prepared these teaching resources, the teachers indicated that they sought to provide the appropriate knowledge and activities required by the curriculum and its outcomes, and they sought to address student abilities, interests, age, and stage level. The material copied by the teachers, however, mostly consisted of exercises and activities intended for the students to work on unassisted.

Student Reading

Typically the lessons of the novice teachers proceeded with the teacher introducing and previewing the material to be covered with the students. Students then read the material silently or aloud around the classroom. Discussion ensued to highlight key concepts or ideas, and then students completed tasks set out in the materials. The novice teachers rarely read to the class themselves or modeled reading strategies. Three of the teachers used reading aloud around the classroom as a way of focusing student attention on the content and structure of the lesson. Although some group work was observed students were only observed to read in groups in one lesson.

Teaching and Learning Strategies Observed

In four of the lessons observed, including the three where photocopied textbook chapters were used, textbooks formed the basis of the structure of the lesson. The teachers first introduced the content and outcomes of the lessons, and then provided a brief review of the subject matter to be learned. The remainder of the lessons concentrated on exploring the information provided in the texts and completing the activities that were included in them. In two of the lessons, teachers prepared their own photocopied text material based on their own research into the topic. In both cases schools had not purchased new textbooks for the students and the teachers were not prepared to use old textbooks with old knowledge. Also in both cases the teachers used new textbooks and internet sources to construct teaching notes with activities for the students. These were photocopied and distributed to all students.

The teachers also prepared photocopied text materials in three other lessons. In one of the lessons, a history teacher prepared photocopied sheets consisting of multiple knowledge sources, charts, diagrams, pictures, source documents, and illustrations. These were collated from a number of textbooks and selected to provide a collage of sources that the students investigated in collaborative groups. In another lesson, the teacher produced a photocopied sheet of exercises and activities for the students in her class. The students in this class had access to textbooks and other knowledge sources but the teacher regarded them as too difficult and as not meeting the learning needs of her students. The new photocopied tasks and activities also had a greater literacy focus than those in the available textbook. Finally in an art lesson, the teacher compiled and produced a collage of illustrative material for her students. She used this to explain key understandings to students and to provide them with multiple knowledge sources.

ANALYSIS OF THE FINDINGS

The study demonstrates that novice teachers spend considerable time and energy in locating, selecting, and preparing text resources for their lessons. There were, however, many differences in the way these teachers used these resources when compared to the expert teacher. Although the novice teachers also scaffolded student use of text material and learning resources through various activities, they spent far less time in this scaffolding process than the expert teacher, and the nature of their scaffolding differed from that of the expert teacher. A significant proportion of the time novice teachers spent in scaffolding and prereading activities was spent in focusing student attention and explaining to students the purpose and structure of the lesson. There was less emphasis on alerting students to the underlying structure of the

knowledge sources and teaching and learning materials, and significantly more emphasis on the topic and content that formed the outcomes of the lessons. The expert teacher's scaffolding, on the other
hand, was far more focused on using the materials to help students
understand the knowledge to be learned. Novice teachers scaffolding
was far more focused on the content itself.

These differences in scaffolding strategies also reflect differences in the
materials selected, procured and photocopied for lessons by expert and
novice teachers. The expert teacher, with greater pedagogic experience
and knowledge, chose teaching and learning material that best represented disciplinary understandings and which met the learning needs of
her students; often these consisted of multiple sources of knowledge and
were presented in collage format. She rarely made use of activities or
exercises from textbooks. While the novice teachers also made use of multiple sources from texts, they made much greater use of textbook activities, exercises, problems, or questions. This reflected their more limited
pedagogical experience and knowledge. The expert teacher, on the other
hand, had her personal fund of activities and exercises which she could
draw upon as needed.

There were also significant differences in the use made of textbooks
and learning resources by expert and novice teachers. Novice teaching
strategies often featured students working individually to complete activities and tasks while the expert teachers' teaching focussed on collaborative and group use of texts and learning resources. In novice teacher
classrooms there was far less emphasis on teaching and learning strategies
that scaffolded and unpacked the teaching and learning materials for students, far less time was spent on teaching students to deconstruct the lit-
erary and structural aspects of knowledge sources, and far less
collaboration and joint construction of meaning took place between the
teacher and the students and amongst students themselves.

From the perspective of a sociocultural analysis of expert and novice
teacher use of textbooks, it is clear that novice teachers were much less
concerned with using texts and learning resources to enculturate students
into the academic disciplines taught. While the expert teacher used text
material to provide students with essential disciplinary knowledge,
including multiple knowledge sources, novice teachers mostly used texts
and learning resources as sources of activities and exercises for students.
Novice teachers provided students with much less scaffolding than expert
the expert teacher, and the nature of this scaffolding differed in important ways. Novice teachers were also much less likely to use collaborative
teaching and learning approaches than the expert teacher, and they were
much more likely to have students working individually and unassisted in
their classes. This suggests that novice teachers were much less likely to

create zones of proximal development for their students so that their students were much more likely to be working in the zone of actual development.

STUDY 3 AN ANALYSIS OF COPYRIGHT AGENCY LIMITED (CAL) SCHOOL PHOTOCOPYING RECORDS

Background to the Study

Each year the Copyright Agency Limited (CAL) commissions an independent copyright survey in 120 schools in three states in Australia. The survey is representative of urban and rural, private and government schools, and is conducted throughout the entire year. The results of the survey are subsequently statistically adjusted to provide national photocopying data. In 2001, for instance, the survey showed that on average 243 per primary student and 203 per secondary were copied—76% from books, mostly textbooks, with artistic and other works making up the remainder of the percentage. These records are used to assign the funds that are collected by CAL to the authors and publishers of the photocopied works. The photocopying data collected by CAL provides a rich source of data on teacher selection of resources for use in teaching and learning but is not generally available to researchers.

During 1998 CAL undertook legal action to increase the amount of funds received per photocopied page under the Copyright Act to reflect the increased costs of publishing educational materials. In preparation for this action individual school and textbook title records from the 1997-98 surveying period were made available to the second author who acted as an expert witness for CAL. Subsequently the 50 most photocopied textbooks from the 1997-1998 period were identified and categorized by school level and subject area, and the most commonly copied pages from these texts were identified. The most commonly photocopied pages were subsequently analyzed to determine the nature of the teaching and learning activities photocopied by schools.

This large scale study of school photocopying study of the pages copied was followed up by small scale observational and interview research. Three teachers, two primary and one secondary, identified by the photocopying survey and known to TREAT researchers were contacted. They were interviewed and their use of the photocopies in their classrooms were observed and analyzed.

Commonly Photocopied Teaching and Learning Resources

The 50 most commonly photocopied textbooks in the CAL 1997-1998 survey were identified and the five books at the top of this list are presented in Table 5.2. The table shows that the most commonly photocopied book was a primary title, *Heinemann's Observational Survey of Early Literacy Achievement*, which was copied in 44 schools with a total of 3,451 copies of pages made. This resulted in the distribution of almost 20,000 Australian dollars to the authors and publishers of this work alone. The next most copied books, also primary books, were *Signpost Maths 6* and *Mission 2000: Daily Meditations* which were copied in 115 and 37 schools respectively. The two remaining books in the list were secondary mathematics books which were copied in 81 and 69 schools respectively. The great volume of photocopying of textual material in schools is, however, demonstrated by the fact that the number of pages copied from these five books ranged from 3,451 at the top to 2,605 at the bottom of the list.

As indicated previously, the 50 most photocopied textbooks from 1997-1998 were analyzed by school level (primary/secondary) and subject area and the most photocopied pages from these books were subject to content analysis to determine the extent to which they consisted of the following:

- tasks and activities for students
- knowledge to be used as the basis for teaching
- knowledge and tasks together
- assessment instruments to measure student outcomes
- teaching and learning support such as homework contracts or forms
- teacher resource materials such as guidebooks on teaching

Table 5.2. The Five Most Commonly Photocopied Textbooks

Total Pages Copied	Instances	Title of Text	Publisher
3,451	44	Heinemann Observational Survey Of Early Literacy Achievement	Heinemann
3,028	115	Signpost Maths 6	Pascal Press
2,667	37	Mission 2000: Daily Meditations	Tabor Publishing
2,634	81	8 Plus Maths	Longman Cheshire
2,605	69	7 Plus Maths	Longman Cheshire

This photocopying data showed that the majority of the most copied 50 textbooks were primary titles; there were 34 primary textbooks compared to 16 secondary books. This large preponderance of primary books may reflect the fact, as is the case in New South Wales, that primary government and nongovernment schools are not allocated funds specifically for teaching and learning materials. Consequently primary teachers have a much greater need to photocopy text materials for their classes. There were significant differences, as can be seen in Tables 5.2 and 5.3, in the textbook subject areas photocopied in primary and secondary schools. In primary schools, English textbooks were most copied while in secondary schools mathematics textbooks were most copied. In primary schools, mathematics books were the next most copied followed by LOTE books and books containing contract material for independent student work. In secondary schools, English and science books were the next most copied followed by LOTE and other books.

Analysis of the content of photocopied pages indicated, for the most part, similar material was copied in primary and secondary schools. The majority of the copied material in both cases consisted of activities, exercises, questions and tasks for lessons, and possibly for homework. Descriptive or expository knowledge text was copied to much lesser extent, although more copying of this type of material occurred in secondary schools. Smaller amounts of photocopying reflected teacher need for teacher support and resource materials, although more of this material was copied in primary schools than secondary schools.

Teacher Interviews and Observation

In this extension of the photocopying study, two primary school teachers and one secondary teacher involved in the national survey and known to TREAT researchers were interviewed and observed in relation to their use of photocopied materials. Two of the primary teachers interviewed used the same photocopied page, page 83, from *Signpost Maths 6* in different ways. One teacher photocopied a class set of the page and distributed the page to students for homework. This use reflected this teacher's use of text materials in much of her mathematics teaching. The teacher typically conducted mathematics lessons by demonstrating to students how to complete a mathematical problem and then set seatwork and tasks where students could practice individual solutions to the problems. Much of her photocopying was to provide homework and unassisted student work. The other teacher used this page in a different way, using the photocopies as the basis of collaborative problem solution. She also photocopied a class set of the page but made on overhead projection of the page and

Table 5.3.   Most Copied Primary Books

Subject	Total	Activities/ Tasks	Knowledge	Assessment	Teacher Support	Teacher Resource
English	17	10			4	3
Math	8	7				1
Science	4	2	1			1
LOTE	3	1			1	1
Contract	2			2		

Table 5.4.   Most Copied Secondary Books

Subject	Total	Activities/ Tasks	Knowledge	Assessment	Teacher Support	Teacher Resource
English	2					2
Maths	10	9			1	
Science	2	1	1			
LOTE	1	1				
Other	1		1			

worked with the class to jointly construct an answer to problem one. Then students worked in groups to complete some of the other problems. Tasks not finished in class were then assigned for homework.

The secondary teacher taught Italian and used photocopies from *Avanti*, the 27th most photocopied title in the study. This teacher had a textbook available, not *Avanti*, for use with her class but photocopied pages 81, 106 and 107 from *Avanti* for her students. In using page 106 she argued that the activities in *Avanti* for this outcome better suited the ability and interests of her class. She used page 107 for role play activity and conversation based upon the diagram provided for the lesson in *Avanti*. The teacher also noted that in one class in previous years she had used page 107 for unassisted student activity.

ANALYSIS OF FINDINGS

There are several points to note in relation to this study. First, it is the first major study of the teaching and learning resources photocopied by teachers from textbooks and other text-based sources. As such, it provides important insights into the amount of material copied by teachers and allows inferences about the possible use made of this material by them.

The study demonstrates the very large amount of photocoping under-taken by teachers in Australian schools and therefore highlights the importance of photocopied textual material in their teaching. The great majority of this material consisted of individual activities, exercises, and questions in both primary and secondary classrooms; this finding suggests that these materials are predominantly used by teachers for independent work on the part of individual students. This inference is supported by the observations of three teachers in the extension of this study as well the observational studies of expert and novice teachers reported earlier; This inference suggests that students working on these materials are working in the zone of actual development. Some photocopied material, however, had been designed for co-operative student learning activity and was therefore presumably used by teachers for collaborative student work and the creation of zones of proximal development. The finding that exposi-tory material is copied by primary and secondary teachers also supports the findings of the two earlier observation studies and suggest that this is an important resource in their teaching. Second, the study of the three teachers emphasizes the fact that different teachers use the same materi-als in very different ways or that themselves also use the same materials in different ways. This finding underscores the importance of research into textbook pedagogy; at the same time this finding suggests that caution needs to be exercised when attempting to draw inferences about the use of photocopied textual materials in the absence of actual observations of their use.

OVERALL CONCLUSIONS

The three studies reported in this chapter clearly demonstrate that teach-ers make great use of textbooks and other learning resources and that they photocopy considerable quantities of textual material for use in their classes. These findings suggest that studies of teaching effectiveness have ignored, or given insufficient attention, to this significant aspect of teach-ing. All of the studies demonstrate that textbooks and textual materials play an important role in enculturating students into academic practices in general, and, in the case of senior students, into more specific aca-demic disciplinary knowledge and practices.

The observational studies of teachers also demonstrate the main con-tention of textbook pedagogy, that is that teachers use textbooks and other learning materials in very different ways. Thus, textbook research which focuses on the optimal design of texts (Chambliss & Calfee, 1998) or on the content of textbooks, while important in its own right, ignores the important issue of the use made of texts. Furthermore, the different uses made of textbooks and learning resource materials can be analyzed from the perspective of sociocultural theories. This analysis suggests that some teachers, expert or more experienced teachers, are more likely to use these materials in ways which promote student learning and development through the creation of zones of proximal development while others, less experienced or novice teachers, are more likely to use these materials for unassisted learning in the zone of actual development. This differentiation in use is believed to be related in important ways to teachers' pedagogical knowledge and experience, a relationship which needs explicit investigation in future research.

All of the studies reported in the chapter demonstrate that, from a sociocultural perspective, textbooks and other textual materials are important classroom artifacts or tools and that teachers, as well as students, play an important mediating role in their classroom use.

REFERENCES

Altbach, P. G., Kelly, G. P., Petrie, H. G., & Wiess, L. (Eds.). (1991). *Textbooks in American society: Politics, policy, and pedagogy*. Albany: State University of New York Press.

Alverman, D. (1987). The role of textbooks in teachers' interactive decision making. *Reading Research and Instruction, 26*, 115-127.

Alverman, D. (1990). Teacher-student mediation of content area texts. *Theory into Practice, 27*, 142-147.

Anderson, T. H., & Armbruster, B. B. (1984). Content area textbooks. In R. C. Anderson, J. Osborn, & R. J. Tierney (Eds.), *Learning to read in American schools: Basal readers and content texts* (pp. 193-226). Hillsdale, NJ: Erlbaum.

Armbruster, B. B., & Ostertag, J. (1993). Questions in elementary science and social studies textbooks. In B. K. Britton, A. Woodward, & M. Brinkley (Eds.), *Learning from textbooks: Theory and practice* (pp. 69-94). Hillsdale, NJ: Erlbaum.

Ayres, P., Sawyer, W., & Dinham, S. (2004). Effective teaching in the context of grade 12 high stakes external examination in New South Wales, Australia. *British Educational Research Journal, 30*, 141-165.

Berliner, D. C. (1994). Teacher expertise. In T. Husen & T. Postlethwaite (Eds.), *The international encyclopedia of education* (2nd ed., pp. 6020-6026). Oxford, England: Pergamon.

Brown, A. L. (1997). Transforming schools into communities of thinking and learning about serious matters. *American Psychologist, 52*, 399-413.

Brown, A. L., & Campione, J. C. (1994). Guided discovery in a community of learners. In K. McGilly (Ed.), *Classroom lessons: Integrating cognitive theory and classroom practice* (pp. 229-272). Cambridge, MA: MIT Press.

Chall, J. S., & Conrad, S. S. (1991). *Should textbooks challenge students? The case for easier or harder books*. New York: Teachers College Press.

Chambliss, M., & Calfee, R. (1998). *Textbooks for learning: Nurturing children's minds.* Oxford, England: Blackwell.

Ciborowski, J. (1992). *Textbooks and the students who can't read them: A guide to teaching content.* Cambridge, MA: Brookline Books.

Elliott, D. L., & Woodward, A. (1990). *Textbooks and schooling in the United States: Eighty-ninth yearbook of the National Society For the Study of Education: Part 1.* Chicago: The University of Chicago Press.

Engestrom, Y. (1987). *Learning by expanding: An activity-theoretical approach to developmental research.* Helsinki, Finland: Orienta-Konsultit.

Greeno, J. G., & The Middle-School Mathematics Through Applications Project Group. (1998). The situativity of knowing, learning, and research. *American Psychologist, 53,* 5-26.

Horsley, M. (2001). Emerging institutions and pressing paradoxes. In M. Horsley (Ed.), *The future of textbooks? Research about emerging trends* (pp. 35-52). Sydney, Australia: TREAT

Horsley, M. (2002). Homage to the handout. In M. Horsley (Ed.), *Perspectives on textbooks* (pp. 57-71). Sydney, Australia: TREAT.

Horsley, M., & Lambert, D. (2001). The secret garden of classroom and textbooks. In M.Horsley (Ed.), *The future of textbooks? Research about emerging trends* (pp. 8-24). Sydney: Australia: TREAT.

Horsley, M., & Laws, K. (1993, June). *Textbooks in the practicum.* Paper presented at the Fifth National Practicum Conference, Macquarie University, Australia.

Horsley, M., & Laws, K. (1993, July). *Textbooks aren't terrible. Textbook use in the classroom: The gap between theory and practice.* Paper presented at the Australian Teacher Education Association Conference, Perth, Australia.

Horsley, M., & Walker, R. (2003, September). *Textbook pedagogy: A sociocultural approach.* Invited keynote address to the biennial conference of the International Association for Research on Textbooks and Educational Media, Bratislava, Slovakia.

Indiana Department of Education (1999). *Textbook funding survey.* Retrieved June 16, 2004, from http://www.doe.state.in.us/legwatch/1999/99appendixD.html

John-Steiner, V., & Mahn, H. (1996). Sociocultural approaches to learning and development: A Vygotskian framework. *Educational Psychologist, 31,* 191-206

Lambert, D. (1999). Exploring the use of textbooks in KS3 geography classrooms: A small scale study. *The Curriculum Journal, 10,* 85-105.

Lambert, D. (2000). Textbooks and the teaching of geography. In C. Fisher & T. Binns (Eds.), *Issues in Geography Education* (pp. 108-119). London: Routledge.

Lambert, D. (2002). Textbook pedagogy. In M. Horsley (Ed.), *Perspectives on textbooks* (pp. 18-33). Sydney, Australia: TREAT.

Levin, J. R., & Mayer, R. E. (1993). Understanding illustrations in text. In B. K. Britton, A. Woodward, & M. Brinkley (Eds.), *Learning from textbooks: Theory and practice* (pp. 95-114). Hillsdale, NJ: Erlbaum.

Miller, P. J., & Goodnow, J. J. (1995). Cultural practices: Toward an integration of culture and development. In J. J. Goodnow, P. J. Miller, & F. Kessel (Eds.), *Cultural practices as contexts for development* (pp. 5-16). San Francisco: Jossey-Bass.

Murilla, B. (2004). Use of science textbooks in Kenyan classes. In A. Peacock & A. Cleghorn (Eds.), *Missing the meaning* (pp. 121-132). New York: Palgrave Macmillan.

Peacock, A., & Cleghorn, A. (Eds.). (2004). *Missing the meaning*. New York: Palgrave Macmillan.

Pressick-Kilborn, K., & Walker, R. A. (2002). The social construction of interest in a learning community. In D. McInerney & S. Van Etten (Eds.), *Research on sociocultural influences on learning and motivation* (Vol 2, pp. 153-182). Greenwich, CT: Information Age.

Pingel, F. (1999). *UNESCO guidebook on textbook research and textbook revision*. Hannover, Germany: Verlag Hahnsche Buchhandlung.

Reynolds, D., Bollen, R., Creemers, B., Hopkins, D., Stoll, L., & Laagerweij, N. (1996). *Making good schools*. London: Routledge.

Rogoff, B. (1994). Developing understanding of the idea of communities of learners. *Mind, Culture. and Activity, 1*, 209-229.

Rogoff, B. (1998) Cognition as a collaborative process. In W. Damon, D. Kuhn, & R. Siegler (Eds.), *Handbook of child psychology, Vol. 2* (5th ed., pp. 679-744). New York: Wiley.

Rogoff. B., Matusov, B., & White, S. (1996). Models of teaching and learning: participation in a community of learners. In D. Olson & N. Torrance (Eds.), *The handbook of cognition and human development* (pp. 388-414). Oxford, England: Blackwell.

Sartor, A. (2004). *Modifying texts for classroom use*. Unpublished manuscript, University of Sydney, Australia.

Shulman, L. (1987). Knowledge and teaching: Foundations of the new reform. *Harvard Educational Review, 15(2)*, 1-22.

Sikorova, S. (2003, September). *Transforming curriculum as teacher's activity*. Paper presented to the biennial conference of the International Association for Research on Textbooks and Educational Media, Bratislava, Slovakia.

Sleeter, C. E., & Grant, C. A. (1991). Race, class, gender and disability in current textbooks. In M. W. Apple & L. K. Christian-Smith (Eds.), *The politics of the textbook* (pp. 78-110). Routledge: New York.

Singer, H., & Donlan, D. (1989). *Reading and learning from text* (2nd ed.). Hillsdale, NJ: Erlbaum.

Valsiner, J. (1987). *Culture and the development of children's action*. Chichester, England: Wiley.

Valsiner, J. (1997). *Culture and the development of children's action: A theory of human development* (2nd ed.). New York: Wiley.

Vygotsky, L. S. (1978). *Mind in society*. Cambridge, MA: Harvard University Press.

Watson, R. (2000). *Relation between school book spending and school results*. Report for the UK Publisher's Association, London.

Zahorik, J. (1990). Stability and flexibility in teaching. *Teaching and Teacher Education, 6*, 69-80.

Zahorik, J. (1991). Teaching style and textbooks. *Teaching and Teacher Education, 7*, 185-196.

CHAPTER 6

MOTIVATIONAL AND COGNITIVE ASPECTS OF CULTURALLY ACCOMMODATED INSTRUCTION

The Case of Reading Comprehension

Robert Rueda

Several years ago, I worked on a research project investigating literacy development of Latino bilingual students in special education settings. The particular classroom I was observing was a combined fourth-fifth grade special education "pull-out" classroom where students spent part of their school day. The classroom, school, and community were heavily populated by low-income Spanish-speaking students. Low English proficiency, pervasive poverty, gang problems, poorly trained teachers, and other factors all characterized this setting, and academic achievement was noticeably low.

Effective Schools, 135–156
Copyright © 2006 by Information Age Publishing

Part of the task in this project was to observe the dynamics of the classroom and the work in which students engaged. Most of the work in literacy was taken from packaged commercial programs on a piecemeal basis, for example specific worksheets and exercises. On the particular day that I was observing, the task was to write a one paragraph essay about Abraham Lincoln. Rather than focus on the quality of the narrative, or an understanding of the significance of Lincoln's life, or connections to relevant concepts such as democracy and freedom, points were awarded for specific structural features such as use of capital letters, headings, indenting paragraphs, and use of proper punctuation. While these writing conventions are clearly important to academic success, the academic work of these students was almost entirely focused on these low level mechanics. The nature of the topic, or connections to other areas of the curriculum or to literacy, was apparently not seen as necessary. What was missing from these repetitive exercises, from the students' perspective, was purpose and connections to existing knowledge and interests. Without these features, the exercises were meaningless activities done, if at all, for teacher approval. One student in particular was especially disruptive in the classroom, often joking, moving around the room, conversing with other students. The three-sentence paragraph he produced in response to the Abraham Lincoln prompt was torturously produced in the span of 45 minutes, but with a great deal of teacher monitoring and threatening. Even in Spanish, which the teacher allowed, there were many errors in the student's text.

Several days later, the same student came to class looking very sad and upset. Since the teacher was not present at that moment, the paraeducator, an older Latina female who had a "grandmotherly" style with the students, asked what was wrong. The student indicated that there had been a gang-involved robbery the prior evening, and that a close cousin had been shot. While he was reluctant to talk about the incident, she asked if he would sit down and write about what had happened and his feelings. The student went to a corner and began to write, producing a long-hand description of what had happened and his reactions to the events. The document that he produced was over seven pages long. Moreover, he did not look up from his desk the entire hour and a half that he wrote, stopping only when asked to go to lunch by the teacher. While grammatical and spelling errors were frequent, the change in engagement and effort between the two contexts was striking.

How do we understand this example from a motivational and/or cognitive perspective? What are the specific factors and processes that can produce such a change in behavior? Why do so many students with backgrounds similar to this student do poorly in school and fail to engage in academic tasks on a consistent basis? What are the characteristics of students in urban public schools and how should schools think about addressing cultural and other differences? The remainder of the chapter will briefly describe past efforts to deal with cultural issues in classroom settings, and propose some motivational and cognitive considerations in specifying possible mechanisms which might be used to guide such efforts in the future. Before doing that, it is useful to quickly examine the characteristics of the students under consideration because they exemplify the rapid and significant changes which have transformed many urban public school settings.

A Brief Look at the Changing Student Population

In the United States the nature of the school age population is changing as a result of immigration, local economic conditions which impact mobility, and other factors. For example, the 100 largest urban school districts in the U.S. represent less than 1% of all school districts but educate 23% of all public school students. The percentage of students who were other than White, non-Hispanic in these districts was 69%, compared to 42% in all school districts. Forty-six percent of the students were eligible for free and reduced-price lunch, compared to 37% of students in all schools (Sable & Hoffman, 2005).

In 2003, the 42% of public school students who were considered to be part of a racial or ethnic group was significantly greater than the 22% reported in 1972. A large part of the increase was driven by growth in the proportion of students who were Hispanic, from 6% in 1972 to 19% in 2003. In the Western part of the United States, ethnic and racial group enrollment exceeded White enrollment in 2003. The percentage of public school reporting enrollment consisting of other than White, non-Hispanic membership was 98.2% in 2003 (Livingston & Wirt, 2005).

At the same time, there remain systematic and long-standing differences in achievement for certain groups who differ in language and cultural backgrounds. This is especially true in reading and literacy. Typically, Anglo American and many Asian groups do relatively well in U.S. schools; Latinos, African Americans, Native Indians, and Pacific Islander tend do much less well. There is of course great variability within any group. The National Assessment of Educational Progress (NAEP) has provided data from Grades 4 and 8, indicating that in both grades Anglo and Asian/Pacific Islander students had higher average scores than American Indian, Black, and Latino students. At both grade levels, poverty (as measured by free or reduced-price lunch eligibility) was negatively associated with student achievement (Livingston & Wirt, 2005). While more extensive documentation could be provided, the general patterns have been outlined. It should be recognized that there is considerable within-group diversity in the achievement levels of different groups of students, but relatively regular patterns among groups. In any case, virtually all schools now deal with a more diverse population, many of whom do not succeed academically, and thus schools must decide how to contend with cultural differences in achievement. How have schools addressed this issue? There is an established body of work in the area of school effectiveness that forms the backdrop for this discussion.

School Effectiveness Research

While a comprehensive treatment of educational reform efforts that have tried to address low academic achievement is beyond the scope of this chapter, it is informative to briefly look at the major trends since they form the backdrop for the current discussion. There have been recognizable "waves" of reform in the United States, beginning with the publication of *A Nation at Risk* (National Commission on Excellence in Education [NCEE], 1983) continuing to the current No Child Left Behind (NCLB). The school effectiveness literature has shifted from the examination of effective school correlates (Brophy & Good, 1986; Levine & Lezotte, 1990) following simple input-output models, to school restructuring efforts (Murphy, 1991), to comprehensive school reform (Datnow & Kemper, 2002; Stringfield et al., 1997) (See also Ellett & Teddlie, 2003, for a comprehensive overview of the historical development of this work). As this work has developed over time, more focus has been placed on examining contextural effects relevant to school improvements. These include investigating school effects across different school contexts, trying to account for varying dimensions such as socioeconomic status, age/grade levels, and type of community. In addition, recent work has been characterized by the use of more sophisticated mathematical modeling tools. The general factors that have been identified in the effective schools research are the following: (a) effective instructional arrangements and implementation; (b) a focus on student acquisition of central learning skills; (c) productive school climate and culture; (d) high operationalized expectations and requirements for students; and (e) appropriate monitoring of student progress (Levine & Lezotte, 1990).

In spite of the considerable amount of school effectiveness research, a recent survey of superintendents from large urban school districts indicated that the achievement differences between minority and nonminority students re-examined one of their major concerns (Huang, Reiser, Parker, Muniec, & Salvucci, 2001). It is interesting to note that while culturally and linguistically diverse students have often been the targets of efforts to reform schools (Stringfield, Datnow, & Ross, 1998), the treatment of cultural differences per se have received much less attention. As Stringfield et al. note, with the exception of *Éxito Para Todos*, the Spanish version of *Success For All* (Slavin, Madden, & Wasik, 1996), there is little research on even program implementation, let alone on subsequent improvements in student achievement, in multilingual, multicultural contexts. Most importantly, with few exceptions (Bennett et al., 2004) culture and sociocultural factors in learning have not been systematically addressed other than as defining characteristics of the students under consideration. There is, hence, a need to begin more systematic exploration of the specific learning-related mechanisms that underlie cultural factors—especially in critical areas such as reading comprehension that are known to mediate later school success.

Cultural Issues in Classroom Settings

Early attempts to identify social and cultural factors influencing minority students' literacy development came from the observation that many of these children (and ethnic minority children in general) do relatively poorly in school, as noted above. Language-related factors were addressed with the creation of bilingual programs, but other efforts focused on the social dimensions of diverse students' lives and experiences in out of school contexts (California State Department of Education, 1986; Jacob & Jordan, 1987). These efforts attempted to move beyond the default approach, which is to ignore differences, often with the stated or implied assumption that whatever pre-existing knowledge skills children and their communities bring to school is deficient or irrelevant and could safely be ignored (Valencia, 1997). The most common alternative approach to address cultural differences has been some form of cultural accommodations in instructional settings. These approaches are varied, but the common thread is that they attempt to reduce presumed student-classroom mismatches in terms of the sociocultural features of the classroom, for example in the types of instructional activities, materials, and discourse/interactional characteristics commonly found in classrooms settings. Often, the rationale for this approach has been couched in arguments about social equality (Au & Mason, 1991). See the following for another example:

> Only when teachers understand the cultural backgrounds of their students can they avoid ... culture clash. In the meantime, the ways in which teachers comprehend and react to students' culture, language, and behaviors may create problems. In too many schools, students are, in effect, required to

leave their family and cultural backgrounds at the schoolhouse door and live in a kind of "hybrid culture" composed of the community of fellow learners. (Cole, 1995)

A common practice in many school settings is the provision of teacher professional development that focuses on monolithic or general cultural factors with the assumption that these will lead to more sensitive or responsive teaching practices. "Learning styles" is a common approach with several variants in which attempts are made to assess a learner's preferred learning style and then match it with instruction. This particular form of accommodation has been heavily criticized on conceptual and measurement grounds (Gutierrez & Rogoff, 2003; Irvine & York, 1995; Stahl, 1999). Other common approaches include the use of culturally familiar reading materials (Abu-Rabia, 1996; Jimenez, 1997; Kenner, 1999, 2000; McCarty, 1993); culturally familiar content ("funds of knowledge") (Moll & González, 2004), or accommodation to students' discourse and interactional features (McCarty, Wallace, Lynch, & Benally, 1991; Wilkinson, Milosky, & Genishi, 1986).

While a complete review of the work in this area is beyond the scope of the chapter, one of the best known and most well-documented efforts in this area is represented in the work at the Kamehameha Schools in Hawaii (Au & Mason, 1981; Tharp, 1982). This project is of special interest because it specifically focused on reading comprehension. The Kamehameha Early Education Program (KEEP) researchers systematically studied the out-of-school cultural and discourse practices of native Hawaiian students, and then attempted to incorporate these features into classroom reading instruction. Some of these features included self-selected turns by students, overlapping speech, and the absence of explicit and overt control of the interaction by the teacher. Unlike the conversational patterns typical of most classrooms where the teacher grants permission for student talk, a pattern much more like that found in students' homes was used whereby students were permitted to engage in interactions with each other and with the teacher freely and spontaneously without waiting for teacher permission.

Careful documentation of the classroom indicated that when classroom reading instruction was compatible with interaction patterns in Hawaiian children's native culture, students demonstrated higher levels of achievement-related behaviors (defined as academic engagement, topical and correct responses, number of idea units expressed, and logical inferences) all went up during the reading lesson. However, it is difficult to know how much of the observed effects were due to cultural accommodations since additional features such as a specially designed reading program, individual teacher mentoring, intensive professional development, and a laboratory school setting were all part of the overall intervention. However, this work has been widely cited as an empirical foundation for cultural modifications in instruction.

Existing Theory

In one of the few efforts to systematically spell out the elements of cultural factors in learning, Tharp (1989) included both culturally variable as well as more universal constants. These "psychocultural variables" represented factors that schools must take into account in order to create positive educational outcomes for various cultural groups. These included:

- *Social organization*—how people organize themselves in groups or as individuals; for example, if they have an individualistic or group-oriented approach to accomplishing tasks;
- *Sociolinguistics*—the conventions of interpersonal communication different groups follow, such as wait time, proximity, rhythm and flow of conversation, and how turn-taking is organized;
- *Cognition*—patterns of thought that can influence learning new skills and knowledge, such as specific cognitive abilities or cognitive styles; and
- *Motivation*—values, beliefs, expectations, and aspirations that influence how, whether, and why individuals approach and persist at specific goals or tasks.

Tharp also identified two "constants" that were deemed important regardless of student culture, including *focus on language development* and *contextualized instruction*. The main hypothesis is that implementation of these factors should produce culturally compatible learning environments and thus improved student outcomes. The question remains as to whether these cultural accommodations are effective. It is commonly assumed that this is the case:

> Research has shown that students learn more when their classrooms are compatible with their own cultural and linguistic experience.... [Students' learning is disrupted] when the norms of interaction and communication in a classroom are very different from those to which the student has been accustomed.... The aspects of culture that influence classroom life most powerfully are those that affect the social organization of learning and the social expectations concerning communication. (Saravia-Shore & Garcia, 1995, p. 57).

However, the question of effectiveness is a difficult one to answer, and more appropriate for another review (Demmert & Towner, 2003; Rueda, 2003). It is fair to say that there is not an abundance of well-designed research to draw from, but there are other problems including difficulty in agreeing upon, defining, and operationalizing key constructs. Much of the work is descriptive and not detailed enough to know what specifically was done; studies focus on many diverse areas and mix several approaches so that the effects of any one factor are not known.

One complicating factor in this area of work is that culture is not an easily quantifiable variable, and not unexpectedly, much of the existing work has been qualitative and descriptive in nature. What is clear is that the research on this topic is not well-developed, and it is not well-organized especially in terms of providing guidance to teachers and researchers. Another likely factor contributing to the state of the research is the lack of conceptual models which attempt to specify what the relevant factors are and how they might operate to produce desired academic outcomes. There are no comprehensive or well-articulated theoretical models that have outlined how such factors might be important in reading instruction in general or reading comprehension specifically. A central unanswered question is, How might cultural accommodations work? The remainder of the chapter examines some of the possible mechanisms with a special focus on motivational and learning processes in order to foster the creation of more meaningful theoretical models to guide research and theory building.

UNDERSTANDING CULTURAL ACCOMMODATIONS: WHAT CAN WE DRAW ON FROM EXISTING RESEARCH AND THEORY

Since this is a beginning effort, the focus will be on the most likely avenues rather than on trying to provide an exhaustive account of all possible factors. In order to focus the task a bit, and because of its importance in school success (Garcia, 2003; National Reading Panel, 2000; RAND Reading Study Group, 2002; Snow, Burns, & Griffin, 1998) reading and reading comprehension in particular will be targeted.

Reading Comprehension

The Rand Reading Study Group (2002) offered the following definition of reading comprehension:

the process of simultaneously extracting and constructing meaning through interaction and involvement with written language. Comprehension has these elements: the reader, the text, and the activity, or purpose for reading. These elements define a phenomenon—reading comprehension—that occurs within a larger sociocultural context that shapes and is shaped by the reader and that infuses each of the elements. All are influenced by the broader context. (p. xi)

In discussing the role of the reader, the report goes on to say:

The reader brings to the act of reading his or her cognitive capacities (attention, memory, critical analytic ability, inferencing, and visualization), motivation (a purpose for reading, interest in the content, self efficacy as a reader), knowledge (vocabulary, domain, and topic knowledge, linguistic and discourse knowledge, knowledge of comprehension strategies), and experiences. (pp. xi-xii)

Where might comprehension break down for students from diverse language or cultural backgrounds? A preliminary list might include the following:

- Attention—there may be differences in the cues students attend to in classroom instruction or they may not attend because of reasons related to other factors.
- Encoding—the input from text, the teacher, or peer discussions may not be comprehensible because of language differences or because of differences in genre or vocabulary, or the formal register used in academic contexts or "academic English" (Bailey, in press) or typical discourse patterns (Cazden, 1988; Mehan, 1979).
- Strategic Processing—because of the complex interplay among race, ethnicity, and socioeconomic status, students from some households may not have been exposed to large numbers of schooled adults who could model strategies useful in processing text.
- Background knowledge—the knowledge and skills that students have acquired may not map easily on to that in curriculum materials or books or activities.
- Motivation—students may come to school with different learning *goals* (Goldenberg, Gallimore, Reese, & Garnier, 2001; Ogbu & Simmons, 1998), poor self-efficacy due to past academic experiences, or low task value because the structure or purpose of instructional activities do not map on to known experiences and abilities and interests.

While the points above clearly suggest some of the sociocultural influences that might impact the process of reading comprehension, they do not specify how such factors might operate specifically for students from diverse language and cultural backgrounds. What place do cultural accommodations in instruction play in reading comprehension? What are the mechanisms through which they might impact comprehension? From a learning perspective, there are two main avenues proposed here through which cultural accommodations might operate to influence student outcomes. One is cognitive, and the other is motivational. In the following paragraphs, these questions will be explored.

A Cognitive Basis for Cultural Accommodations

One likely avenue for exploring cultural accommodations, from a cognitive perspective, is based on current notions of the information processing system, in particular the capacity limitations of working memory. Cognitive load theory (Paas, Renkl, & Sweller, 2003; Sweller, 1998; Sweller, van Merriënboer, & Paas, 1998) focuses on how constraints in working memory help determine what types of instruction are effective.

A basic tenet of cognitive load theory is that learning activities that are the most desirable minimize processing and/or storage requirements that are not directly relevant for learning in order to avoid taxing working memory capacity. Effective learning activities may "get around" working memory limitations by enabling the use of schemas, stored in long term memory (LTM), to process information more efficiently. LTM contains huge amounts of domain-specific knowledge structures, which can be described in terms of hierarchically organized schemas, that allow one to categorize different problem states and decide the most appropriate solution moves. Controlled use of schemas requires conscious effort, and therefore working memory resources. After sufficient practice, however, schemas can operate under automatic rather than controlled processing. Automatic processing of schemas requires minimal working memory resources and allows problem solving to proceed with minimal effort. A basic assumption of cognitive load theory is that schema construction and automation are the major goals of instruction.

Categories of Cognitive Load

One of the features of cognitive load theory is that it proposes different types of cognitive load. *Intrinsic cognitive load* refers to the demands on working memory capacity intrinsic to the material being learned. Different materials differ in their levels of element interactivity and thus intrinsic cognitive load, and they cannot be altered by instructional manipulations. Only a simpler learning task that omits some interacting elements can be chosen to reduce the load. The omission of essential, interacting elements will compromise sophisticated understanding but may be unavoidable with very complex, high-element interactivity tasks. Subsequent additions of omitted elements will permit understanding to occur. Simultaneous processing of all essential elements must occur eventually despite the high-intrinsic cognitive load because only then does "understanding" commence. The cognitive architecture (working memory—where all conscious cognitive processing occurs, can handle no more than two or three novel interacting elements, and LTM - comprised of *schemas*, or cognitive constructs that incorporate multiple elements of information into a single element with a single function) help lighten the load – bringing in the schema from LTM into working memory means only one element must be processed, even though the schema may incorporate many interacting elements. Thus schemas accomplish the same purpose as a factor analysis in a statistical context—simplifying many things into fewer so it is simpler to understand.

Culture can be thought of, for our purposes, as automated schema that helps simplify cognitive demands in everyday tasks and activities. If every behavior or thought or sentence were novel, the cognitive demands would be very high—familiar schema lighten this load. When these are *automated*, it further reduces the cognitive load. Thus, being in a culturally familiar setting is relatively effortless compared with being in a strange cultural setting. A culturally unfamiliar text (because of unfamiliar text structure or unfamiliar concepts or ideas) could impose intrinsic cognitive load even if the text were able to be decoded.

Extraneous or *Ineffective cognitive load*, which is due to the manner in which information is presented or the nature of the learning activities, imposes an unnecessary cognitive load and interferes with schema acquisition and automation. Most instructional design work has focused thus far on extraneous cognitive load because it is amenable to manipulation through instructional modifications. Extraneous cognitive load is primarily important when intrinsic cognitive load is high because the two forms of cognitive load are additive. If intrinsic cognitive load is low, levels of extraneous cognitive load may be less important because the *total cognitive load* may not exceed working memory capacity. Likewise, when element interactivity is low, instructional design intended to reduce the load on working memory have little or no effect.

Germane or effective cognitive load refers to demands placed on working memory capacity that are imposed by mental activities that contribute directly to learning, that is, schema acquisition and automation. Germane cognitive load enhances learning, and is influenced by instructional design. Also, increases in effort or motivation can increase the cognitive resources devoted to a task. If these additional resources are relevant to schema acquisition and automation, it also constitutes an increase in germane cognitive load.

Intrinsic, extraneous, and germane cognitive load are additive. That is, the total load cannot exceed working memory resources available if learning is to occur. The relations among the three types are asymmetric. Intrinsic load is the base, and cannot be reduced other than by constructing additional schemas and automating previously acquired schemas. Any working memory resources that are left after dealing with intrinsic cognitive load can be allocated to deal with extraneous and germane load. If learning is improved by an instructional design that reduces extraneous cognitive load, the improvement may have occurred because the additional working capacity freed by the reduction in extraneous cognitive load has now been allocated to germane cognitive load. As a consequence of learning, through schema acquisition and automation, intrinsic cognitive load is reduced. A reduction in intrinsic cognitive load reduces total cognitive load, thus freeing working memory capacity. The freed working memory capacity allows the learner to use the new learned material in acquiring more advanced schemas, and over many cycles of this advanced learning and skills may be acquired.

Applications to Cultural Accommodations and Reading Comprehension Instruction

The applications of cognitive load theory to conceptualizing cultural accommodations and reading comprehension are relatively straightforward. In essence, culturally unfamiliar reading materials and texts, reading-related activities, and even ways of talking and speaking during reading instruction may represent sources of extraneous cognitive load. It should be recalled that the different types of cognitive load are additive. Therefore, as the total cognitive load surpasses the capacity of the cognitive system, specifically working memory, comprehension will be diminished. While accommodations of the type being discussed here are often thought of in terms of the *social* processes they are thought to involve, the proposal here is that they may involve critical *cognitive* processes as well. In short, cognitive load theory suggests an important cognitive mechanism through which cultural unfamiliarity might impact teaching and learning environments and materials for reading comprehension instruction for students whose prior knowledge and experience differ from that of the classroom. Children whose cultural understandings and practices match those of the classroom or teacher can be hypothesized to be relatively advantaged with respect to reading comprehension processes insofar as they already possess the automated schema that help simplify ongoing cognitive demands. Conversely, students who do not possess these schema can be hypothesized to be relatively disadvantaged unless steps are taken to either increase their knowledge base, provide reading materials or activities which draw on existing "funds of knowledge" (Moll & González, 2004), or modify one or more aspects of instruction or materials to reduce extraneous cognitive load.

The processes just described might heuristically be called a *Facilitative Encoding Model*. That is, this model hypothesizes that cultural compatibility in the context of reading comprehension instruction produces effects mainly by emphasizing familiarity and connections to students' existing (cultural) knowledge or automated schema. It refers to situations, activities, or settings in which culturally-familiar content, activities, or language are used to connect new information to existing experience, prior knowledge and structures; that is, it helps the learner encode new information. This model hypothesizes that cultural compatibility produces effects mainly by making tasks more comprehensible and accessible. Interestingly, a somewhat related concept, comprehensible input, has long been posited as a factor in second language acquisition (Krashen, 1982), although specific cognitive processes or mechanisms have not been addressed in this work. If the above claims are correct, teachers of students from diverse backgrounds need to focus on the nature of reading materials, instructional activities, and other aspects of comprehension instruction that might unduly increase cognitive load to the point where comprehension breaks down. This would involve more attention to students' existing schema and prior knowledge and ways that it can be used to facilitate rather than impede comprehension processes.

Motivational Factors

The field of motivation is complex and multi-dimensional (Pintrich, 2003) with many constructs and models that address one or more of the relevant dimensions of culturally accommodated instruction. Pintrich outlined substantive questions which frame current work in motivation: What do students want? What motivates students in classrooms? How do students get what they want? Do students know what they want or what motivates them? How does motivation lead to cognition and cognition to motivation? How does motivation change and develop? What is the role of context and culture?

What distinguishes contemporary approaches to motivation from earlier conceptualizations is that the focus is on self-, task-, and context-related beliefs rather than inborn and unmalleable traits. In a comprehensive review of current work and issues in motivation, Pintrich (2003) outlined key motivational generalizations based on current understandings. These include:

- Adaptive self-efficacy and competence beliefs motivate students
- Adaptive attributions and control beliefs motivate students
- Higher levels of interest and intrinsic motivation motivate students
- Higher levels of value motivate students
- Goals motivate and direct students (p. 672).

Of relevance to the present undertaking, Pintrich and Schunk (2002) usefully outline three indices that distinguish motivational problems from other types of problem such as inadequate knowledge. These indices include active choice, persistence, and mental effort, all of which are assumed to impact achievement. Clearly, these are areas of focus and concern for students who are most often the target of cultural accommodations in the classroom. More importantly, it is highly plausible that these indices might be implicated in helping understand how cultural accommodations might serve to impact learner outcomes. Returning to the example of the student at the beginning of the chapter, his writing behavior exhibited significant changes in all three dimensions when the task was more relevant. A change in the nature of the writing task significantly changed his goals for writing and greatly impacted his task value and interest for writing compared to more traditional writing assignments.

It is possible to look at many different aspects of the motivation literature in the attempt to understand the possible mechanisms underlying the use and potential effects of culturally accommodated instruction. However, for heuristic purposes, the work in expectancy-value theory forms the focus here because it includes a number of potentially relevant motivational constructs that might have a plausible link to cultural accommodations, especially as these accommodations apply to reading comprehension.

An Expectancy-Value Account of Motivation

The most well-known embodiment of expectancy-value theory is based on work of Eccles and Wigfield and their colleagues (Eccles, 1983, 1987, 1993; Eccles & Midgley, 1989; Wigfield, 1994; Widgield & Eccles, 1992,

2000). In the complete model (Pintrich, 2002), achievement is a function motivated behavior (active choice, persistence, mental effort), which is impacted by motivational beliefs (task value components and expectancy components), individuals' cognitive processes (perceptions of the social environment and causal attributions), and finally, aspects of the social world (cultural milieu, socializers' behaviors, and past performances). The critical motivational components in expectancy-value theory are, however, represented by the constructs of expectancy and value. The value component of the theory focuses on beliefs related to the question, "Why should I do this task?" and includes the constructs of interest, importance, utility, and cost. In contrast, the expectancy component of the theory focuses on beliefs related to the question, "Am I able to do this task?" (Eccles, 1983) and focuses on the constructs of self-efficacy, perceived task difficulty, and causal attribution. The proposal here is that the hypothesized effects of cultural accommodations are mediated through impact on one or several expectancy variables and/or value variables leading to effects on motivational indices and thus achievement. The processes just described might heuristically be called a *Facilitative Motivation Model.*

In the context of reading comprehension instruction, researchers have noted that students such as those who are the focus here may not have had exposure to literate adults who use literacy in school-like ways, even though they may use literacy to accomplish everyday demands. These students may not share the same task value or utility for reading as the teacher or students who have had exposure to interesting and varied texts, or questions and discussions about the meaning of texts, such as those that characterize the backgrounds of many students from middle class homes. Minority students may also not have had the same opportunities to develop self-efficacy related to understanding complex texts. Thus cultural accommodations, especially as they impact on expectancy and value motivational variables, may facilitate engagement and thus promote reading comprehension processes.

Consideration of an expectancy-value motivational framework facilitates the development of specific testable hypotheses and provides some guidance about relevant constructs to assess and/or manipulate when considering reading comprehension instruction. For example, some questions of interest are: "Does the systematic use of culturally relevant texts produce higher student outcomes (greater interest and task value, thus impacting the choice to read more, to persist at reading tasks, to exert more effort with challenging text, and finally to increased comprehension)?" More generally, "Does culturally accommodated instruction lead to higher self-efficacy?" or "How do features of culturally accommodated instructional routines or activities increase student interest, importance, and utility, thus impacting choice, persistence, or effort?" These and many other related questions have not been systematically explored to date. As a result, instructional and curriculum designers are left to rely on intuition or educated guesses regarding if, when, and how to design and implement cultural accommodations. Systematic work drawing on current understandings of learning and motivation promises to help unravel these questions. The example at the beginning of the chapter suggests that persistence, choice, and effort *can* be significantly modified under the right conditions. They are not factors intrinsic to individual children, but rather reside in the interaction between the student and the environment. Thus, educators who try to facilitate reading comprehension processes with students from nontraditional backgrounds need to systematically consider the motivational implications of the classroom activities and materials they provide.

FUTURE DIRECTIONS FOR THEORY, RESEARCH, AND PRACTICE

Sociocultural factors in motivation have gained increasing attention in the field of learning and motivation (McInerney & Van Etten, 2001, 2002, 2003, 2004; Pintrich, 2003; Urdan, 1999). In the context of reading and literacy, especially those aspects which require effortful cognitive activity such as comprehension, the general proposition is that cultural accommodations may be an important instructional scaffold for certain students whose cultural beliefs and practices may not cleanly map on to the classroom context. Currently, there is widespread belief that culturally-accommodated approaches are effective and useful. However, there is little systematic evidence with well-defined outcomes that provide evidence for this belief, and there are no learning-related theoretical accounts of how or why these approaches might work. This chapter has outlined plausible theoretical mechanisms related to learning and motivation that suggest how such instructional accommodations might operate to produce achievement outcomes.

Potential Problems

There are potential problems and issues in pursuing work in the areas outlined above. Among the first and most important of these is that there are no widely agreed upon definitions (and more importantly, operational definitions), of key constructs such as "culturally relevant" or even "culture" (Erickson, 2003). In addition, many urban classrooms are increasingly heterogeneous. Unlike the well-known KEEP classrooms in Hawaii, which were relatively ethnically and linguistically homogenous, many classrooms now contain students from multiple cultural and linguistic backgrounds. An even greater obstacle is the lack of a comprehensive set of data on which to draw to determine *what* to accommodate in "accommodated" instruction because there are big gaps in what is known about the everyday lives and motivational orientations of diverse students from low socioeconomic backgrounds. Perhaps the most pressing need, however, is to demonstrate in a clearer and more systematic way that these accommodations *can* be important instructional scaffolds.

A Note on the Treatment of Culture

It is critical to keep in mind that much research in the past has treated culture as an independent variable, often used interchangeably with racial or ethnic categories. However, culture is much more complex than relatively "simple" racial or ethnic categories (Erickson, 2003; Gutierrez & Rogoff, 2003; Rogoff, 2003). It is much more defensible, therefore, to examine the cultural practices and beliefs of a specific individual or class as a basis for instructional modifications rather than relying on generalizations about an entire culture, and then making inferences about how those generalizations apply to an individual who happens to be a member of the culture. It is not the abstract cultural models, beliefs, and practices of an entire group that matters; it is the cultural beliefs and practices of individual students in a specific classroom context (Gallimore & Goldenberg, 2001).

Linking Accommodations With Instructional Goals

One criticism of some general multicultural approaches is that they often target awareness or understanding around issues of culture and power relationships, but are relatively disconnected from, or only weakly connected to, long term academic instructional goals and outcomes. Achieving awareness, understanding, and the acquisition of coping skills are neither trivial nor negative goals, but if student academic outcomes are also a desired outcome, then sociocultural factors need to be tied to instructional goals as well. In short, the proposal is that if academic goals are to be achieved through the use of cultural accommodations, then these accommodations should be *strategic* and *instructionally linked*. Strategic is meant here to emphasize that not every feature of a home culture or background merits consideration for accommodation, nor does the entire classroom have to be transformed from the bottom up, especially in classrooms where multiple cultural groups are present. The best understandings of culture suggest that cultural conventions are learned and can be negotiated (Tharp & Gallimore, 1988; Rogoff, 2003). Thus decisions should be selective and purposefully made.

Just as important in achieving academic outcomes is the creation of instructional linkages between cultural accommodations and academic goals. If academic goals are to be achieved, then consideration must be given to how instructional accommodations are linked to, and how they promote, these academic goals. It should be clear here that a narrow definition of achievement indexed solely by standardized test scores is not being promoted. Rather, it is deep understanding and the ability to use knowledge (in this case reading and literacy) to achieve learning goals both in and out of school that is being promoted. But such understanding does not happen at random, and thought needs to be given to the connections between accommodations and eventual learning goals.

As a final word, it should be noted that there now exist excellent models that target motivation (in this case, reading engagement) and that are theoretically and empirically grounded, for example the CORI (Concept Oriented Reading Instruction) approach developed by Guthrie and colleagues (Guthrie, Wigfield, & Perencevich, 2004). Future work on instructional accommodations should, thus, integrate and build upon the significant work that currently exists. While this existing work has not targeted cultural factors specifically, it does provide many important implications for research from sociocultural perspectives.

The intersection of motivation, culture, and reading is, then, fertile ground for both research and practice. However, we still do not have good answers to the question: "Do cultural accommodations work?" And, if so: "Which accommodations are the most important and how do they work?" This chapter is a start at outlining some key factors and processes that may provide guidance in answering these questions.

REFERENCES

Abu-Rabia, S. (1996). Druze minority students learning Hebrew in Israel: The relationship of attitudes, cultural background, and interest of material to reading comprehension in a second language. *Journal of Multilingual & Multicultural Development, 17*(6), 415-426.

Au, K. H.-P., & Mason, J. M. (1981). Social organizational factors in learning to read: The balance of rights hypothesis. *Reading Research Quarterly, 17*(1), 115-152.

Bailey A. L. (in press). From Lambie to Lambaste: The conceptualization, operationalization and use of academic language in the assessment of ELL students. In T. Wiley & K. Rolstad (Eds.), *Academic language*. Mahwah, NJ: LEA.

Bennett, A., Bridglall, B. L., Caude, A. M., Everson, H. T., Gordon, E. W., Lee, C. D., et al. (2004). *All students reaching the top: Strategies for closing academic achievement gaps. A report of the National Study Group for the Affirmative Development of Academic Ability.* Naperville, IL: Learning Point Associates.

Brophy, J. E., & Good, T. L. (1986). Teacher behavior and student achievement. In M. Wittrock (Ed.), *Third handbook of research on teaching* (pp. 328-375). New York: Macmillan.

California State Department of Education (1986). *Beyond language: Social and cultural factors in schooling language minority students.* Los Angeles: Evaluation, Dissemination and Assessment Center, California State University.

Cazden, C. B. (1988). *Classroom discourse.* New York: Heinemann.

Cole, R. W. (1995). *Educating everybody's children: Diverse teaching strategies for diverse learners: What research and practice say about improving achievement.* Alexandria, VA: ASCD.

Datnow, A., & Kemper, E. (2002, March). *From statehouse to schoolhouse: The implementation of comprehensive school reform in the era of CSRD.* Report prepared as a deliverable to OERI, U.S. Department of Education for CRESPAR Project 4.2.

Demmert, W., & Towner, J. (2003). *A review of the research literature on the influences of culturally based education on the academic performance of Native American students.* Retrieved August 1, 2005, from http://www.nwrel.org/indianed/cbe

Eccles, J. (1983). Expectancies, values and academic behaviors. In J. T. Spence (Ed.), *Achievement and achievement motives* (pp. 75-146). San Francisco: Freeman.

Eccles, J. (1987). Gender roles and women's achievement-related decisions. *Psychology of Women Quarterly, 11*, 135-172.

Eccles, J. (1993). School and family effects on the ontogeny of childrens' interests, self-perceptions, and activity choice. In J. Jacobs (Ed.), *Nebraska symposium on motivation: Developmental perspectives on motivation* (pp. 145-208). Lincoln, NE: University of Nebraska Press.

Eccles, J. S., & Midgley, C. (1989). Stage-environment fit: Developmentally appropriate classrooms for young adolescents. In C. Ames & R. Ames (Eds.), *Research on motivation in education* (Vol. 3, pp. 139-186). San Diego, CA: Academic Press.

Ellett, C. D., & Teddlie, C. (2003). Teacher evaluation, teacher effectives and school effectiveness: Perspectives from the USA. *Journal of Personnel Evaluation in Education, 17*(1), 101-128.

Erickson, F. (2003). Culture in society and in educational practices. In J. A. Banks & C. A. McGee Banks (Eds.), *Multicultural Education: Issues and perspectives.* (5th ed., pp. 31-60). New York: Wiley.

Gallimore, R., & Goldenberg, C. (2001). Analyzing cultural models and settings to connect minority achievement and school improvement research. *Educational Psychologist, 36*(1), 45-56.

Garcia, G. G. (2003). *English learners: Reaching the highest level of English literacy.* Newark, DE: International Reading Association.

Goldenberg, C., Gallimore, R., Reese, L., & Garnier, H. (2001). Cause or effect? A longitudinal study of immigrant Latino parents' aspirations and expectations and their children's school performance. *American Educational Research Association Journal, 38*, 547-582.

Guthrie, J. T., Wigfield, A., & Perencevich, K. C. (2004). *Motivating reading comprehension: Concept-oriented reading instruction*. Mahwah, NJ: Erlbaum.

Gutierrez, K. D., & Rogoff, B. (2003). Cultural ways of learning: Individual styles or repertoires of practice. *Educational Researcher, 32*, 19-25.

Huang, G., Reiser, M., Parker, A., Muniec, J., & Salvucci, S. (2003). *Institute of Education Sciences findings from interviews with education policymakers*. Retrieved December 2, 2005, from http://www.ed.gov/rschstat/research/pubs/findingsreport.pdf

Irvine, J. J., & York, D. E. (1995). Learning styles and culturally diverse students: A literature review. In J. A. Banks (Ed.), *handbook of research on multicultural education* (pp. 484-497). New York: Simon & Schuster.

Jacob, E., & Jordan, C. (Eds.). (1987). Explaining the school performance of minority students (Theme issue). *Anthropology and Education Quarterly, 18*(4).

Jimenez, R. T. (1997). The strategic reading abilities and potential of five low-literacy Latina/o readers in middle school. *Reading Research Quarterly, 32*(3), 224-243.

Kenner, C. (1999). Children's understandings of text in a multilingual nursery. *Language and Education, 13*(1), 1-16.

Kenner, C. (2000). Biliteracy in a monolingual school system? English and Gujarati in South London. *Language Culture & Curriculum, 13*(1), 13-30.

Krashen, S. (1982). *Principles and practice in second language acquisition*. New York: Pergamon Press.

Levine, D. U., & Lezotte, L. W. (1990). *Unusually effective schools: A review and analysis of research and practive*. Madison, WI: The National Center for Effective Schools Research and Development.

Livingston, A., & Wirt, J. (2005). *The condition of education 2005 in brief: U.S. Department of Education, National Center for Education Statistics* (NCES 2005-095). Washington, DC: U.S. Government Printing Office.

McCarty, T. L. (1993). Language, literacy, and the image of the child in American Indian classrooms. *Language Arts, 70*(3), 182-192.

McCarty, T. L., Wallace, S., Lynch, R. H., & Benally, A. (1991). Classroom inquiry and Navajo learning styles: A call for reassessment. *Anthropology & Education Quarterly, 22*(1), 42-59.

McInerney, D. M., & Van Etten, S. (Eds.). (2001). *Research on sociocultural influences on motivation and learning* (Vol. 1). Greenwich, CT: Information Age.

McInerney, D. M., & Van Etten, S. (Eds.). (2002). *Research on sociocultural influences on motivation and learning* (Vol. 2). Greenwich, CT: Information Age.

McInerney, D. M., & Van Etten, S. (Eds.). (2003) *Research on sociocultural influences on motivation and learning* (Vol. 3). Greenwich, CT: Information Age.

McInerney, D. M., & Van Etten, S. (Eds.). (2004). *Research on sociocultural influences on motivation and learning* (Vol. 4). Greenwich, CT: Information Age.

Mehan, H. (1979). *Learning lessons: The social organization of classroom instruction*. Cambridge, MA: Harvard University Press.

Moll, L. C., & González, N. (2004). Engaging life: A funds of knowledge approach to multicultural education. In J. Banks & C. McGee Banks (Eds.), *Handbook of research on multicultural education* (2nd ed., pp. 699-715). New York: Jossey-Bass.

Murphy, J. (1991). *Restructuring schools: Capturing and assessing the phenomena*. New York: Teachers College Press.

National Commission on Excellence in Education (1983). *A nation at risk: The imperative for educational reform*. Washington, DC: U.S. Government Printing Office.

National Reading Panel (2000). *Report of the National Reading Panel: Teaching children to read—an evidence-based assessment of the scientific research literature on reading and its implications for reading instruction* (NIH Publication No. 99-4769). Jessup, MD: National Institute for Literacy.

No Child Left Behind Act of 2001, Pub. I. No. 107-110, 115 Stat 145 (2002).

Ogbu, J., & Simmons, H. D. (1998). Voluntary and involuntary minorities: A cultural-ecological theory of school performance with some implications for education. *Anthropology and Education Quarterly, 29*(2), 155-188.

Paas, F., Renkl, A., & Sweller, J. (2003). Cognitive load theory and instructional design: Recent developments [Special issue]. *Educational Psychologist, 38*(1), 1-4.

Pintrich, P. R. (2003). A motivational science perspective on the role of student motivation in learning and teaching contexts. *Journal of Educational Psychology, 95*(4), 667-686.

Pintrich, P. R., & Schunk, D. H. (2002). *Motivation in education: Theory, research, and applications*. Upper Saddle River, NJ: Merrill Prentice Hall.

RAND Reading Study Group. (2002). *Reading for understanding: Toward an R&D program in reading comprehension*. Santa Monica, CA: RAND Education.

Rogoff, B. (2003). *The cultural nature of human development*. New York: Oxford University Press.

Rueda, R. (2004, March). *Preliminary findings of the National Literacy Panel*. Paper presented at the annual meeting of the California Association for Bilingual Education (CABE), San Jose, CA.

Sable, J., & Hoffman, L. (2005). *Characteristics of the 100 largest public elementary and secondary school districts in the United States: 2002-03*. (NCES 2005-312). U.S. Department of Education, National Center for Educational Statistics. Washington, DC: U.S. Government Printing Office.

Saravia-Shore, M. & García, E. (1995). Diverse teaching strategies for diverse learners. In R. Cole, (Ed.), *Educating everybody's children: Diverse strategies for diverse learners* (pp. 47-74). Alexandria, VA: Association for Supervision and Curriculum Development.

Slavin, R. E., Madden, N. A., & Wasik, B. A. (1996). Roots and Wings: Universal excellence in elementary education. In S. Stringfield, S. M. Ross, & L. Smith (Eds.), *Bold plans for school restructuring: The New American Schools designs* (pp. 207-231). Mahwah, NJ: Erlbaum.

Snow, C. E., Burns, M. S., & Griffin, P. (1998). *Preventing reading difficulties in young children*. Washington, DC: National Academy Press.

Stahl, S. A. (1999). Different strokes for different folks? A critique of learning styles. *American Educator, 23*(3), 27-31.

Stringfield, S., Datnow, A., & Ross, S. M. (1998). *Scaling up school restructuring in multicultural, multilingual contexts: Early observations from Sunland County.* Retrieved December 2, 2005, from http://repositories.cdlib.org/crede/rsrchrpts/rr02

Stringfield, S., Milsap, M. A., Herman, R., Yoder, N., Brigham, N., Nesselrodt, P., et al. (1997). *Urban and suburban/rural special strategies for educating disadvantaged children. Final Report.* Washington, DC: U.S. Department of Education.

Sweller, J. (1988). Cognitive load during problem solving: Effects on learning. *Cognitive Science, 12,* 257-285.

Sweller, J., van Merriënboer, J. G., & Paas, F. G. (1998). Cognitive architecture and instructional design. *Educational Psychology Review, 10,* 251-296.

Tharp, R. G. (1982). The effective instruction of comprehension: Results and descriptions of the Kamehameha Early Education Program. *Reading Research Quarterly, 17,* 503-527.

Tharp, R. G. (1989). Psychocultural variables and constants: Effects on teaching and learning in schools. *American Psychologist, 44*(2), 349-359.

Tharp, R. G., & Gallimore, R. (1988). *Rousing minds to life: Teaching, learning, and schooling in a social context.* New York: Cambridge University Press.

Urdan, T. (Ed.). (1999). *Advances in motivation and achievement, Volume 11: Motivation in context.* Stamford, CT: JAI Press.

Valencia, R. R. (1997). *The evolution of deficit thinking: Educational thought and practice.* The Stanford Series on Education and Public Policy. London: Falmer Press.

Wigfield, A. (1994). Expectancy-value theory of motivation and achievement: A developmental perspective. *Educational Psychology Review, 6,* 49-78.

Wigfield, A., & Eccles, J. (1992). The development of achievement task values: A throretical analysis. *Developmental Review, 12,* 265-310.

Wigfield, A., & Eccles, J. (2000). Expectancy-value theory of achievement motivation. *Contemporary Educational Psychology, 25,* 68-81.

Wilkinson, L. C., Milosky, L. M., & Genishi, C. (1986). Second language learners' use of requests and responses in elementary classrooms. *Topics in Language Disorders, 6*(2), 57-70.

Part III

ON TEACHERS

CHAPTER 7

SOCIAL INFLUENCES AND THE QUEST FOR EXCELLENCE

A Sociocultural Perspective on Teacher Effectiveness

La Tefy Schoen

This chapter explores ways in which teacher effectiveness is impacted by factors associated with the social context of the school. Teaching is inherently a social activity, and there are numerous forces acting upon teachers which influence their behavior and thereby their effectiveness. Moreover, teachers routinely make social as well as educational decisions about the way they teach (Angelides & Ainscow, 2000; Broadway, 1999; Brown, 2002; Remillard, 1999, 2005; Zembylas, 2003). An analysis of the literature reveals three types of social concerns which impact the work of teachers. These include psycho-social factors at work within the teacher/employee (Ashton & Webb, 1986; Brief & Aldag, 1981; Broadway; Zembylas; Newmann, Rutter, & Smith, 1989), sociocultural factors at work within the school/workplace (Angelides & Ainscow; Deal & Kennedy, 1983; Deal & Peterson, 1999; Loup, 1994; Rosenholtz, 1985; Rosenholtz, Bassler, & Hoover-Dempsey, 1986; Schein, 1985, 1992; Schoen, 2005), and sociopo-

Effective Schools, 159–184

litical factors at work in the community (Conley & Bodone, 2002; Spillane, 2000).

When teachers and administrators notice a dissonance between a new situation and their usual routines, they use their personal and collective experience to make sense of the new demands (Brown, 2002; Coburn, 2001; Louis, Febey, & Schroeder, 2005; Remillard, 1999). Weick (1993) describes this sense-making as an ongoing process focused on extracted clues, driven by plausibility, and tied to identity construction. In this chapter we will explore a fictionalized account of how two veteran teachers grapple with the interplay between several levels of social forces when asked to implement a new curriculum which requires very different instructional methods. Through this vignette we will consider how some of these social factors might impact teacher behavior.

TEACHER KNOWLEDGE AND TEACHER EFFECTIVENESS

It has long been acknowledged that teacher knowledge of both content and pedagogy influence teacher effectiveness (Schulman, 1987). It is a foregone conclusion that an individual who does not posses the precursory foundational knowledge of subject content will be unable to adequately guide students into mastering that which they themselves do not comprehend. This is the concern behind the move to require that teachers demonstrate subject area mastery. An example of this is found embedded in mandates that schools be accountable for hiring "Highly Qualified" teachers (No Child Left Behind [NCLB], 2002).

Other factors impacting teacher performance are more oblique. Pedagogical knowledge is one such area. There is much literature documenting that high levels of teacher pedagogical knowledge are associated with more effective instruction in the classroom (Brophy & Good, 1986; Brookover Schweitzer, Schneider, Beady, Flood, & Wisenbacher, 1978; Darling-Hammond, 1990, 1993; Elmore, 1992, 1996; Little, 1993). The move towards teacher professionalization is built upon the premise that highly informed professionals are more capable of reflecting on practice (Kruse, 1997; Schon, 1983) evaluating data, planning and executing high quality instruction. Proponents of teacher professionalization (e.g., Darling-Hammond, 1990, 1995; Khmelkov, 2000) stress professional development as a means of creating more collaborative work cultures for teachers (Boyle, Lamprianou, & Boyle, 2005; Corcoran, 1995b; Hargreaves & Fullan, 1992). Collegial/collaborative faculties tend to exhibit higher levels of teacher professionalism and effective classroom instruction (Lieberman, 1996; Little; Bryk, Camburn, & Lewis, 1999).

However, teacher knowledge of "best practices" (DuFour & Eaker, 1998) does not always equate to better teaching and learning in the classroom (Hargreaves, 1991; Hargreaves & Goodson, 1996; Lieberman, 1995; Little, 2001; Schoen, 2005). Nor can we assume that the possession of knowledge and skills will automatically translate into efficacious action upon that knowledge (Bandura, 1986). This awareness suggests that factors besides teacher knowledge may have an impact upon teaching behavior. Sociocultural theory (Vygotsky, 1978) holds that knowledge is socially constructed and its meaning is subjectively determined (Van der Veer & Valsiner, 1991; Stetsenko, 2002). This implies that social factors may influence the way teachers make sense of new information and interpret its value and utility for them.

Teaching is both an art and a science (Bolman & Deal, 1997; Deal & Kennedy, 1983; DuFour & Eaker, 1998; Eisner, 1994). The science of teaching involves the application of established technical knowledge to produce desired effects (DuFour & Eaker; Levine & Lezotte, 1990). The scientific practice of teaching requires that teachers acquire both content and pedagogical knowledge and skills. Many researchers have stressed the importance of professional growth and development in this process (Boyle, Lamprianou, & Boyle, 2005; Lieberman, 1996; Little, 1982, 1993; Mortimore, 1991; Shulman & Sparks, 1992; Teddlie & Stringfield, 1993).

The art of teaching involves teachers individually navigating their way through the barrage of "ought to"s simultaneously inundating them from multiple directions (Fullan, 1993; McCarthy & Peterson, 1989; McLaughlin & Pfeifer, 1988) to arrive at a unique expression of how the job "should be" performed. Knowledge is interpreted by teachers within a social framework, within which teachers assesses the value and utility of new information. Individual and group judgments are made about whether new ideas will "work" for them. When teachers receive pressures and stimuli from various sources, they prioritize these and "artfully" process the demands in a way that they deem most appropriate. Teacher judgments impact whether they significantly change their practices, implement incremental changes, or resist change (Bandura, 1986; Gold, 2002; Louis & Dentler, 1988; Louis, Febey, & Schroeder, 2005). To illustrate this point, consider the case of Mrs. Lewis and Miss Clark, two well educated, veteran teachers who teach the same subject and grade level at the same school. Both teachers underwent the same training but responded very differently.

A Tale of Two Teachers

Miss Stephanie Clark smiled as she looked across the crowded room and spotted a familiar face. Three tables over sat her friend and colleague, Regina Lewis. The teachers were there to participate in an intensive summer training program in hands–on science instruction. The summer session was a part of a district wide effort to restructure science education. The school district had opted to implement an inquiry based science curriculum; therefore, rather than replacing dated textbooks and related materials, teachers were being trained in methods of managing discovery learning and provided with science kits to help them implement the new curriculum.

Following the session orientation, teachers broke into smaller groups, sorted by grade level taught. This meant that Stephanie and Regina would be working together, since they both taught the same grade. This pleased both teachers who had worked cooperatively on a number of projects in the past. As the friends greeted each other, Stephanie could tell that Regina was as excited as she was. The district was not only paying for the training, but they were each being paid a handsome stipend and would receive graduate credit for their participation, not to mention the promise of new "stuff" to use in the classroom.

The training lived up to their expectations. The two participated in hands-on activities from the new curriculum and discussed methods and materials to use with this new approach. They worked together in small collaborative groups to plan and present sample lessons to their group of grade level cohorts. Both Stephanie, who was nearing the completion of her master's degree, and Regina, who had recently completed a master's plus 30 graduate hours, found this format stimulating. The two were competitive by nature and excelled at their assigned tasks. In fact, as the course progressed, they became known as "The Beckley Bunch," a reference to the school that employed them.

All too soon, the break came to a close and the contrived world of the training session gave way to the realities of preparing for a new school term. Stephanie felt energized and inspired by the experience and could not wait to try out some of the things she had learned. She and Regina vowed to stay in contact more over the school year so that they could support each other during the transition to this new program.

However, as was always the case, the opening of the school year brought with it many demands on their time. The teachers rarely found time to discuss applying the things they had learned, despite their best intentions. This frustrated Stephanie who spoke to the principal about the need for a collaborative planning period. The principal was supportive, but was only able to free up 45 minutes twice a month for the two to talk. However, this was better than nothing, so Stephanie was satisfied. A month into the school year the promised hands-on kits arrived. The teachers were thrilled. Now they were armed with new ideas, new "things," and time to collaborate. Everything was in place to successfully implement the program ... or so it would seem.

As Stephanie and Regina began to meet to discuss the program, it was more awkward than they had imagined, without the structure of the workshop. Neither quite knew what to say or where to begin. It was not that they were inexperienced in teamwork; the Beckley teachers were accustomed to working cooperatively on projects, but this was different somehow. Eventually Stephanie found herself taking the lead by inquiring what Regina had experimented with thus far, and sharing her own experiences.

However, Stephanie perceived reluctance on Regina's behalf when they met to plan. Her partner seemed considerably less enthusiastic about the program than she had been during the training. Knowing that Regina was somewhat of a perfectionist, Stephanie decided that it was probably due to the extra preparation required to execute this method of instruction. After all, changing old habits and established ways of doing things was hard on anyone. She imagined that someone like Regina, who wanted everything to be "just perfect," would have a hard time with the trial and error required to learn such a radically different method. Regina had a reputation for being a very good teacher. In the past, her classes, like most at their school, had been characterized by traditional teacher-centered direct instruction and this new program was anything but that. Though Regina said nothing, her lack of enthusiasm led Stephanie to wonder how things were really going.

Later that year, as Stephanie was in the hall on an errand, she passed Regina's room and noticed that Regina was talking to the class and had out one of the new Science kits. The door of the classroom was slightly ajar, allowing Stephanie to see and hear without being entirely conspicuous, so she hesitated to observed her colleague implementing the activity they had planned, hoping to glean some small skill from the veteran teacher. But as she lingered, she began to realize that the way Regina was using the materials and addressing the content was diametrically opposed to the discovery methods that they had been trained in. Suddenly she understood Regina's hesitation when they talked. She recalled how Regina had so readily let her take the lead, and had contributed very little. Of, course she had little to share if she was not actually *doing* the program!

Regina had simply adapted (Remillard, 2005; Hennessy, Ruthven, & Brindley, 2005) the new content and materials to her established way of teaching. Her instructional methods had actually changed very little since the training. This puzzled Stephanie who had watched Regina excel in the course they had shared together; she knew Regina understood the philosophy of the program and how to implement it. This same training had brought radical changes to her own classroom and revolutionized the entire way she taught. Stephanie was perplexed, but resigned herself that she would have to go it alone. Subsequently, at an informal social gathering, Stephanie decided to broach the subject by asking what Regina *really* thought of the new program. Regina's response was very telling. She said that she was uncomfortable with the new methods advocated by this program. She had never taught that way and it just did not fit with her notion of good teaching or a well run classroom. She explained that while the training was good, she still had doubts about how she was supposed to be doing things. With a sigh, she concluded, "I just wasn't brought up that way; I was taught with traditional methods and I believe that's the best way to teach—at least for me."

Sociocultural Influences on Behavior

Unseen social forces act upon teachers and can have an impact on job performance (Argyris, 1964; Argyris & Schon, 1976; Bandura, 1997; Little, 1982, 1993; Louis, Febey, & Schroeder, 2005; Mayo & Kajs, 2005; Schein, 1992). Such was the case with Regina Lewis, whose professional training did not fit with her past experiences. When she discovered the two were incompatible she was forced to decide how to best execute her work. Curriculum theorists have studied "the enacted curriculum" (Brown, 2002; Remillard, 1999, 2005) and found that a number of internal personal characteristics interact with the formal curriculum, to yield the enacted curriculum (i.e., what is actually done in the classroom). Mrs. Lewis' response to Miss Clark's inquiry about the new curriculum reveals that Mrs. Lewis' personal values, (which are socially derived and reinforced) influenced her, and were to some extent responsible for her resistance to the new curriculum.

The extensive funding that was allocated to support a change in Mrs. Lewis' teaching methods (i.e., the training, the stipend, the new materials and schedule adjustments to allow for collaborative planning) did not achieve its intended purpose. Every day teachers, like Mrs. Lewis and Miss Clark make decisions regarding many aspects of their own practice (Blasé & Kirby, 2000; Pearson & Moomaw, 2005; Remillard, 1999, 2005). Instructional decisions made by teachers are influenced by many factors, not the least of which are social and cultural forces which may or may not be obvious to teachers or their supervisors (Deal & Peterson, 1999; Little, 1982, 1993; Schoen, 2005; Schein, 1985, 1992).

Social and cultural influences on teacher behavior are often so taken for granted as to escape the conscious awareness of teachers and administrators; however, they exhibit powerful controls over the way in which teachers actually perform their work (Argyris & Schon, 1976; Schein, 1985, 1992; Schoen & Teddlie, 2005a). Deeply held social constructions such as self-efficacy, basic assumptions, and espoused values can dramatically alter the effectiveness of teacher behavior in the classroom despite educational background or training (Bandura, 1986; Schoen, 2005). This chapter examines three sources of sociocultural influences on teachers and offers suggestions for utilizing the social context of the school to maximize teacher effectiveness.

SOURCES OF SOCIAL INFLUENCES ON TEACHERS

Social influences upon teachers can be categorized as emanating from three different sources: (1) *psycho-social* influences which are internal to individual teachers (Argyris, 1964; Ashton & Webb, 1986; Bandura, 1977, 1999; Fullan, 1993), (2) *Sociocultural influences* which are exerted within the culture of the school (Deal & Peterson, 1999; Schein, 1992; Schoen, 2005) and (3) *Sociopolitical* influences which teachers perceive from the larger societal context beyond the school (Scott, 1995; Jespersen, Nielsen, & Sognstrup, 2002). Mrs. Lewis was simultaneously responding to stimuli from all three levels of sociocultural influences. First, she was haunted by doubts about her own ability to be effective using methods that she was inexperienced with (self-efficacy). Furthermore, the culture of the school reinforced more traditional methods by favoring direct instruction over discovery learning. Finally, she was bothered that this new curriculum did not fit with internalized generalizations about school based upon her own personal experiences as a student (institutional norms). These forces affected her motivation to adopt the new curriculum (Brief & Aldag, 1981) and proved to have a stronger impact over her behavior than her training, despite the fact that she possessed the knowledge to execute the curriculum. In the end, she did not adopt the new philosophy, but rather found ways to conform new curriculum and materials to her existing beliefs, values, and practices.

Psycho-Social Influences: The Internal Guide to Good Teaching

Theories-in-use

In their classic book on professional effectiveness, Argyris and Schon (1976) differentiate between what they refer to as "theories-in-use" and "espoused theories." In lay terms this roughly translates to "what I do at work" and "what I should do." Theories in use are basically sets of tacit if-then assumptions derived from experience which prescribe how to react in various situations on the job. They form unwritten scripts based on what teachers have observed or participated in, and assist in making decisions about how to behave in various situations.

Basic Assumptions

Edgar Schein (1985, 1992) describes a similar guiding force over the behavior of individuals in organizations which he calls "basic assumptions." Basic assumptions, like theories-in-use, are generalizations derived from past experiences of the individual which consist of internalized perceptions of the nature of persons or objects (including ideas) in the work environment. These generalizations prescribe how to relate to people in various roles and how to act in given circumstances.

While basic assumptions are held by all individuals, they are covert and typically escape the conscious awareness of individuals. These conceptions held by individual teachers, hidden beneath the surface, exert a powerful controlling force over professional behavior (Schein, 1985, 1992). Schon (1983) stresses the importance of self-reflection in discovering one's generalized assumptions and making them explicit. He identifies self-reflection as a key component of an effective professional practice. Professional reflection is an underutilized tool which has the potential for helping teachers to examine the congruence between their knowledge, their values and their actions.

Espoused Beliefs

In addition to the basic assumptions held by individuals, each teacher has an internalized set of espoused beliefs or values which are derived from many sources. These espoused beliefs differ from basic assumptions in that individuals formulate these values at a conscious level. Espoused beliefs are the guiding principles that individuals and organizations aspire to (Schein, 1985, 1992) and may be found in statements of goals or philosophies. Espoused beliefs are essentially understandings about the "right way" of doing things. Espoused beliefs may or may not be congruent with behavior or theories-in-use. Awareness of inconsistencies between espoused beliefs and personal behavior can create internal disequilibrium, and force individuals to alter either their beliefs or their behavior (Gold, 2002; Louis & Dentler, 1988). An example of this is seen in the case of Mrs. Lewis, who at some point became aware that the philosophy of the new program conflicted with what she believed about teaching and learning. When forced with the choice of altering her espoused beliefs or her behavior, she opted to act in a manner consistent with her internal beliefs. Thus, the new philosophy was rejected in favor of existing espoused beliefs.

Teacher Self-Efficacy

Another individual factor at work influencing teacher behavior is a teacher's sense of self-efficacy (Ashton & Webb, 1986). This is essentially a personal feeling of confidence in one's ability to perform competently

(Bandura 1977, 1999). Mrs. Lewis had a demonstrated track record of effectiveness using the methods with which she was familiar; therefore her sense of self-efficacy with these established methods was high. She was comfortable with them, in part, because she was confident in her ability to teach using these tried and true methods. However, this new program was something altogether different. She was uncertain of her ability to teach effectively in this new paradigm, thus, she faced a personal paradox: execute the program despite doubts about whether the students were actually learning as she felt they should, or continue to do what she was familiar and confident with. This anxiety contributed to her reluctance to accept the new program whole heartedly. Therefore, she settled for surface level compliance, which allowed her to save face professionally, but avoid the insecurity associated with fundamentally altering established patterns of behavior.

This scenario is consistent with research on teacher self-efficacy in educational contexts (e.g., Ashton & Webb, 1986; Dembo & Gibson, 1985; Newmann, Rutter, & Smith, 1989; Rosenholtz, 1985). Bandura (1986) asserts that self-efficacy is not a global disposition, but is situation specific and socially constructed. Likewise, Raudenbush, Rowan, and Cheong (2005) found that high school teachers reported feeling more efficacious in some classes than others. Self-efficacy is also linked to motivation to accept change in work situations (Brief & Aldag, 1981). If we apply these insights to our scenario with Mrs. Lewis we can begin to understand how she had high self-efficacy for traditional instruction, but low self-efficacy for using the new methods.

The understanding that self-efficacy, like knowledge (Vygotsky, 1978), is socially constructed has important implications for educational reformers. These precepts of sociocultural theory have found their way into the literature on teacher development and drive many educational reform initiatives (Schulman, 1987; Sparks, 1994). Educational researchers and practitioners alike have begun to recognize the importance of social interactions in the professional growth of teachers (Leithwood, Dart, Jantzi, & Steinbach, 1991; Lieberman, 1990; Little, 1982, 1993; Rosenholtz, 1989). Activities which support social/collegial interaction between teachers are highly recommended by many as the best way to scaffold teacher learning and thereby accomplish meaningful improvements in instruction. Such activities as focused study groups, teacher networking, mentoring, coaching, brainstorming, or collaborative problem solving can provide valuable opportunities for teachers to think about and discuss topics over an extended period (Arbough, 2003; Loucks-Horsley, Hewson, Love, & Stiles, 1998). Studies of teachers involved in these types of collegial learning experiences report that having a social support system was important in increasing their sense of sense of self-efficacy (Little, 2001; Loup, 1994).

Returning to our vignette, we can begin to see how these concepts have a bearing on Mrs. Lewis' feelings about the new curriculum. Perhaps Mrs. Lewis' self-efficacy would be enhanced if the curriculum were being implemented school wide, with regular opportunities for teachers to interact. However, since the program is only being piloted by a select few, social reinforcement for the new behaviors is limited. As it is, Beckley's culture is socially reinforcing maintenance of the existing instructional norms. This is providing Mrs. Lewis with little opportunity to make-sense of the new curriculum in light of her own experience (Louis, Febey, & Schroeder, 2005) or to build her own self-efficacy for using the new methods.

Sociocultural Influences: School Culture as the Official "Unofficial Rule Book"

School culture refers to the established ways of doing things that have evolved and prevail in a particular school (Bower, 1966; Schoen, 2005). School culture is built upon shared understandings about priorities and "the best ways to get the job done" in a given school (Deal & Kennedy, 1983). Culture is the means by which a school establishes and maintains its identity and is an integral part of all school processes. The culture of the school is the frame through which new persons, ideas, and programs are viewed and interpreted (Deal & Peterson, 1999; Hargreaves, 1994; Owens, 2001).

Each school has its own distinctive culture (Sarason, 1996; Stoll & Fink, 1996). School culture can be broken down into four separate but overlapping dimensions: The Professional Orientation of the Faculty, The Organizational and Leadership Structure, The Quality of the Learning Environments, and The Student-Centered Focus (Schoen, 2005; Schoen & Teddlie, 2005a). Norms of teacher behavior exist within each of these dimensions. School culture perpetuates a set of collective values and exerts a constant influence over teachers to conform to accepted norms of behavior (Deal & Peterson, 1999; Owens, 2001; Sarason). The strength of prevailing norms varies from dimension to dimension within a school and between schools. Therefore, what is very important to teachers in one school, may be inconsequential for teachers at a nearby school. The culture of the school influences teacher behavior in a number of ways and can impact teacher effectiveness. Let us consider the impact of Beckley's culture on Mrs. Lewis.

Beckley is a school with a moderately strong professional orientation. Consequently, Mrs. Lewis' natural inclination towards studiousness and meticulous planning caused her to fit in well and achieve some degree of respect among her colleagues. Beckley also has a traditional approach to leadership and discipline with the principal and a number of teachers leaning towards more autocratic and authoritarian patterns of behavior. Mrs. Lewis' no nonsense approach and firm classroom discipline are typical of school norms. She does what she is asked at the school, but perceives that her role is to maintain order and to deliver a set curriculum to the students; nothing more, nothing less. Quality instruction, for her, consists of making sure the students are attentive and complete their assigned tasks. This, too, is a behavioral norm exhibited by most of the teachers at Beckley. The school, in general, has a low standard of student-centered focus with few special programs offered for students not officially qualifying for special education services. Instructional differentiation in the regular education classroom is rare at Beckley. The principal tracks student achievement from one year to the next, but no effort is made to disaggregate the data and track the performance of subpopulations or individuals. Feedback for teachers consists of how well the students performed by grade level or subject area on standardized tests. Program evaluation is performed at the district level and teachers have very little input.

In all, there is little in Beckley's culture that reinforces a decision on Mrs. Lewis' behalf to adopt the new curriculum. In fact, the new program introduced in the summer training actively violates norms in several dimensions of Beckley's culture. To implement the program successfully Mrs. Lewis would need to change behavior established over a period of time and widely accepted as "the right way of doing things" by most of her colleagues. To teach in the ways recommended by this program, would, without a doubt, invite numerous raised eyebrows and critical comments from her colleagues. Sarason (1996) noted that "change is greeted with suspicion and reluctance when expectations for behavior embedded in a new practice do not coincide with existing conceptions of the way school life is or should be." This seems to be the case with Mrs. Regina Lewis, who ultimately opts for the path of least social resistance, rather than the path of "the lone social reformer."

The culture of the school exerts a powerful influence over teacher behavior by socially reinforcing one set of behaviors over others. In some situations, school culture can actually coerce teachers to alter ineffective behavior by socially reinforcing positive instructional behavior (Hargreaves & Goodson, 1996; Senge, 1990). Numerous researchers have underscored the importance of school culture in accomplishing change (Chrispeels, 1992; Deal & Peterson, 1999; Halsall, 1998; Hargreaves,

1994, 1997; Schein, 1985; Stoll & Fink, 1996). Conversely, even the most theoretically sound and well funded reforms can fail when they neglect to address issues faced by the teachers responsible for implementing the changes (Fullan, 1993; Little, 2001; Remillard, 2005); chief among these are social and cultural concerns.

Sociopolitical Influences: Pressures From the Outside

Policy Compliance

Sociopolitical influences on teachers are those gleaned from the larger social context, beyond the realm of the individual school. One source of sociopolitical influence on teachers is the expectation that they act in accordance with district, state, and national policies. These concerns influenced the manner in which Mrs. Lewis responded to the new science program. She found herself in a precarious place that confronts many teachers when official policy changes, but personal and school values do not. She was faced with finding a way to comply with new mandates without substantially changing old ways (Gold, 2002). A recent study of school change in six elementary schools in the United States (Schoen, 2005) found that at schools resistant to change, teachers can be quite resourceful and adept at finding ways to adapt to new policies and programs without making substantial changes. Schoen found that in nonimproving schools involved in change initiatives, the faculties went through the motions of adopting the reform, but in actuality the teachers found creative ways of avoiding meaningful behavioral change by layering aspects of the new program on top of existing norms; this was referred to as the *layering on effect*. Similar findings have been documented in the implementation of new curricula in mathematics (Remillard, 2005) and Technology (Hennessy, Kenneth, Ruthven & Brindley, 2005). In all of these studies teachers "artfully" molded the new ways around the old, so that very little substantive change actually occurred. Curriculum theorists also allude to this by establishing different meanings for the word curriculum (Gehrke, Knapp, & Sirotnik, 1992). For example, the *formal curriculum* refers to the goals and activities outlined in school policies or textbooks, whereas the *enacted curriculum* is what is actually taught in the classroom (Gehrke et al.).

In our scenario, Mrs. Lewis has decided that she does not really want to change the way she teaches for psycho-social reasons as well as sociocultural ones. Hence, she develops what Argyris and Schon (1976) would call a "theory of action" that tries to fuse the new with the old in the least disruptive manner. She finds ways to use the new materials in ways consistent with her preexisting basic assumptions and espoused beliefs. However, Mrs. Lewis is mindful of district policy and expectations for compliance, so she goes through the motions of implementation, such as meeting with Miss Clark, but her compliance is surface level. Fullan (1993) noted that this survival skill is common in situations where teachers are expected to demonstrate change without being given adequate time or support. In Mrs. Lewis' case, she possesses the requisite knowledge and skills to implement the new curriculum, but has opted not to for a variety of socially derived reasons. Despite her internal resistance to change, she is aware that there could be repercussions for openly rejecting established policy. Therefore, in response to sociopolitical concerns, possibly associated with fear of job or status loss, she goes through the motions in order to appear compliant to supervisors. Her resistance to the new curriculum, therefore, remains subtle and passive.

Institutional Norms

Institutional norms exist in all social institutions and create "social identities in which scripts emerge that guide action" (Weick, 1979). Individuals tend to mimic or imitate those they perceive as successful within the social institution. Thereby, institutional forces exert pressures upon individuals to behave in a manner consistent with established form. This phenomenon is referred to as structural isomorphism and it functions to stabilize the role of an institution in society (Scott, 1995). Schooling is a fairly stable societal institution, and as such certain expectations and standards have evolved in conjunction with it (DiMaggio & Powell, 1983). Some institutional norms are regional in nature, such as the extent to which the state funds education. Most, however, tend to be more universal in nature, such as roles and responsibilities associated with schools, and the relationship between student and teacher (Murphy, 1991). While there is little research on the impact of institutional norms on the behavior of teachers, the presence of institutional norms is well documented (DiMaggio & Powell; Jespersen, Nielsen, & Sognstrup, 2002; Scott).

Teachers' awareness of institutional norms may have an impact upon the way in which they perform their job. Each individual, teacher, administrator, or parent in the schooling relationship has past experiences with other schools, and has had the opportunity to formulate concepts about what it means to go to school and to teach school. These expectations are present, at some level, in any school context. Institutional norms in general, tend to provide some degree of stability and continuity across various organizations (i.e., schools) within an institution. In general, the influence exerted by the institutional context tends to be conservative, reinforcing more traditional behaviors routinely associated with the prescribed institutional roles (Gupta, Dirsmith, & Fogarty, 1994). This influence occurs through past associations with schools who have adhered to these traditional practices, and through awareness that contemporaries still follow these "time honored" practices. Thus, institutional norms influence teachers to "stick with the tried and true" and can have a negative impact on any change effort that seeks to break with norms of the institution at large. Examples of some reforms that have broken institutional norms are attempts at nongraded schools, year round schools, or schools that follow a nonstandard curriculum. While these types of reforms can be successful, they tend to not enjoy as much popular support, in part, because these ideas do not adhere to the mental image most people have when they think of "school." Implementing programs outside of institutional norms may require large investments in time, money, and effort in order to gain the necessary internal and external public support. Policymakers would be wise to consider how well proposed changes fit with the social conceptions of teachers and parents before embarking on dramatic school change initiatives.

Community Expectations

The final arena of sociopolitical influence over teacher behavior is local traditions indigenous to the community in which the school is located. Schools do not exist in isolation from the rest of society, but are an integral part of it. Teachers are frequently members of the community in which they teach, or are at least familiar with local traditions. An example of teacher responsiveness to community expectations can be found by delving a little deeper into Miss Clark's experience at Beckley Elementary School.

Miss Clark's background is urban and suburban in nature. She was hired to work at Beckley because of her outstanding credentials, but is not a member of the rural community immediately surrounding Beckley. When she began teaching at Beckley she believed firmly in the importance of homework for students, thus she assigned a goodly amount on a daily basis. Her lesson plans were written to build upon the homework from the night before, but she soon encountered a problem. Substantial numbers of her students, even the best students, were not completing the tasks assigned to them in the evenings. She reacted by implementing harsh penalties, but it seemed to have little impact. When a student invited her to attend his soccer game she was surprised to see how many school people she recognized.

After attending a few of these sporting events and observing how well attended they were and how involved the students and their families were in these activities, she began to realize the importance of athletics to the community. Subsequent to this she had an opportunity to visit casually with one of her colleagues who was a native of Beckley and had several school aged children involved in sports. She spoke harshly of insensitive teachers who assigned "unnecessary" homework. Miss Clark found this an odd statement from a teacher; from her perspective, academics should take precedent. It was not until she befriended a coach and history teacher at the local high school that she understood. He explained to her that this was a working class community whose primary form of socialization was involvement in recreational sports. The area has historically had a strong athletic tradition and has produced a number of professional athletes who now live affluently. He also explained that area high school students received more athletic scholarships than academic scholarships. Therefore, though there was otherwise strong public support for education, the parents resented homework because they felt it hurt their child's chances of excelling in sports. She learned that most teachers had learned to work around this. In light of understanding the strength of this local tradition, Miss Clark, too, adapted her instructional plans to include less homework.

This scenario highlights how differences in the contextual setting can influence the instructional decisions and behavior of teachers. Examples of sociopolitical influence from the community might include community pressure for a school near a military base to implement strict disciplinary policies, people in affluent areas expecting schools to offer enriched/accelerated content, or expectations that schools in high crime areas implement drug and violence prevention programs. Miss Clark's experience in the ballpark illustrates how informal interactions with colleagues and community members can help teachers make sense of and respond to (Louis, Febey, & Schroeder, 2005) community expectations.

USING SOCIAL AND CULTURAL FORCES TO ENHANCE TEACHER EFFECTIVENESS

The preceding section has described three sources of sociocultural influences on teachers: (1) psycho-social influences internal to teachers, (2) sociocultural influences internal to the school, and (3) sociopolitical influences derived from the larger society. The extent to which these influences impact individual teachers or schools is not known. Nor is it known which of these social realms exerts greater control over teacher behavior or teacher motivation to change behavior related to instruction. These are questions for future research.

Helpful insights regarding social mechanisms at work in the behavioral change of teachers have been gained by researchers in the fields of psychology, education, and sociology. It is through application of knowledge bases in all of these areas that we can begin to understand the complexities of teacher effectiveness, and the forces at work when we attempt to implement instructional change. Social forces at the individual/

intrateacher level, the organizational/interpersonal level and the societal level simultaneously act on teachers, shaping the way teachers act upon acquired knowledge and skills. Awareness of these social influences on teachers may help administrators create social conditions in the school that are conducive to effective teaching.

In recent years advances have been made in the study of school improvement, among these is the emergence of a situative perspective (Borko, 2004) which acknowledges that education is a multidisciplinary field of practice whose tools of inquiry are diverse in nature and are derived from many epistemologies and traditions (Chatterji, 2002). This influence is seen in calls for school reform models which meet both the needs of the teacher as an individual and as a member of a social group (Fullan, 1993). The remainder of this chapter is devoted to discussing researched based ways in which the culture of the school might be altered to create a social context conducive to enhancing teacher effectiveness.

Psycho-Social Considerations

Teacher Self-Efficacy: The Can do Attitude That Makes the Difference

Sometimes teachers cling to the familiar because they are unsure of their ability to perform successfully within the new system (Fuller, Wood, Rapoport, & Dornbusch, 1982; Loup, 1994). Low self-efficacy can impact a teacher's willingness or motivation to engage in new behaviors (Ashton & Webb, 1986; Brief & Aldag, 1981; Choi & Price, 2005; Loup, 1994). Studies of effective (Ashton & Webb, 1986; Reynolds, Creemers, Stringfield, Teddlie, & Schaffer, 2002; Reynolds, Teddlie, Hopkins, & Stringfield, 2000; Rosenholtz, 1985; Teddlie & Stringfield, 1993) and improving schools (Schoen, 2005) have established that teacher efficacy in these schools is high. Teachers have a "can do" attitude and are resourceful in finding ways to increase student learning. Therefore, the success of school improvement efforts may be related the extent to which the initiative offers opportunities for teachers to interact and build individual and collective teacher efficacy relevant to the expected changes.

Professional Development: Why it Works

Successful school improvement initiatives include professional growth opportunities at the individual teacher level, as well as at the school level (Fullan, 1993, 1999; Loup, 1994). Teacher training programs or seminars, like the one attended by Mrs. Lewis and Miss Clark, are not uncommon at the launching of a new initiative. Such programs introduce teachers to *what* the initiative entails and *how* it is to be implemented at the classroom level. These components are essential for program success, as teachers must clearly understand what is expected of them in order to execute it. However, a frequently over looked component of such training programs is the *why*.

Teachers need to understand the rationale behind the new initiative (Louis, Febey, & Schroeder, 2005). When they comprehend the intellectual framework for why this program or initiative is believed to be superior to other methods, this provides them with a level of motivation that otherwise may be lacking. Research on school improvement (National Foundation for the Improvement of Education [NFIE], 1996; Senge, 1990, 2000; Schoen, 2005; Schoen & Teddlie, 2005b) has documented the importance of teachers understanding the need for change on teacher motivation and support for school change. Yet, we still see school improvement initiatives launched without providing teachers adequate time to reflect individually and collectively on why it is that change is needed, and how the proposed initiative will impact their teaching.

There is overwhelming consistency among school improvement proponents that improved professional development may be a key to educational reform (National Staff Development Council [NSDC], 1995). Interactive professional development that is sustained in focus and duration and involves teachers in routine structured collaborative interactions about instruction has been recommended by many experts in school reform (Boyle, Lamprianou, & Boyle, 2005; Corcoran, 1995b; Darling-Hammond, 1995; Hargreaves & Fullan, 1992; Lieberman, 1996; Little, 1993; Richardson, 1994; Stiles, Loucks-Horsley, & Hewson, 1996). Teachers who belong to highly collaborative cultures report higher self-efficacy (Raudenbush, Rowan, & Cheong, 2005) which makes sense if we accept that self-efficacy is socially constructed (Mayo & Kajs, 2005). Activities such as teacher study groups, participation in teacher networks across contexts, and action research are believed to build teacher self-efficacy.

Instructional Support and Developing Teacher Efficacy for Change

Even when teachers understand and accept the need for change, and have been provided with the tools to implement changes (e.g., extensive training as to *what* they are to do and *how*, *and* have the necessary materials in hand), there is no guarantee that the program will be executed as intended (Remillard, 2005). In addition to group professional development, teachers also benefit from more individualized sources of social feedback such as mentoring and coaching relationships, formative instructional supervision, and focused reflection. These activities are associated with improved self-efficacy, greater teacher professionalism, and deeper connections between theory and practice (Arbaugh, 2003).

Teacher efficacy in particular, might be enhanced through providing non-threatening in-class instructional supports. Examples of activities which could build teacher efficacy for a new instructional method include:

- Observing and/or team teaching with a knowledgeable teacher
- Planning a lesson collaboratively, being observed teaching it, and receiving feedback from someone proficient in the program
- Receiving training in professional reflection (Schon, 1983) and keeping a reflective log of experiences with the new initiative
- Participating in periodic informal discussions with colleagues who are also trying to implement the new initiative (Sparks, 1994)
- Coaching a new comer or novice teacher in techniques that you have used successfully

It must be emphasized that teacher observations in the early implementation phase of a program should be primarily for the purpose of instructional support and not for formal teacher evaluations. Otherwise, teachers may be reluctant to open up to supervisors and may feel inhibited to experiment (Fullan, 1993). When teachers realize that a period of trial and error is natural and expected, and that observations and interactions are being used to support rather than to evaluate, they may feel less threatened. Teachers are more likely to experience a growth in knowledge and skills in a supportive and interactive social climate. Given that a positive relationship between teacher effectiveness and teacher efficacy has been established, gains in teacher efficacy can also be expected (Ashton & Webb, 1986; Brookover et al., 1984; Brookover & Lezotte, 1979; Levine & Lezotte, 1990; Teddlie, 1993).

Establishing a School Culture That Supports Instructional Change

Research on school and organizational change has established that school culture is strongly associated with change and capacity to change (Deal & Peterson, 1999; Halsall, 1998; Schoen, 2005; Schoen & Teddlie, 2005b). School culture is a normative concept which gives the school and its teachers a sense identity and continuity through a system of unwritten unofficial standards of conduct for school people (a term inclusive of not only personnel, but students, parents, and others routinely a part of "the scene"). These standards prescribe for school people the "correct" or socially acceptable way of doing things at this school. This code of conduct is rarely verbalized, but is perceived from the actions of others, particularly those with high status, popularity or social standing in the group. The cultural code in effect says, "This is who we are and how we do things"; those who adhere strictly to its dictates are accepted as insiders or members.

Not all norms of behavior in a school's cultural code are equally sacred (Rossman, Corbit, & Firestone, 1988; Schein, 1985; Schein, 1996). Some things are profane and can be ignored by members with little or no notice by other members. Other aspects are more sacred because they are strongly tied to basic assumptions strongly held by the group. Violation of sacred traditions can bring harsh social sanctions for teachers who choose not to conform, but act in "out-of–the-box" ways. Hence, school culture exerts a strong controlling force over teacher behavior. Educational researcher, Robert Halsall (1998) asserts that "unless the issue of school culture is addressed, school improvement will never be achieved."

The Dimensions of School Culture and School Change

Research on school culture (Schoen, 2005; Schoen & Teddlie, 2005a) has suggested a four dimensional framework for the construct which includes: Professional Orientation, Organizational and Leadership Structure, Quality of the Learning Environments, and Student-Centered Focus. Early studies using this framework indicated that the Professional Orientation of the faculty and the Organizational Structure of the school have the strongest impact on student achievement (Schoen, 2005). Therefore, schools wishing to implement changes should concentrate on school leadership and developing a professional orientation among the teachers. This is consistent with prior findings by researchers (e.g., Leithwood et al., 1991; Darling-Hammond, 1990, 1993). It is believed that norms in leadership (i.e., the leadership style of the principal, the amount/types of teacher leadership, and the established school routines/traditions) and teacher professional orientation (attitudes and common practices regarding acquiring new knowledge/skills, reflection, and responsibility for student learning) have the most influence over the way teachers think and act in their school setting. The norms of behavior across all dimensions of culture act collectively to exert a strong influence over teacher behavior in a number of ways. Thus, school culture can significantly contribute to or detract from teacher effectiveness.

Transformational school leaders can have a dramatic effect on school culture by inspiring teachers to work toward a collective vision (Deal & Peterson, 1999; Leithwood et al., 1991). Such leadership can facilitate changes, such as implementing greater teacher leadership, restructuring time to allow for increased collaboration, providing instructional support, engaging in routine on-site program evaluation, and facilitating the acquisition of new instructional knowledge and skills in teachers (Newmann, 1996; Reynolds, et al., 2000, 2002; Sashkin & Egermeier, 1992; Senge et al., 2000; Schulman, 1987). Visionary school leadership can be instrumental in encouraging teachers to engage in more professional and effective behavior. Collaborative school cultures are more likely to provide teachers with positive psycho-social and sociocultural influences. They can also generate useful interpretive frames to mitigate perceived sociopolitical influences which can compromise teacher effectiveness.

Establishing a highly effective school culture can take considerable time, 3-5 years by some estimates (Fullan, 1993), but is worth the effort since school culture is believed to be strongly tied to both teacher effectiveness and school improvement (Deal & Peterson, 1999; Halsall, 1998; Hargreaves, 1994; Sarason, 1996; Schoen, 2005, Schoen & Teddlie; 2005a, 2005b; Teddlie & Reynolds, 2000). Once firmly established, school culture tends to become self-perpetuating, and provides a powerful source of social influence over teachers, constantly nudging them to perform their work according to its dictates.

CONCLUSION

There is still much that is unknown about the social influences that impact teacher behavior. This chapter has presented one conceptualization which categorizes them into psycho-social, sociocultural, and sociopolitical influences. Future research might investigate which of these sources of social influence concern teachers more. Qualitative studies of teachers participating in change initiatives might shed light on the particular concerns teachers have when asked to implement new programs, or the decision making processes teachers engage in when they implement planned changes. There is still much to be learned about the extent to which sociopolitical influences from outside the school impact teacher choices. Though they are not seen, social influences should not be overlooked by school leaders, as they may have a very real impact over the way teachers perform their work. Savvy administrators should be aware of the social factors which can influence teachers and make every effort to use social and cultural factors to maximize teacher and school effectiveness.

REFERENCES

Angelides, P., & Ainscow, M. (2000). Making sense of the role of culture in school improvement. *School Effectiveness and School Improvement, 11,* 145-163.

Arbaugh, F. (2003). Study groups as a form of professional development for secondary Mathematics teachers. *Journal of Mathematics Teacher Education 6,* 139-163.

Argyris, C. (1964). *Integrating the individual and the organization.* New York: Wiley.

Argyris, C., & Schon, D. (1976). *Theory in practice: Increasing professional effectiveness.* San Francisco: Jossey-Bass.

Ashton, P. T., & Webb, R. B. (1986). *Making a difference: Teachers' sense of self-efficacy.* New York: Longman.

Bandura, A. (1977). Self-efficacy: Toward a unifying theory of behavioral change. *Psychological Review, 84,* 191-215.

Bandura, A. (1986). *Social foundations of thought and action: A social cognitive theory.* Englewood Cliffs, NJ: Prentice-Hall.

Bandura, A. (1997). *Self-efficacy: The exercise of control.* New York: Freeman.

Bandura, A. (1999). *Self-efficacy in changing societies.* Cambridge, England: Cambridge University Press.

Blasé, J. J., & Kirby, P. C. (2000). Bringing out the best in teachers: What effective principals do (2nd ed.). Thousand Oaks, CA: Corwin Press.

Bolman, L., & Deal, T. E. (1997). *Reframing organizations: Artistry, choice and leadership* (2nd ed.). San Francisco: Jossey-Bass.

Borko, H. (2004). Professional development and teacher learning: Mapping the terrain. *Educational Researcher, 33*(8), 3-15.

Bower, M. (1966). *Will to manage.* New York: McGraw-Hill.

Boyle, B., Lamprianou, I., & Boyle, T. (2005). Longitudinal study of teacher change: What makes professional development effective? Report of the second year of the study. *School Effectiveness and School Improvement, 16*(1), 1-27.

Brief, A. P., & Aldag, R. J. (1981). The "self" in work organizations: A conceptual review. *The Academy of Management Review, 6*(1), 77-88.

Broadway, F. S. (1999). Student teachers' sense-making of an instructional ecology. *Journal of Research and Development in Education, 32,* 234-245.

Brookover, W. B., & Lezotte, L. W. (1979). *Changes in school characteristics coincident with changes in student achievement.* East Lansing: Institute for Research on Teaching, College of Education, Michigan State University.

Brookover, W. B., Schweitzer, J. G., Schneider, J. M., Beady, C. H., Flood, P. K., & Wisenbacher, J. M. (1978). Elementary school social climate and school achievement. *American Educational Research Journal 15,* 301-318.

Brookover, W. B., Beamer, L., Efthim, H., Hathaway, D., Lezotte, L., Miller, S., et al. (1984). *Creating effective schools: An in-service program for enhancing school learning climate and environment.* Holmes Beach, FL: Learning Publications.

Brophy, J., & Good, T. L. (1986). Teacher behavior and student achievement, in Wittrock M. (Ed.), *Third handbook of research on teaching* (pp. 328-375). New York: Macmillan.

Brown, M. W. (2002). *Teaching by design: Understanding the design of curricular innovation.* Unpublished doctoral dissertation, Northwestern University, Evanston, IL.

Bryk, A., Camburn, E., & Louis, K. S. (1999). Promoting school improvement through professional communities: An analysis of Chicago elementary schools. *Educational administration quarterly, 35,* 707-750.

Chatterji, M. (2002). Models and methods for examining standards based reforms and accountability initiatives: Have the tools of inquiry answered pressing questions on improving schools? *Review of educational research, 72*(3), 345-386.

Choi, N. J., & Price, R. H. (2005). The effects of person-innovation fit on individual responses to innovation. *Journal of Occupational and Organizational Psychology, 78,* 83-96.

Chrispeels, J. H. (1992). *Purposeful restructuring: Creating a culture for learning and achievement in elementary schools.* London: Falmer Press.

Coburn, C. E. (2001). Collective sense-making: How teachers mediate reading policy in their professional communities. *Education evaluation and policy analysis, 23,* 145-170.

Conley, D. T., & Bodone, F. (2002). *University expectations for student success: Implications for system alignment and state standard and assessment policies.* Eugene: University of Oregon.

Corcoran, T. B. (1995b). *Transforming professional development for teachers: A guide for state policymakers.* Washington, DC: National Governors' Association.

Darling-Hammond, L. (1990). Teacher professionalism: Why and how. In A. Leiberman (Ed.), *Schools as collaborative cultures* (pp. 25-50). Bristol, PA: Falmer Press.

Darling-Hammond L. (1993). Reframing school reform agenda: Developing capacity for school transformation. *Phi Delta Kappa, 74,* 753-761.

Deal, T. E., & Kennedy, A. (1983). Culture and school performance, *Educational leadership, 40*(5), 140-141.

Deal T., & Peterson, K. (1999). *Shaping school culture: The heart of leadership.* San Francisco: Jossey-Bass.

Dembo, M. H., & Gibson, S. (1985). Teachers' sense of self-efficacy: An important factor in school improvement. *Elementary School Journal 86,* 173-184.

DiMaggio, P. J., & Powell, W. W. (1983). The iron cage revisited: Institutional Isomorphism and collective rationality in organizational fields. *American Sociological Review, 48,* 147-160.

DuFour, R., & Eaker, R. (1998). *Professional learning communities at work: Best practices for enhancing student achievement.* Bloomington, IN: National Educational Service & Association for Supervision & Curriculum Development.

Eisner, E. W. (1994). *The educational imagination: On the design and evaluation of school programs* (3rd ed.). New York: Macmillan.

Elmore, R. F. (1992). Why restructuring alone won't improve teaching. *Educational leadership, 49*(7), 44-48.

Elmore, R. F. (1996). *Staff development and instructional improvement in community school district #2, New York city.* Cambridge, MA: Consortium for Policy Research in Education.

Fullan, M. (1993). *Change forces: Probing the depths of educational reform.* London: The Falmer Press.

Fullan, M. (1999). *Change forces: The sequel.* London: Falmer Press.

Fuller, B., Wood, K., Rapoport, T., & Dornbusch, S. M. (1982). The organizational context of individual efficacy. *Review of Educational Research, 52,* 7-30.

Gehrke, N. J., Knapp, M. S., & Sirotnik, K. A. (1992). In search of school curriculum. *Review of Research in Education, 18,* 51-110.

Gold, B. (2002). *Social construction of urban education: New Jersey whole school reform and teachers' understanding of social class and race.* New York: Pace University.

Gupta, P. P., Dirsmith, M. W., & Fogarty, T. J. (1994). Coordination and control in a government agency: Contingency and institutional theory perspectives on GAO audits. *Administrative science quarterly, 39*, 264-284.

Halsall, R. (1998). *Teacher research and school improvement.* Philadelphia: Open University Press.

Hargreaves, A. (1991). Contrived collegiality: The micropolitics of teacher collaboration. In J. Blase (Ed.), *The politics of life in schools.* Newbury Park, CA: Sage.

Hargreaves, A. (1994). *Changing teachers, changing times: teachers' work and culture in the postmodern age.* London: Cassell.

Hargreaves, A. (Ed.). (1997). *Rethinking educational change with heart and mind.* Alexandria, VA: Association of Supervision and Curriculum Development.

Hargreaves, A., & Fullan, M. G. (1992). *Understanding teacher development.* London: Cassell.

Hargreaves, A., & Goodson, I. (1996). Teachers' professional lives: aspirations and actualities. In I. Goodson & A. Hargreaves (Eds.), *Teachers' professional lives* (pp. 1 27). London: Falmer Press.

Hennessy, S., Ruthven, K., & Brindley S. (2005). Teacher perspectives on integrating ITC into subject teaching: Commitment, constraints, caution, and change. *Journal of Curriculum Studies, 37*(2), 155-192.

Jespersen, P. K., Nielsen, L. M., & Sognstrup, H. (2002). Professionals, institutional dynamics, and the new public management in the Danish hospital field. *International Journal of Public Administration, 25*(12), 1555-1574.

Khmelkov, V. T. (2000). Developing professionalism: Effects of school workplace on organization of novice teachers' sense of responsibility and efficacy. *Dissertation Abstracts International, 61*(04) 1639. (UMI microform AAT 9967316)

Kruse, S. D. (1997). Reflective activity in practice: Vignettes of teachers' deliberative work. *Journal of Research and Development in Education, 31*, 46-60.

Leithwood, K., Dart, B., Jantzi, D., & Steinbach (1991). *Building commitment for change: A focus on school leadership.* Toronto, Ontario, Canada: OISE Report prepared for British Columbia Ministry of Education.

Levine, D. U., & Lezotte, L. W. (1990). *Unusually effective schools: a review and analysis of research and practice.* Madison, WI: National Center for Effective Schools Research.

Lieberman, A. (1990). *Schools as collaborative cultures: Creating the future now.* Bristol, PA: Falmer Press.

Lieberman, A. (1995). Restructuring schools: The dynamics of changing practice, structure, and culture. *The work of restructuring schools: Building from the ground up.* New York: Teachers College Press.

Lieberman, A. (1996). Practices that support teacher development: Transforming conceptions of professional learning. In M. W. Mc Laughlin & Oberman (Eds.), *Teacher learning: New policies and new practices* (pp. 185-201). New York: Teachers College Press.

Little, J. W. (1982). Norms of collegiality and experimentation: workplace conditions of school success. *American educational research journal, 19*(3), 325-340.

Little, J. W. (1990). The persistence of privacy: autonomy and initiative in teachers' professional relations. *Teachers college record, 91*(4), 509-36.

Little, J. W. (1993). Teachers' professional development in a climate of educational reform. *Educational evaluation and policy analysis, 15*(2), 129-151.

Little, J. W. (2001). Professional development in pursuit of school reform, in A. Lieberman & L. Miller (Eds.), *Teachers caught in action: Professional development that matters* (pp. 23-44). New York: Teachers College Press.

Loucks-Horsley, S., Hewson, P. Love, N., & Stiles, K. (1998). *Designing professional development for teachers of science and mathematics.* Thousand Oaks, CA: Corwin Press.

Louis, K. S., & Dentler, R. (1988). Knowledge use and school improvement. *Curriculum Inquiry, 18,* 32-62.

Louis, K. S., Febey, K., & Schroeder, R. (2005). State-mandated accountability in high schools: Teachers' interpretations of a new era. *Educational evaluation and policy analysis, 27*(2), 177-204.

Loup. K. S. (1994). *Measuring and linking school professional learning environment characteristics, teacher self and organizational efficacy, receptivity to change, and multiple indices of school effectiveness.* Unpublished doctoral dissertation, Louisiana State University.

McCarthy, S. J., & Peterson, P. L. (1989, April). *Teacher roles: Weaving new patterns in classroom: Practice and school organization.* Paper presented at the annual meeting of the American Educational Research Association, San Francisco.

McLaughlin, M. W., & Pfeifer, R. S. (1988). *Teacher evaluation: Improvement, accountability, and effective learning.* New York: Teachers College Press.

Mayo, N. B., & Kajs, L. T. (2005). Longitudinal study of technology training to prepare future teachers. *Educational research quarterly, 29*(1), 3-15.

Mortimore, P. (1991). Effective schools from a British perspective: Research and practice. In J. R. Bliss, W. A. Firestone, & C. E. Richards (Ed.), *Rethinking effective schools* (pp. 76-90). Englewood-Cliffs, NJ: Prentice-Hall.

Murphy, J. (1991). *Restructuring schools: Capturing and assessing the phenomena.* New York: Teachers College Press

National Foundation for the Improvement of Education (NFIE). (1996). *Teachers take charge of their learning: Transforming professional development for student success.* Westhaven, CT: Author.

National Staff Development Council (NSDC) & National Association of Elementary School Principals. (NAESP). (1995). *Standards for staff development: Elementary school edition.* Oxford, OH and Alexandria, VA: Author.

No Child Left Behind (NCLB). (2002). *Highly qualified teachers: Scientifically based research.* Retrieved February 17, 2006, from http://www.ed.gov/admins/tchrqual/learn/hqt/edlite-slide026.html

Newmann, F. M., & Associates (1996). *Authentic achievement: Restructuring schools for intellectual quality.* San Francisco: Jossey-Bass.

Newmann, F. M., Rutter, R. A., & Smith, M. S. (1989). Organizational factors affecting school sense of efficacy, community, and expectations. *Sociology of education, 64,* 221-238.

Owens, R. G. (2001). *Organizational behavior in education: Instructional leadership and school reform.* Boston: Allyn & Bacon.

Pearson, C., & Moomaw, W. (2005). The relationship between teacher autonomy and stress, work satisfaction, empowerment, and professionalism. *Educational research quarterly, 29*(1), 37-53.

Raudenbush, S. W., Rowan, B., & Cheong, Y. E. (2005). Contextual effects on self-perceived efficacy of high school teachers. *Sociology of education, 65*(2), 150-167.

Remillard, J. T. (1999). Curriculum materials in Mathematics education reform: A framework for examining teachers' curriculum development. *Curriculum inquiry, 29*(3), 211-246.

Remillard, J. T. (2005). Examining key concepts in research on teachers' use of mathematics curricula. *Review of educational research, 75*(2), 211-246.

Reynolds, D., Teddlie, C., Hopkins, D., & Stringfield, S. (2000). School effectiveness and school improvement. In C. Teddlie & D. Reynolds (Eds.), *The international handbook of school effectiveness research* (pp. 206-231). London: Falmer Press.

Reynolds, D., Creemers, B., Stringfield, S., Teddlie, C., & Schaffer, G. (2002). *World class schools: International perspectives on school effectiveness.* London: Routledge Falmer.

Richardson, V. (Ed.). (1994). *Teacher change and staff development process: A case in reading instruction.* New York: Teachers College Press.

Rosenholtz, S. J. (1985). Effective schools: Interpreting the evidence. *American Journal of Education, 94,* 352-387.

Rosenholtz, S. (1989). *Teachers' workplace.* New York: Longman.

Rosenholtz, S. J., Bassler, O., & Hoover-Dempsey, K. (1986). Organizational conditions of teacher learning. *Teaching and Teacher Education, 2*(2), 91-104.

Rossman, G., Corbett, H., & Firestone, W. (1988). *Change and effectiveness in schools: A cultural perspective.* Albany: State University of New York Press.

Sarason, S. (1996). *Revisiting "The culture of the school and the problem of change."* New York: Teachers' College Press.

Sashkin, M., & Egermeier, J. (1992. April). *School change models and processes: A review of research and practice.* Paper presented at the annual meeting of the American Educational Research Association, San Francisco.

Schein, E. H. (1985). *Organizational culture and leadership* (1st ed.). San Francisco: Jossey-Bass.

Schein, E. H. (1992). *Organizational culture and leadership* (2nd ed.). San Francisco: Jossey-Bass.

Schein, E. H. (1996). Three cultures of management: The key to organizational learning. *Sloan Management Review, 38*(1), 9-20.

Schon, D. (1983). *The reflective practitioner: How professionals think in action.* New York: Basic Books.

Schoen, L. (2005). *Conceptualizing, describing, and comparing school cultures: A comparative case study of school improvement processes.* Unpublished doctoral dissertation, Baton Rouge, Louisiana State University.

Schoen, L., & Teddlie, C. (2005a, April). *A theoretical perspective of school culture as a multi-level multi-dimensional construct.* Paper presented to The American Educational Research Association, Montreal, Canada.

Schoen, L., & Teddlie, C. (2005b, April). *Describing and contrasting school cultures: A comparative case study of differentially improving schools.* Paper presented to The American Educational Research Association, Montreal, Canada.

Schulman, L. S. (1987). Knowledge and teaching: Foundations of a new reform. *Harvard Educational Review, 57*(1), 1-21.

Scott, R. W. (1995). *Institutions and organizations.* Thousand Oaks, CA: Sage.

Senge, P. M. (1990). *The fifth discipline: The art and practice of the learning organization.* New York: Doubleday.

Senge, P., Cambron-McCabe, N., Lucas, T., Smith, B., Dutton, J., & Kleiner, A. (2000). *Schools that learn: A fifth discipline fieldbook for educators, parents, and everyone who cares about education.* New York: Doubleday.

Shulman, L., & Sparks, D. (1992). Merging content knowledge and pedagogy: An interview with Lee Shulman. *Journal of Staff Development, 13*(1), 14-16.

Sparks, D. (1994). A paradigm shift in staff development. *Journal of Staff Development, 15*(4). Oxford, OH: National Staff Development Council.

Spillane, J. (2000). Cognition and policy implementation: District policymakers and the reform of mathematics education. *Cognition and Instruction, 18,* 141-179.

Stetsenko, A., & Arievitch, I. M. (2002). Teaching, learning and development: A post-Vygotskian perspective. In G. Wells & G. Claxton (Eds.), *Learning for life in the 21st century: Sociocultural perspectives on the future of education* (pp. 84-96). London: Blackwell.

Stiles, K., Loucks-Horsley, S., & Hewson, P. (1996). *Principles of professional development for Mathematics and Science education: A synthesis of standards* (NISE Brief, Vol. 1), Madison, WI: National Institutes for Science Education.

Stoll, L., & Fink, D. (1996). *Changing our schools.* Buckingham, England: Open University Press.

Teddlie, C., & Reynolds, D. (2000). *The international handbook of school effectiveness research.* New York: Falmer Press.

Teddlie, C., & Stringfield, S. (1993). *Schools make a difference: Lessons learned from a ten-year study of school effects.* New York: Columbia University, Teachers College Press

Van der Veer, R., & Valsiner, J. (1991). *Understanding Vygotsky: A quest for synthesis.* Oxford, England: Blackwell.

Vygotsky, L. (1978). *Mind in society.* In M. Cole, V. John-Steiner, S. Scribner, & E. Souberman (Eds.), Cambridge, MA: Harvard University Press.

Weick, K. E. (1979). *The social psychology of organizing* (2nd ed.) Reading, MA: Addison-Wesley.

Weick, K. E. (1993). The collapse of sense-making in organizations: The Mann Gulch disaster. *Administrative Science Quarterly, 38,* 628-652.

Zembylas, M. (2003). Interrogating "teacher identity": Emotion, resistance, and self-information. *Educational Theory, 53,* 107-127.

CHAPTER 8

THE GOOD TEACHER

A Cross-Cultural Perspective

David Watkins and Qunying Zhang

Yan was completely devoted to teaching. He spent most of his leisure time helping students with their learning and answering their questions. In order to make it easier for students to approach him, he bought a house on loan near the campus and saved a room where he met his students about their problems.... He loved his students whole-heartedly. Even in the last days of his life, he explained problems to the students who went to see him in the ward.... Within three days after he died of lung cancer there appeared thousands of articles in memory of him on the campus BBS (Bulletin Board Service on Internet). The students voluntarily raised money to publish the corpus of the articles written for him. ("The last class," 2005)

This is a true story that recently happened in China. The hero of the story was a very common yet very good university science teacher. His death evoked a wide social response and provided a basis for discussion on being a good teacher, especially a good university teacher. Whatever opinions people held in the discussion, they all thought highly of him and his deeds. A devoted teacher who not only gives good instruction in class but also extends his or her deep care and love for students outside class has been praised in China for thousands of years.

Effective Schools, 185–204

Today, teachers in China are exhorted to follow in the steps of a teacher such as Yan in the above story. The emphasis is on caring for each student not only in terms of subject knowledge but more importantly in terms of his or her development as a person both within and outside the classroom. Such views of the qualities a teacher should posses are intended to influence Chinese views of what is a good teacher.

However, do Chinese teachers really hold such views? Do other cultures share their opinions? Do these views vary at different levels of education and in different subject areas? Why is it important to try to answer such questions anyway? We will briefly address the last question now while the presentation of research evidence related to the former questions will form the basis of much of this chapter. A further relatively neglected question is whether students and their teachers share a common view of "the good teacher." This issue which will be further examined in this chapter is particularly important in this age of valuing student evaluations of their teachers.

In this chapter, to clarify the issue, the term "China" will refer to the People's Republic of China (PRC) exclusive of Hong Kong which is officially a Special Administrative Area of the PRC. The term "Chinese" will refer to ethnic Chinese people wherever they may live.

THE IMPORTANCE OF CULTURAL PERSPECTIVES

It is now widely recognized that quality of education is related to economic development, so round the world countries from the poorest to the richest see improving education as a necessity for the future success of their nation. Globalization has been a buzzword for economists and educators for at least the last decade. Comparisons of educational achievement such as those conducted by the International Association for the Evaluation of Educational Achievement and the Organisation for Economic and Cultural Development have highlighted large disparities between the performances of students from different countries (e.g., Beaton, Martin, Mulliw, Gonzalez, Smith, & Kelly, 1996a, 1996b). It is now commonplace for countries to bring in international experts to advise how to improve their educational system in areas such as curriculum development; instructional practices; assessment methods; and the professional development and evaluation of teachers at all levels from preschool to postgraduate.

Yet it can be questioned whether different countries actually share a common view of quality teaching and quality teachers. The work of Stigler and Hiebert (1999) suggests that there may well be little such agreement. In their well-known book *The Teaching Gap* these authors were able to describe the nature of the pedagogical flow of educational systems in Germany, Japan, and the United States. After analyzing videotapes of secondary school classrooms in these countries "they were amazed at how much teaching varied across cultures, and how little it varied within cultures" (p. 10). It seemed that each culture had developed its own script and Stigler and Hiebert concluded that superior learning outcomes in Japan were due to a better script rather than due to the actor who delivered it. They concluded that the Japanese teaching script was both more student centered and more focused on higher quality learning outcomes than the American or German scripts. Moreover, the Japanese had built in a quality enhancement mechanism to the educational process. Stigler and Hiebert's findings suggest that before we turn to teachers we first need to explore whether the very nature of teaching may be seen differently in different cultures.

WHAT IS TEACHING?

In every culture it seems clear that the main role of a teacher is to teach. But does "teaching" mean the same thing in every culture? The work of Alexander (2000) comparing primary schools across cultures reported by Berliner (2005, p. 205) further supports the "no" answer:

> A high-quality teacher in India does not allow questioning by the students. Students simply listen for hours on end. The opposite is true in many American classes, where students are expected to raise questions during class. Alexander (2000) found that maintaining discipline is not part of any definition of *quality* in Russia or India because there are almost no discipline problems in their schools. But in the organizationally complex world of American and British schools, with individualization of some activities, promotion of collaboration and negotiation, and a concern for students' feelings, there is a greater incidence of behavior problems. Thus, American and British teachers of high quality must have classroom management skills that are unnecessary in Russia or India.

Chinese Views of Teaching

More than 2500 years ago, the great Chinese thinker Confucius stated that education is an important way for people to acquire knowledge, ability, and virtues and thus it plays a substantial role in personal transformation and enhancement. He maintained that every man can be educated regardless of his social status or class (*You Jiao Wu Lei*). "Confucius himself set an example by never refusing to teach whosoever came with a nominal ceremonial tutorial fee" (*Analects*, VII. 7, cited in Lee, 1996, p. 28).

Of course, one can question whether the words of Confucius and later ancient scholars have relevance today. For many Hong Kong teachers this is clearly the case as shown in the following quotes volunteered by such teachers in the first author's ongoing research:

- The mission of teachers is to teach students how to be a good person. I pay attention to the conduct of students as in a Confucian society, moral values are important.
- Teachers can bring about changes in students, and those changes may last for the whole life. My teacher affected me in my attitudes towards life and I have learnt from him the Confucius philosophy.
- I myself trust in the Confucius ideologies.... I act as a role model for them. I also use personal stories of some famous athletes to teach them the philosophy of life.

Chang (2000) remarks that researching the Chinese people has become "the flavour of the month," among Western cross-cultural researchers (p. 125). Unfortunately, she says, they "find 'Chineseness' in all the wrong places"; it is defined demographically, as an independent variable, while Western derived instruments provide the dependent variables. Thus, Chineseness is in effect defined in terms of deviance from Western norms, and generally as being interestingly different from the world defined by and constructed within mainstream, that is Western, psychology.

According to Watkins and Biggs (2001) the "right places" are where the Chinese identify themselves as being Chinese in places where they normally exist, in classrooms not in laboratories, and who describe themselves using constructs contextualized within their community. Chang refers to such constructs as involving "vernacular Confucianism," that is Confucianism as it may be relevant and interpreted by ordinary Chinese people today. Thus, there is a sense in which Lee Kuan Yew can call Singapore a "Confucian" society, when many of its values are far indeed from what Confucius would even recognize, let alone endorse. In *The Chinese Learner*, Lee (1996) described many educational Confucian values deriving from the *Analects*, yet these are hard to square with the vernacular Confucianism espoused by many Hong Kong teachers today. Watkins and Biggs noted some of these beliefs, such as "no pain, no gain," "scolding builds character" and "failure is the result of laziness." They stem if anywhere from the grim Xun Zi, rather than from the constructivist Confucius described by Lee. But the point is not to which current beliefs about the raising and educating of children can be attributed to what ancient scholars, but the fact itself that these beliefs are current today, within the focus culture, and that they influence what teachers do in present day classrooms. The story at the beginning of this chapter illustrates the view of teaching today's PRC teachers are exhorted to adopt.

According to Confucius, teachers and students have a reciprocal relationship. Feedback from one party is quite valuable to the other. In Chinese culture this relationship is revered: third only in importance to those with the Emperor and the father in Confucian philosophy. Thus most Chinese students automatically show their teachers great respect and treat them as sources of wisdom who should not be questioned (Lee, 1996). In Hong Kong, Chinese school teachers also see their role as extending far more beyond the classroom and far more into moral issues than do most Australian teachers (Ho, 2001). What consistently comes through the research in this area is that teachers in China and Hong Kong believe that they have the role of "cultivating" not only their students' cognitive development but also promoting positive attitudes to society and responsible moral behavior.

This view of teaching came through strongly in the analysis of in-depth interviews and classroom observation of 18 secondary school teachers of physics in Guangzhou, China, from which Gao and Watkins (2001) developed a model of the teaching conceptions held by these teachers. This model was supported in a quantitative study of over 700 such teachers. The model developed involved two higher orientations of Molding (with subareas of Knowledge Delivery and Exam Preparation) and Cultivating (with subareas of Ability Development, Attitude Promotion, and Conduct Guidance). These two orientations have some elements in common with the teacher-centered/content-oriented and student-centered/learning-oriented views identified in Kember's (1997) review of research on Western university teaching but extend the latter to affective and moral areas.

The emphasis on cultivating attitudes and good citizenship is consistent with Chinese cultural values. As one of the respondents of Gao and Watkins (2001, p. 31) put it:

> Teaching should involve far more than knowledge delivery. It should include educating and cultivating students. Help them to learn how to be a person. That's what we call *Jiao Shu Yu Ren* (which means teaching involves developing a good person). This should be more important than other things.

However, it is important to realize that the teaching of such values, supported by virtually all 700 Chinese teachers sampled in the research of Gao and Watkins (2001), is primarily conveyed implicitly in the teacher's performance and teacher-student interaction. The Chinese teacher is expected not only to have good instructional skills but also to be a good moral role model in all areas of life (this is known in China as *Wei Ren Shi Biao*).

It might be argued that this view of teaching would also be commonly held by Western school teachers rather than the university teachers who were the focus of the research reviewed by Kember (1997). However, Ho (2001) in a comparison of Australian and Hong Kong secondary school teachers, found that the former felt their responsibilities ended in teaching the curriculum inside the classroom. The Australians typically did not feel responsible for their student's personal or family problems or even unfinished homework. The Hong Kong teachers saw things very differently, and like their Guangzhou counterparts described above, voiced a pastoral as well as an instructional view of teaching.

The research of Cortazzi and Jin (2001) also depicted a similar view of Chinese teachers. They referred to education as "books and society" and the teacher as a friend and a parent. These authors also argued that this reflects the Chinese holistic view of teaching, where teaching refers not only to the cognitive but also the affective and moral, including teaching children their place in society. Such views were not found in their survey of the views of British teachers.

Western Views of a Good Teacher

> Defining quality in teaching is unusually difficult. Were anyone serious about this issue, they would soon realize that quality is an ineffable concept, as the best-selling book by Pirsig (1974) made clear. Defining quality always requires value judgments about which disagreements abound. (Berliner, 2005, p. 206)

In the United States, the No Child Left Behind Act of 2001 mandated that a highly qualified teacher be in all U.S. classrooms by mid-2005. The supposed principle behind the policy is that if teachers were of a higher quality then education would improve (Berliner, 2005). Of course, the equating of "highly qualified" with "high quality" is simplistic. At best, even if the United States could agree how to define the former. As Berliner pointed out, in terms of formal qualifications such as relevant degrees and teacher training, the current U.S. teaching force is well qualified so what is this Act trying to ensure? Perhaps that students learn more, but again Berliner pointed to clear evidence that the achievement of U.S. students are improving rapidly in major subject areas.

Kottler and Zehm (2000) contended that among the number of attributes that make up the essence of the best teachers are sound subject knowledge, proper methods of instruction, and other related skills. They argued that it was too often overlooked in the Western literature that "it is the human dimension that gives all teachers, whether in the classroom, the sports arena, or the home, their power as effective influencers" (p. 2). The following human characteristics were emphasized by these authors as essential qualities of the best teachers: (1) charisma, (2) compassion, (3) egalitarianism, (4) sense of humor, and (5) additional desirable traits (e.g., smarts, creativity, honesty, emotional stability, patience, ability to challenge and motivate, and novelty) (Kottler & Zehm). Unfortunately, as Berliner (2005) pointed out, such psychological and moral aspects of teaching are hard to measure objectively so are typically ignored in attempts to assess teaching quality.

A study on students' and teachers' cognitions about good teachers in the Netherlands by Beishuizen, Hof, Van Putten, Bouwmeester, and Asscher (2001) involved students of different age groups (7, 10, 13, and 16 years of age) and primary and secondary school teachers in the task of writing an essay on the good teacher. Their analysis identified two dimensions:

> The first dimension reflected the preference of students and teachers for describing the good teacher in terms of either personality or ability characteristics. The second dimension was interpreted as an orientation in the essays towards either attachment to, detachment from or commitment to school and teachers. (Beishuizen et al., 2001, p. 185)

They found that primary school pupils perceived good teachers basically as competent instructors, focusing on transmitting knowledge and skills. Secondary school students laid much weight on relational aspects of good teachers, which was similar to the teachers' perceptions of establishing personal relationship with their students. Hence, disagreements between secondary school students and teachers were smaller than those between primary school pupils and teachers.

Chinese Views of Good Teaching

Before we further examine the conceptions held by modern Chinese teachers and students, we need to consider traditional Chinese beliefs in this regard because their influences on the present, implicitly or explicitly, may be great.

Confucius believed that a good teacher should be completely devoted (*Hui Ren Bu Juan*) and should teach students in accordance with their aptitude (*Yin Cai Shi Jiao*). Han Yu, one of the most celebrated litterateurs and educators in the Tang Dynasty wrote in his book *Shi Shuo* (On Teachers): "What is a teacher? A teacher is the one who shows you the way of being human, teaches you knowledge and enlightens you while you are confused" (Liu, 1973, cited in Gao & Watkins, 2001, p. 461). Good teachers in China should not only promote students' intellectual or academic development, but also enhance their conduct or moral behavior. Some other relevant influential Chinese sayings are: "Teach by personal example as well as verbal instruction" (*Yan Chuan Shen Jiao*), "Teaching as well as cultivating good persons" (*Jiao Shu Yu Ren*), and "Profound knowledge makes teachers, upright behavior makes models" (*Xue Gao Wei Shi, Shen Zheng Wei Fan*). The latter is the accepted doctrine of many normal universities and teacher-training institutes in China today.

With respect to the conceptions of a good teacher held by modern Chinese people, the related research is very limited. Cortazzi and Jin (1996) asked 135 Chinese university students in Tianjin about their perceptions of good teachers by asking them to write essays on this topic. Sixty-seven percent of the students wrote that a good teacher *has deep knowledge* or a similar phrase, 25% of them thought a good teacher *is patient*, 23.7% *is humorous*, and 21.5% *is a good moral example* and *shows friendliness*.

CROSS-CULTURAL STUDIES

School Teachers

Some cross-cultural studies further illuminate Western-Chinese differences. For example, on the basis of the type of essay analysis mentioned above, Jin and Cortazzi (1998) developed a questionnaire which was administered to 129 university students in China and 205 comparable respondents in Britain to explore cross-cultural differences in conceptions of a good school teacher. They found significantly different emphases between Chinese and British students in the conceptual items indicative of a good teacher. In particular good Chinese teachers were more often considered to "have deep knowledge," "have an answer to students' questions" and to "be good moral examples"

The above research supported the conceptions of "knowledge delivery" and "conduct guidance" identified by Gao and Watkins (2001) in their model of conceptions of teaching in China introduced earlier. The first conception of teaching takes learning as a process in which knowledge is transferred from teachers to students. Therefore, deep knowledge and sound academic competence count a lot in valuing a teacher. The latter conception of "conduct guidance" requires a teacher to teach students good behavior and values and to pay attention to their moral development. In contrast, good British teachers are held to "arouse students' interest" "explain clearly" "use effective teaching methods" and "organize a variety of classroom activities."

Jin and Cortazzi (1998) further interviewed some Tianjin primary teachers on the same topic. They typically said that good teachers: "'love their job and love children,' 'have professional morality and responsibility,' 'must have good knowledge, including knowledge of methods to help pupils learn,' 'must be models... write clearly, speak and stand well, have good deeds,' 'develop children's expectations, train children in routines from the very beginning'" (p. 752). Although no parallel interviews were carried out, the researchers surmised that British teachers would agree with the comments given by the Chinese teachers but the degree of emphasis would vary across cultures.

A follow-up study by Lai (2000) examined the perceptions of a good teacher held by secondary school students and teachers in Hong Kong. The findings were compared with those derived from the study of Jin and Cortazzi (1998). It was found that the Hong Kong teachers' and students' views were different from those of both the mainland Chinese teachers and students and the British participants obtained in the latter study. Hong Kong students did not consider teaching methods as important unlike the Chinese and the British students. They preferred the teacher to explain everything clearly so that they can acquire knowledge in the fastest way. They did not care whether the teacher helped them to learn independently or not. The Chinese students admired teachers with deep knowledge but the British and Hong Kong students did not. Consistent with the influence of traditional Confucian thinking, the Chinese and Hong Kong students typically thought that a good teacher should be a moral example but the British students disagreed. The British students believed that good teachers should be able to control discipline but the Chinese and Hong Kong students did not think this as important. This finding is in accord with many previous studies that concluded that high discipline was observed in China, even in very large language classes (e.g., Jin & Cortazzi). Neither the Chinese and Hong Kong teachers nor students considered discipline a big concern.

Student Evaluation of University Teachers

At university level, Lin, Watkins, and Meng (1994) used the "applicability paradigm" proposed by Marsh (1986) to compare perceptions of good and bad teachers in seven different countries or regions, namely Australia, New Zealand, China, Hong Kong, Nepal, the Philippines, and Taiwan. The paradigm required students in these settings to evaluate teachers on an instrument which combined items from several student evaluation of teaching questionnaires. The students in each setting were asked to indicate which 5 of the 55 items were most important for differentiating "good" from "bad" lecturers. The two most important items in all seven settings were whether the teaching style held their interest and whether the lecturer gave clear explanations. There were also differences across the settings. Nepalese students were quite concerned that their teachers allowed them to share ideas in class whereas the Australian, New Zealand, China, and Taiwanese respondents considered the teacher's enthusiasm and the interest they could generate in the students as far more important. The Hong Kong and Filipino students were concerned more about the learning outcomes they achieved. Lin et al. (1994) also examined the similarity in the pattern of the most important items across the seven settings. It was found that the two Western countries, New Zealand and Australia, with quite similar cultural, geographical, and educational systems had the most similar pattern of importance ratings (a similarity index of 0.86). The three Chinese culture settings were more similar to each other than the other countries but with indices of only 0.52 between Hong Kong and Taiwan, 0.60 between Hong Kong and China, and 0.71 between China and Taiwan.

NEW RESEARCH

The above research suggests similar cultural differences within different Chinese culture settings and Western countries. Three as yet unpublished studies which throw further light on the issue of cross-cultural differences in student and teacher views of the good teacher at school and university levels are described below.

Study 1 (Kelly & Watkins, 2002)

The focus of this study was views of an effective university teacher. The research involved four components: (1) a survey of 27 Western and 54 Hong Kong Chinese lecturers from four Hong Kong universities using open-ended questions; (2) focus group interviews with 24 lecturers from three Hong Kong universities; (3) a survey of 405 second and third year Chinese undergraduates from seven departments from the same universities as in (1) above; and (4) focus group discussions with 11 Chinese students from nine departments in three universities. The questions were designed to elaborate on issues raised in the survey.

Analysis showed that the main aims of expatriate and Chinese lecturers were very similar, namely, to develop their students' capabilities in problem solving and critical and analytical thinking. However, when the ways the lecturers reported trying to achieve these goals were examined clear differences emerged. The Western lecturers typically emphasized what the researchers termed a "professional model" of effective teaching. A common theme was that they showed how they cared for their students by their careful preparation of lecturers and the use of good instructional methods. The following quotes illustrate this view:

> The critical thing is to have a professional approach to the relationship in the learning environment. (*ex-pat lecturer; interview response*)

> So I'm caring in the classroom, like I give them lecture notes, OK. I write lecture notes and these are very special showing I'm interested in this unit ... so that's how caring I can be. Anyway so that's how caring I am, and besides that I am pretty cool. I wouldn't have a party with them. When they ask me to take a picture with me I will say "Are you sure?" So that's this anonymity thing, I put that on a similar level. I don't want to know their names. (*ex-pat lecturer; interview response*)

> My attitude towards whether I think that I care for students is whether I believe that I have what I would call a professional approach ... that means they know what is expected of them, they know that I will deliver to them, and they know that what I do in terms of assessment is going to be fair. In terms of my business of caring for them if I do that properly then I believe that I'm caring for them. (*ex-pat lecturer; interview response*)

Only the rare expatriate teachers wanted a more personal relationship:

> So to me it's vital that you establish that human contact and get them comfortable enough so that they can start appreciating themselves ... It really hurts me when you look at an exam result, and you think "oh no, I know she is trying so hard and I know it's difficult for her," but it's like having kids. You know, ... it's exactly like being a parent—that you have to do things that are painful and that are hard. I think if you care, if your students know that you have this in the back of your mind, that what you are doing is really for them.... We are the parents, you know. (*ex-pat lecturer; interview response*)

Responses of this latter type were much more commonly given by the Chinese lecturers. Typically they reported that they cared for their students not just by using good instructional methods but particularly by the relationships they developed with them:

> I emphasize personal contact in my teaching and believe in the effectiveness of staying close to your teacher (i.e., the teacher makes herself available to her students). (*Chinese lecturer; survey response*)

I think it depends on what our needs are and you mentioned the personal interaction. They (students) need caring teachers. They're insecure and incompetent. I think that's partly what one can do in a small group or one-to-one basis ... you have different people giving different people giving different lectures, they need that one (person) for personal care. (*Chinese lecturer; interview response*)

The students also consistently commented on the role of student / teacher relationships in their description of effective teaching:

He established a close relationship with students so, during lessons, students pay more attention to the lecture and dare to ask questions. (*survey response—student*)

He is concerned about students' feelings. During tutorial classes he listened to students attentively and gave feedback. In addition he sometimes makes an appointment to talk to students after class. (*survey response; student*)

Such good relationships were more common with Chinese lecturers:

The Chinese way of teaching is ... not just restricted to knowledge ... but also the students, students' life, students' future. They are concerned about these things. But western teachers are only concerned about students' knowledge in the field of study. They focus on the subject discipline. (*interview response; student*)

It depends on whether they have the heart to understand Hong Kong students ... but if some lecturers can chat with students after talking about the assignments, they can understand more about their students. Some Western lecturers only know that we are young adults. If they put in more effort, I think they can understand more about Hong Kong students. (*interview response; student*)

Study 2 (Watkins & Sachs, 2005)

The views of students have been relatively neglected in research on the 'good teacher' described above. The aim of Study 2 was to compare the perceptions of the "good teacher" held by primary or secondary students from either one of two American International schools in Hong Kong or from one of two typical Chinese public secondary school in Hong Kong. It should be noted that all students in the public schools were of Chinese ethnicity as were the majority of respondents from the international schools. So strictly the comparisons were between students studying in different cultural educational contexts rather than of different cultures. Following the findings of Beishuizen et al. (2001) the perceptions of students from primary and secondary schools and possible interaction effects were also investigated.

One hundred and twenty-eight students agreed to take part in this study. Of these 40, 40, 18, and 30 were from the U.S. international primary (Grade 4, average age of 10 years) and secondary (Grade 10, average age of 16 years) schools and like aged Chinese primary and secondary schools, respectively. Virtually equal numbers of males and females were involved in each group.

All participants were asked to write a short essay at home (no more than one-page) about what they thought a good teacher should be. Following the procedure of Beishuizen et al. (2001) they were also told not to think about any one teacher but rather the good teacher in general. The advantage of the essay approach as used here and some other research reported in this chapter is that it allows the participants to express their own views rather than having the researcher setting the agenda as in standardized questionnaires. We feel that this is particularly appropriate in a cross-cultural study where participants from different cultural backgrounds may not share some perceptions. Students at the international schools wrote in English while those at the Chinese schools in Chinese. The latter essays were transcribed into English by one of four pairs of Hong Kong Chinese part-time graduate students, all experienced secondary school teachers. These same four pairs of Master of Education students acted as judges through the remainder of the analysis. The essays were first divided randomly into four piles of equal size. Each pair of "judges" after analyzing a few essays together to agree on how to proceed, then identified 35 conceptual items used by the respondents to describe the good teacher. The "judges" then worked in pairs again to rescore each essay in their pile according to the presence or absence of the items in that essay: coded as "1" or "0," respectively. They then swapped with another pair of judges to check the reliability of the coding. Over 90% agreement was reached and cases of disagreement were settled by discussion of the judges as a group.

These essay scores were then entered into the computer along with the school context (international versus Chinese) and type (primary versus secondary). The dimensions of these scores were then identified by dual scaling, similar but statistically superior to correspondence analysis (Nishisato & Nishisato, 1998). Each participant's responses were then rescored according to their position on these dimensions, and the ensuing scores analyzed by School Context by School Type ANOVA.

The data analyzed here identified three main dimensions underlying views of the good teacher held by the student respondents. Although many of the students from the former schools were in fact Chinese it seems that, presumably due to the American-based educational environment they found themselves in, they had rather different views of good teachers than their peers attending traditional Chinese schools. Dimension 1 was the one which clearly differentiated between the responses of students from these different school contexts. The international school students generally supported the view that their teachers should not get upset with their students nor make them work too hard while the Chinese school students usually disagreed and emphasized rather that a good teacher should be honest, responsible, and keep their promises.

This supports the findings reported by Watkins and Biggs (2001) that Chinese students tended to expect their teachers to be strict but caring. Further qualitative research may allow us to identify the characteristics of the school environments which promote such different views. We also hope to replicate this study with Western and Chinese students attending schools in their own country to provide a clearer cultural perspective on these findings. Yet it appears that different perceptions of good teachers can be promoted within different school contexts within the same country.

Study 3 (Zhang, 2005)

The above two studies focus on views of good teachers in general. However, Kember (1997) pointed out that conceptions of teaching are likely to vary in terms of the learning context. This study compared the views of Chinese teachers and students and Western teachers involved in English language courses at universities in China.

After reviewing Western and Chinese views of English as a foreign and as a second language (EFL and ESL) teaching some cross-cultural discrepancies emerged and they were summarized by the second author (Zhang, 2005). Four skills are necessary for English language mastery in the eyes of Western educators (reading, listening, speaking, and writing) whereas one more skill (translating) is stressed by Chinese educators. The latter also put much emphasis on laying a solid linguistic foundation for students in early stages of English learning. Cultural appreciation is included in both Western and Chinese practices of English teaching but with different degrees of emphasis. As a matter of fact, it is usually neglected by Chinese educators.

The present teaching approach adopted by EFL tertiary teachers in China is an eclectic approach which is based on the grammar-translation method but integrates many elements of the communicative approach (Cortazzi & Jin, 1996). Such a mixture of teaching methods is adopted because the traditional grammar-translation method is believed to have hindered the development of English language teaching and learning in

China and meanwhile the application of a pure communicative approach has met a lot of problems. Compared with the Western approach, this eclectic approach is more likely to be consistent with teacher-centered, knowledge-based language activities. Guided by the notion of development of communicative skills, student learning assessment using the Western approach is communication-oriented while examination-oriented assessment is dominant in China:

> In many [Western] language classrooms, the major focus is on the development of skills for communication. Much attention is paid to learning contexts and student needs, to creative and appropriate expression. Classroom environments are influenced by learner-centered notions and a task-based or problem-solving approach, for both linguistic and cultural learning.... There is a strong focus on classroom interaction and student participation as ways of learning and developing skills related to the functions and uses of language. (Cortazzi & Jin, 1996, p. 103)

A recent study by Ng (2003) explored teacher and student perceptions of good language teachers in Hong Kong secondary schools. Fourteen English teachers and 148 students participated in the study by writing a short essay on that topic. Five areas of conceptions (personal qualities and personalities, professional development and academic requirement, roles of English teachers, classroom practices, and relationship with students) were identified and differences in the distribution of the conceptions emerged after comparing the teachers' and the students'. The 16 most frequently mentioned conceptual items were obtained from the teachers' and the students' essays respectively.

Ng (2003) concluded that the teachers' perceptions emphasized teaching roles and professional skills whereas the students' perceptions focused on teaching practices in the classroom. This indicates that a gap exists between Hong Kong teachers' and students' perceptions regarding ESL teaching-related activities.

Zhang's (2005) research also involved writing essays as in Study 2 and some of the other research reported in this chapter. The topic this time was the "good tertiary English language teacher." The participants were 100 Chinese undergraduate English language students and 20 Chinese and 20 Western teachers of such students. Each was asked to write a short essay as described above.

The essays were content analyzed based on the combined sample of students and teachers. Identification of conceptual items from all the essays was initially done independently by the researcher and a consultant who had worked as a tertiary English teacher in the PRC for 7 years. All difficult cases were then thoroughly discussed and refinements were made as necessary. As a result of this process a preliminary coding scheme which contained 54 items was developed. Two other educationists were approached next to check the coding. First the researcher randomly selected three essays from the full sample and trained the coders on how to use the coding scheme. Then they were asked to code another 14 randomly selected essays independently without consultation or guidance from the researcher. Based on their responses, the coding scheme was refined.

Forty-nine items were finally retained. The two coders were then asked to analyze another randomly selected sample of 30 essays (21.4% of the full sample) based on which the intercoder reliability for the full sample was assessed. Calculation of Cohen's kappa showed the intercoder reliability for the full sample was high. Then the full sample was analyzed by the three judges and the researcher. All the responses were then assigned the values "0" or "1" according to the "absence" or "presence" of particular items in each essay. Exploratory factor analysis of this data was conducted. Visual inspection of the scree plot of the eigenvalues (Cattell, 1966) supported a seven-factor model which explained 35.55% of the total variance. These factors were identified as follows (1) is highly disciplined; (2) has team spirit and copes with diversity; (3) displays high standards of behavior and responsibility; (4) has sound pedagogical content knowledge; (5) is practical in teaching; (6) interacts with students; and (7) develops the whole student.

MANOVA was employed to examine the mean differences in the seven dimensions of conceptions of a good EFL teacher among the three major groups-Chinese students, Chinese teachers, and Western teachers. It was found that the Western teachers significantly more often supported the second dimension, namely "has team spirit and copes with diversity" and the fifth dimension, "is practical in teaching" than the Chinese teachers and students. The Chinese teachers supported the fourth dimension, "has pedagogical content knowledge," significantly more than the Western teachers and Chinese students.

The second and fifth factors explained many of the cross-cultural differences found in conceptions of a good tertiary English teacher because the items that loaded highly on both factors were emphasized by many foreign teachers in their essays but not by the Chinese participants. These items included "be a good team worker," "get along well with colleagues," "be adaptable to different environments/cultures," "be able to cope with large class size," "connect teaching content to real life," "provide practical knowledge" and so on. The following comments in the Western teachers' essays illustrate these differences:

> Some Chinese colleagues seem to have felt quite threatened at first, and very suspicious. All had read from those Chinese/English cultural texts that

there is a large range of subjects that foreigners don't like talking about. So for the first 18 months (till I heard about this idea) they just didn't know what we could talk about, so some didn't talk to me at all.... However, I have formed some relationships with some teachers and I believe that with more effort and more time from my side, we might be able to have more methodological discussions and sharing together. (*Western teacher 2*)

Chinese students come to class with Confucian values, and if we were more prepared for those before taking on a job in China we would perhaps be better equipped from the beginning.... To stand a chance to learn about Chinese society and the way the Chinese think, Westerners have to devote more time learning about Confucianism.... I don't know how to teach large classes in China, and the communicative Western methods are not always workable in large classrooms where all you can do anyway is "chalk and talk!"... Adapting what we conceived of/how we approached language teaching to Chinese settings is very important. (*Western teacher 10*)

The teacher needs to give practical knowledge. If a teacher gives the students something they will never use or rarely use, the time is wasted. Language learning is a matter of gaining something usable. The teacher needs to provide chances for students to use their knowledge. (*Western teacher 5*)

CONCLUSIONS

The three studies reported here for the first time generally support the Chinese view of a good teacher as portrayed in the story introducing this chapter, in the traditional Chinese literature, and in the limited previous research. For Chinese students and teachers, whether in Hong Kong or Mainland China, a teacher is expected to be caring, to want to get to know his or her students as individuals away from the classroom, and to be a good moral example (and for their students to do well in external exams, of course). Our review of the Western literature and relevant cross-cultural research shows such aspects of teaching are downplayed in the West compared with the need for a good teacher be "professional" in terms of their preparation, teaching skills, and fairness of assessment (see Table 8.1 for a summary of the different emphases in Chinese and Western views).

These cross-cultural differences seem to be found from primary through to tertiary levels of educations. However, there may well be disciplinary specific differences in perceptions of good teachers. While the senior PRC secondary school physics teachers interviewed by Gao and Watkins (2001) fit nicely to the above portrayal of Chinese teachers, Zhang's EFL teachers and students did not.

In the latter study, the Western teachers emphasized that a good tertiary English teacher in their teaching context should fit well into a

**Table 8.1.   Summary of Emphases in Chinese and
Western Views of a Good Teacher**

Western Views	Chinese Views
Has good subject knowledge	Has deep knowledge in general
Uses effective teaching methods	Has deep subject knowledge in particular
Prepares lessons carefully	Focuses on knowledge delivery
Is well qualified	Cares about students' personal problems
Has a professional attitude	Develops close relations with students
Encourages creativity and student activity	Is a good moral guide
Can arouse student interest	Promotes positive attitudes to society
Can control misbehavior	Cultivates good citizenship
Assesses fairly	Students do well in public examinations

"team" with other teachers and needed to be able to adapt to a different learning environment and culture. Not surprisingly the Chinese respondents did not see much need to be concerned with such issues. The Western teachers also emphasized that language teaching should be practical whereas the Chinese teachers considered that sound pedagogical subject knowledge was more salient: underlying this difference may be the communicative versus grammar teaching approach dispute reported in the EFL literature. These results suggest additional research is required in other specific areas of teaching before we can generalize views of the good teacher further.

Such differences in views have implications for the cross-cultural generalizability of notions of educational reform. Currently it is common for reformers in one country to point to how things are done differently elsewhere and advocate importing the other approach. Often this is done without adequate consideration of the cultural values, traditions, and context which have led to the development of their own system in the first place. As in Hong Kong (Watkins & Biggs, 2001) well meaning innovations often fail because the teachers charged with implementing the new approach do not believe in it because they have different views of how they should be teaching.

The views of students were shown to be somewhat different from their own teachers even within their own culture. This may be reflected in the ratings of teachers provided by student as an indicator of teaching competence. Expatriate teachers should also be aware of the more 'caring' attitude expected by their students if they are to be successful in teaching Chinese students.

Future research in other cultures may uncover different views of the good teacher which may have implications for improving educational outcomes in those cultures.

REFERENCES

Alexander, R. (2000). *Culture and pedagogy: International comparisons in primary education.* Oxford, England: Blackwell.

Beaton, A. E., Martin, M. O., Mulliw, I. V. S., Gonzalez, E. J., Smith, T. A., & Kelly, D. L. (1996a). *Science achievement in the middle school years: IEA Third International Mathematics and Science Study.* Chestnut Hill, MA: Center for the Study of Testing, Evaluation, and Educational Policy, Boston College.

Beaton, A. E., Martin, M. O., Mulliw, I. V. S., Gonzalez, E. J., Smith, T. A., & Kelly, D. L. (1996b). *Mathematics achievement in the middle school years: IEA Third International Mathematics and Science Study.* Chestnut Hill, MA: Center for the Study of Testing, Evaluation, and Educational Policy, Boston College.

Beishuizen, J. J., Hof, E., Van Putten, C. M., Bouwmeester, S., & Asscher, J. J. (2001). Students' and teachers' cognitions about good teachers. *British Journal of Educational Psychology, 71,* 185-201

Berliner, D. C. (2005). The near impossibility of testing for teaching quality. *Journal of Teacher Education, 56,* 205-213.

Cattell, R. B. (1966). The scree test for the number of factors. *Multivariate Behavioral Research, 1,* 245-276.

Chang, W. C. (2000). In search for the Chinese in all the wrong places! *Journal of Psychology in Chinese Societies, 1*(1), 125-142.

Cortazzi, M., & Jin, L. (1996). Cultures of learning: Language classrooms in China. In H. Coleman (Ed.), *Society and the language classroom* (pp. 169-206). Cambridge, MA: Cambridge University Press.

Cortazzi, M., & Jin, L. (2001). Large classes in China: "Good" teachers and interaction. In D. A. Watkins & J. B. Biggs (Eds.), *Teaching the Chinese learner: Psychological and pedagogical perspectives* (pp. 115-134). Hong Kong & Australia: Comparative Education Research Centre & Australian Council for Educational Research.

Gao, L., & Watkins, D. A. (2001). Identifying and assessing the conceptions of teaching of secondary school physics teachers in China. *British Journal of Educational Psychology, 71,* 443-469.

Ho, S.-P. A. (2001). A conceptual change approach to university staff development. In D. A. Watkins & J. B. Biggs (Eds.), *Teaching the Chinese learner: Psychological and pedagogical perspectives* (pp. 239-254). Hong Kong & Australia: Comparative Education Research Centre & Australian Council for Educational Research.

Jin, L., & Cortazzi, M. (1998). Dimensions of dialogue: Large classes in China. *International Journal of Educational Research, 29,* 739-761.

Kelly, E., & Watkins, D. A. (2002, April). *A comparison of the goals and approaches to teaching of Expatriate and Chinese lecturers at universities in Hong Kong.* Paper presented to Hong Kong branch of the Higher Education Research and Development Society of Australasia, City University of Hong Kong.

Kember, D. (1997). A reconceptualisation of the research into university academics' conceptions of teaching. *Learning and Instruction, 7*(3), 255-275.

Kottler, J. A., & Zehm, S. J. (2000). *On being a teacher* (2nd ed.). Thousand Oaks, CA: Corwin.

Lai, W. -C. R. (2000). *Perceptions of "A good Teacher" by teachers and students in Hong Kong—their cultural implications.* Unpublished MEd thesis, The University of Hong Kong, Hong Kong.

Lee, W. O. (1996). The cultural context for Chinese learners: Conceptions of learning in the Confucian tradition. In D. A. Watkins & J. B. Biggs (Eds.), *The Chinese learner: Cultural, psychological, and contextual influences* (pp. 25-41). Hong Kong & Australia: Comparative Education Research Centre & Australian Council for Educational Research.

Lin, W. Y., Watkins, D. A., & Meng, Q. M. (1994). A cross-cultural investigation into students' evaluation of university teaching. *Education Journal, 22*(2), 291-304.

Liu, Z. (1973). *Shi Dao (The Way Of Teachers).* Taipei, Taiwan: Chung Hwa.

Marsh, H. W. (1986). Applicability paradigm: Students' evaluations of teaching effectiveness in different countries. *Journal of Educational Psychology, 78*, 465-473.

Ng, Y. -Y. C. (2003). *What makes a "Good Language Teacher?" Teachers' and students' perceptions of "Good Language Teachers" in Hong Kong secondary schools.* Unpublished MEd thesis, The University of Hong Kong., Hong Kong.

Nishisato, S., & Nishisato, I. (1998). *DUAL3 for Windows (version 4.10+).* Toronto, Canada: MicroStats.

Pirsig, R. M. (1974). *Zen and the art of motorcycle maintenance.* New York: William Morrow.

Stigler, J., & Hiebert, J. (1999). *The teaching gap.* New York: The Free Press.

The last class of a university lecturer from Shanghai Jiaotong University (Shanghai jiaotong daxue yiwei jiangshi de zuihou yike) (n.d.). Retrieved May 31, 2005, from http://www.southcn.com/edu/xinwenbobao/200504050526.htm

Watkins, D. A., & Biggs, J. B. (2001). The paradox of the Chinese learner and beyond. In D. A. Watkins & J. B. Biggs (Eds.), *Teaching the Chinese learner: Psychological and pedagogical perspectives* (pp. 3-23). Hong Kong & Australia: Comparative Education Research Centre & Australian Council for Educational Research.

Watkins, D. A., & Sachs, J. (2005). *Comparing concepts across cultures: The application of dual scaling to analyse perceptions of the "good teacher."* Unpublished manuscript.

Zhang, Q. (2005). *Conceptions of a good tertiary English teacher in PRC: A cross-cultural perspective.* Unpublished manuscript.

Part IV

ON LEARNING ENVIRONMENTS

CHAPTER 9

CHANGING CLASSROOM
ENVIRONMENTS THROUGH
EFFECTIVE USE OF
TECHNOLOGY

**Deborah L. Lowther, Steven M. Ross,
Fethi A. Inan, and J. Daniel Strahl**

Classroom environments in high-poverty schools often reflect instructional practices that do not adequately prepare students to perform well on standardized achievement tests or to achieve success in today's high-tech workforce. In this chapter, we discuss these issues by presenting data that reveal what typically happens in high-poverty classrooms with regard to the role of teachers, students, and technology. Next, we present our research from two state technology initiatives by introducing the integration models used by both programs, then showing how application of the models resulted in promising trends of changed classroom environments. Specifically, observation data from random visits to classrooms revealed that teachers with "integration model" training used significantly more student-centered, technology-supported strategies than teachers without the training. However, the trained teachers were observed implementing these strategies only rarely to occasionally. The chapter concludes with a

Effective Schools, 207–233
Copyright © 2006 by Information Age Publishing
All rights of reproduction in any form reserved.

discussion of the implications of increasing technology integration to enhance student learning for teachers in high-risk schools.

CLASSROOM ENVIRONMENTS IN HIGH-POVERTY SCHOOLS

Children from high-poverty families not only face the harshness of insufficient funds for food, clothing, and safe homes, but also living in home environments that offer no or limited opportunities for educational growth (Bartlett, 1998; Jackson, 2003). For example, the parents or adult caretakers typically do not have the time, resources, and sufficient knowledge to help their children with reading or homework; to take them to museums; or discuss current events (Evans, 2004). It is commonly assumed that school is the answer to these issues because children are under the guidance of educated teachers. However, the classroom environments in high-poverty schools often fall short of expectations because the instructional practices within these settings are most frequently traditional, teacher-centered, and involve very limited use of technology (Center for Research in Educational Policy [CREP], 2005). In other words, teachers tend to implement strategies designed to collectively rather than individually meet student needs—a perception, that as will be seen in the following paragraphs, is verified in recent research studies.

Direct observation data from over 10,000 K-12 classrooms in predominately high-risk schools are reported in Table 9.1. The data revealed very traditional classroom environments as direct instruction and independent student seatwork were the most commonly observed instructional strategies (CREP, 2005). In contrast, student-centered activities such as cooperative learning, project-based learning, and independent inquiry were seen much less frequently. Classroom use of computers was equally disappointing, as computers were observed being used as delivery tools (e.g., drill and practice) occasionally too extensively in only 28% of the elementary and 10% of the high school classrooms. By comparison, students were observed using computers as learning tools in only 21% of the elementary and 17% of the high school classrooms (Ross et al., 2004).

The prevalence of teacher-centered environments are not limited to high-poverty schools, as revealed in survey responses from over 90,000 teachers from schools representing a cross-section of income levels (Newman, 2002; U.S. Department of Education [DOE], 2003). The survey results indicated that the teachers most frequently used a teacher-centered approach and most often had students use computers for low-level learning tasks or as a reward for early completion of work. These low levels of technology use occurred even though reports from high-poverty schools indicated that access to computers was not a problem. Specifically,

Table 9.1. School Observation Measure (SOM): National Elementary and Secondary School Norms

The Extent to Which Each SOM Strategy was Used or Present in the Schools		Grade Level	Percent None	Percent Rarely	Percent Occasionally	Percent Frequently	Percent Extensively
Instructional orientation	Direct instruction (lecture)	Elem.	3.0	10.4	23.7	34.8	28.1
		HS	1.6	8.7	19.0	44.0	26.6
	Team teaching	Elem.	49.8	32.3	11.9	5.6	0.4
		HS	64.1	30.3	5.4	0.3	0.0
	Cooperative/collaborative learning	Elem.	38.1	41.8	13.1	5.2	1.9
		HS	35.7	36.5	23.2	4.4	0.3
	Individual tutoring (teacher, peer, aide, adult volunteer)	Elem.	44.6	31.8	16.1	5.2	2.2
		HS	76.5	17.8	1.9	3.0	0.8
Classroom organization	Ability groups	Elem.	36.3	22.5	15.7	12.7	12.7
		HS	40.1	29.8	13.3	7.3	9.5
	Multiage grouping	Elem.	70.1	15.7	7.5	4.1	2.6
		HS	53.7	10.6	8.9	17.1	9.8
	Work centers (for individuals/groups)	Elem.	27.3	27.7	26.2	15.4	3.4
		HS	69.4	23.0	7.3	0.3	0.0
Instructional strategies	Higher level instructional feedback to enhance student learning	Elem.	28.0	36.2	26.5	7.1	2.2
		HS	25.1	24.9	25.7	18.1	6.2
	Integration of subject areas (interdisciplinary/thematic units)	Elem.	58.3	20.7	7.6	3.0	0.4
		HS	66.1	21.7	8.9	1.4	1.9

Project-based learning	Elem.	75.4	15.8	5.0	3.8	0.0
	HS	51.1	35.1	10.6	2.4	0.8
Use of higher-level questioning strategies	Elem.	19.5	32.7	32.0	12.4	3.4
	HS	19.2	29.0	32.8	17.1	1.9
Teacher acting as a coach/facilitator	Elem.	7.1	20.2	28.5	34.5	9.7
	HS	3.8	16.3	27.9	28.5	23.6
Parent/community involvement in learning activities	Elem.	75.3	18.4	6.0	0.4	0.0
	HS	93.0	6.0	1.1	0.0	0.0
Student activities	Independent seatwork (self-paced worksheets, individual assignments)	Elem.	4.1	13.7	39.6	31.1	11.5
		HS	1.1	9.8	26.0	39.6	23.6
	Experiential, hands-on learning	Elem.	30.5	36.4	24.9	6.3	1.9
		HS	44.0	36.4	14.7	4.6	0.3
	Systematic individual instruction (individualized assignments)	Elem.	64.9	26.5	5.6	2.2	0.7
		HS	76.1	20.9	2.7	0.3	0.0
	Sustained writing/composition (self-selected or teacher-generated topics)	Elem.	56.0	32.8	7.8	2.2	1.1
		HS	54.5	33.2	10.4	1.6	0.3
	Sustained reading	Elem.	43.3	31.9	18.5	4.1	2.2
		HS	52.5	36.0	10.7	0.8	0.0
	Independent inquiry/research on the part of students	Elem.	82.8	13.1	2.6	1.5	0.0
		HS	67.7	24.5	7.1	0.8	0.0
	Student discussion	Elem.	46.0	24.5	16.6	9.1	3.8
		HS	65.7	17.2	8.7	4.6	3.8

Technology use	Computer for instructional delivery (e.g., CAI, drill, & practice)	Elem.	35.2	37.1	20.6	6.7	0.4
		HS	49.6	40.1	8.1	2.2	0.0
	Technology as a learning tool or resource (e.g., Internet, spreadsheets)	Elem.	49.6	29.9	16.4	3.4	0.7
		HS	45.5	37.9	11.9	4.6	0.0
Assessment	Performance assessment strategies	Elem.	66.4	16.4	9.9	5.7	1.5
		HS	59.2	26.8	11.8	2.7	0.0
	Student self-assessment (portfolios, individual record books)	Elem.	72.9	18.7	5.7	2.7	0.0
		HS	77.7	171	4.1	1.1	0.0
Summary items	High academically focused class time	Elem.	0.4	1.5	17.1	38.3	42.8
		HS	0.0	1.6	23.4	59.4	15.5
	High level of student attention/interest/engagement	Elem.	0.4	3.0	20.1	48.3	28.3
		HS	0.0	3.3	42.0	46.9	7.9

N = 688 Elementary observations (approx. 6,880 classrooms); 370 high school observations (approx. 370 classrooms)

the computer to student ratio of instructional computers was 1: 3.9 students in high-poverty schools and 1: 3.8 students in nonhigh poverty schools (Fox, 2005).

These findings raise concerns because schools are not adequately preparing our at-risk children with the higher-order knowledge and skills needed to achieve success on today's standardized tests (U.S. DOE, 2004b) *or* in the workplace of tomorrow (CEO Forum, 2001; Partnership for 21st Century Skills, 2003). Attempts to raise achievement often involve offering high-poverty students a limited (basic skills) curriculum taught through "rigid" traditional methods, which, regrettably, has been shown to hinder learning and the development of complex thinking skills (Hixson & Tinzmann, 1990; Means, Chelemer, & Knapp, 1991). Research-based practices suggest that the greatest opportunities for successful learning occur in student-centered environments that are challenging and engage students in meaningful, technology-supported learning activities (Bransford, Brown, & Cocking, 1999; Bruner, 1996; Cradler, McNabb, & Burchett, 2002). McCombs and Whisler (1997) offer the following definition of this environment:

> Learner-centered learning is the perspective that couples a focus on individual learners (their heredity, experiences, perspectives, backgrounds, talents, interests, capacities and needs) with a focus on learning (the best available knowledge about learning and how it occurs and about teaching practices that are most effective in promoting the highest levels of motivation, learning and achievement for all learners). (p. 9)

Yet, understandably, the problem then becomes one of preparing teachers in high-poverty schools to create these seemingly "ideal" learner-centered environments (Education Week, 2004; Ross & Lowther, 2003). Our research has shown that when used as the foundational components of instruction, the *en-Gauge-Range of Use* model (North Central Regional Educational Laboratory [NCREL], 2004) and the iNtegrating Technology for inQuiry model (*N* classroom pedagogy, student performance, and teacher attitudes and beliefs (Lowther Ross, Wang, & Strahl, McDonald, 2004; Lowther, Ross, & Morrison, 2003; Ross Lowther, Walter, McDonald, & Wang, 2002). The following sections will briefly describe each model then discuss two applied studies that demonstrate the specific impact of utilizing this approach.

The en-Gauge-Range of Use Model

The *en-Gauge-Range of Use* model proposes that basic software applications or "production" tools offer the greatest opportunities to achieve higher-level thinking in a constructivist environment (NCREL, 2004). The basic premise of the model demonstrates how the level of three components found in instructional environments changes according to the type of computer activities in which students are engaged. As seen in Figure 9.1, the three components and their associated range of implementation are as follows: instructional approach to learning (didactic, coaching, constructivist); authenticity of learning (artificial, real world); and complexity of learning (basic skills, higher-order thinking). Following are examples of how the three components interact when students use various forms of technology.

When students use drill-and-practice software, typically in the form of educational games, the program provides all the information (which is artificial), while the primary goal for students is memorization of the content. Again, this is of concern given that application of rote skills is not the focus of today's standardized tests. Yet as reported earlier, drill and

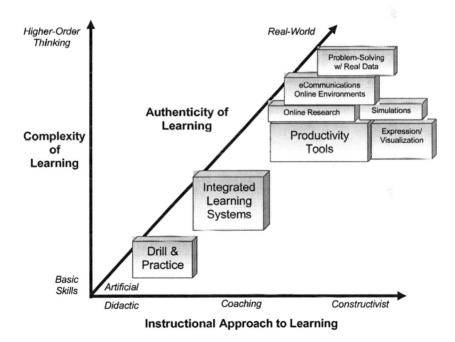

Figure 9.1. The *en-Guage-Range of Use* chart (NCREL, 2004).

practice was the most commonly observed computer activity in which students were engaged (Ross et al., 2004).

The next level involves the use of integrated learning systems (ILS), which are "packages of networked hardware and software ... [that] embodies a mastery learning approach to instruction" (Holum & Gahala, 2001). These systems provide improved opportunities as compared to drill and practice because progression through the program is based on individual performance. However, most ILS activities still focus on lower levels of learning such as knowledge acquisition and simple comprehension (Bloom & Krathwohl, 1984).

The types of computer activities that yield the greatest benefits are those that involve students in the use of production tools to not only learn core content, but also to learn problem-solving methodologies while improving computer skills (Jonassen, 1994; Moursund, 1996). For example, students can create a spreadsheet of daily weather reports to help them better understand the interactions of barometric pressure, temperature, and humidity. From this information they can plot the relationships, then use graphs to summarize their findings in a report or presentation. Students completing this lesson gain a deeper understanding of weather systems because they used the processing power of computers to examine the information from multiple perspectives (Bransford, Brown, & Cocking, 1999; Bruner, 1996; Cradler, McNabb, & Burchett, 2002). In contrast, students using a "weather" game might be presented with descriptions of different weather conditions and told to move the humidity bar to discover what happens. Practice would typically involve rote questions regarding definitions of weather terms or identifying the tools used to collect weather data. Thus, the use of games does not help students perform better on achievement tests that require application of higher-level skills or gain experience in using computers as problem-solving tools in ways that reflect workplace practices.

As seen, the key to the *en-Gauge-Range of Use* model is to have students construct deep levels of learning in the core content areas through the use of higher-order thinking skills to investigate real-world data (NCREL, 2004). This type of learning does not require the development of elaborate units, because high levels of student engagement can happen in everyday activities. However, it does require teachers to know how to plan and implement effective technology integration lessons. One approach, the *NTeQ* model, has proven to be successful for this purpose.

The NTeQ Model

The *NTeQ* model uses an easy 10-step problem-based lesson plan that has five components unique to a lesson that integrates student use of computers: (1) Computer Functions (2) Data Manipulation, (3) Activities During Computer Use, (4) Activities Before Computer Use, and (5) Activities After Computer Use (see Figure 9.2) (Morrison & Lowther, 2005). The five planning components are briefly described below.

Computer Functions

The first step for any lesson plan is to identify the lesson objectives. When using the *NTeQ* lesson, the next step is to align computer functions with the action portion of the objectives (e.g., analyze, compare, describe, illustrate, organize, sequence), keeping in mind that student use of computers may not be appropriate for some objectives. Computer function refers to the basic processes of production software. For spreadsheets the basic functions include storing data, performing calculations, and creating graphs. Whereas, the basic functions of databases are storing data in records, sorting, matching, merging, and creating specialized reports (Morrison & Lowther, 2005).

Data Manipulation
After the computer functions are chosen, the next step is to determine the specific ways that students will manipulate the data. For instance, if the student learning objective is to "compare and contrast past presidents based on their political party," the teacher would identify the specific information students will be comparing or contrasting, for example, key accomplishments, previous careers, number of terms. Or if the objective

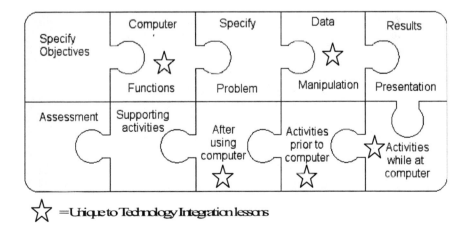

Figure 9.2.   NTeQ 10-Step lesson plan.

were for students to create an animated illustration of the water cycle, the teacher would identify the specific components that should be animated, for example, evaporation, transpiration, and precipitation. Even though this step has the teacher identify the specific forms of data manipulation for the lesson, in many cases the students will be given the opportunity to "identify" the key factors to be manipulated as part of the problem-solving process. The teacher will use his/her facilitation skills as the students "identify" the predetermined factors to ensure the selections align with the planned criteria.

Activities During Computer Use

Now that the computer functions are identified and the specific data manipulation methods are selected, the actual computer activities need to be decided. If we return to the weather example, the teacher would need to plan how the students will create a spreadsheet for the data records, which graphs would best represent the relationships between barometric pressure, temperature, and humidity, and how a word-processed report or presentation would be structured. The *NTeQ* model encourages teachers to create a sample student product to ensure the plans are workable and also to serve as a prototype example to show students.

Activities Before Computer Use

After the computer activity is planned, the teacher decides how students can prepare for computer use. This step is necessary even in a laptop classroom with one computer per student, because learning begins as students complete the planning activities. For example, preparation for the database of past presidents might involve selecting key search terms to find specific presidential information on the Internet, choosing field names, and determining how to configure data in each field to ensure manipulations will be consistent.

Activities After Computer Use

The last planning component defines what students do after they complete computer work. The *NTeQ* model suggests using a "Think Sheet" to guide students through this phase by asking lesson-specific higher-level questions. For example: What trends do you see between past military experience and increased funding for military? What interactions did your team observe as changes occurred between barometric pressure and temperature? If you could add more data to your spreadsheet, what would you add and why? The main consideration for designing after computer activities is to ensure that student learning of the objectives is reinforced.

Does NTeQ Work?

Findings from applied research studies have revealed dramatic changes in teacher practices after they have been trained to design and implement *NTeQ* lessons (Lowther, Ross, & Morrison, 2003; Lowther et al., 2005; Lowther et al., 2004; Ross et al., 2002). Highlights from two investigations conducted in high-poverty schools are presented below.

TWO APPLIED STUDIES

The research that we will be discussing in the remainder of the chapter was focused on investigating the overall effectiveness of two state technology programs targeted to reach high-poverty students through the Tennessee (TN) Department of Education's: Technology Literacy Challenge Fund (TLCF) and Ed'lech Launch (ETL), a No Child Left Behind (NCLB) Title II-D grant (U.S. Department of Education [DOE], 2001). The state used a competitive application process for funding 39 economically disadvantaged schools: 26 in TLCF and 13 in ETL. The primary goals of the TLCF and ETL programs were to increase student learning and achievement through student use of technology. In an effort to reach these goals, both programs implemented a comprehensive professional development approach that provided ongoing, embedded support through on-site technology coaches. The theoretical foundation of the professional development was based on the two integration models presented above, *en-Guage* (NCREL, 2004) and *NTeQ* (Morrison & Lowther, 2005). Below are brief descriptions of TLCF and ETL, which are followed by a discussion of the study methodology and key findings related to the focus of this chapter.

Technology Literacy Challenge Fund (TLCF)

The Technology Literacy Challenge Fund (TLCF) required the 26 participating schools to develop a building-level, 12-month program that was supported by a full-time technology coach and utilized at least 50% of the funds given to each school ($200,000) for professional development (Ross et al., 2002). The technology coach was to be a certified teacher selected by each school. The specific purpose of TLCF grant was achievement of the following four goals:

1. All teachers will have the training and support they need to help students learn using computers and the information superhighway.

2. All teachers and students will have modern multimedia computers in their classrooms.

3. Every classroom will be connected to the information superhighway

4. Effective software and online learning resources will be an integral part of every school's curriculum (Ross et al., 2002, p. 10).

EdTech Launch

The 13 EdTech Launch (ETL) schools were each awarded $300,000 to implement an 18-month school-wide initiative that utilized full-time, school-based technology coaches to plan and implement comprehensive, on-site professional development programs for teachers in their own schools (Lowther et al., 2004). The intent of ETL's professional development was to equip teachers with the knowledge and skills to better prepare students to meet state academic standards through effectively integrating student use of technology into their curriculum and instruction. The specific program goals were:

1. All students will be educated in learning environments that have access to educational technology used in support of academic achievement.

2. All students will demonstrate technology literacy by the end of eighth grade.

3. All students will be taught by teachers qualified to use technology for instruction (Lowther et al., 2004, p. 10).

TLCF and ETL Methodology

Presentation of the methodology varies somewhat from the traditional approach, in that the research designs for the two programs differed. The TLCF utilized a pre postdescriptive design that involved two data collection periods in the 26 participating schools: fall (pre or baseline) and spring (post). The ETL study utilized a matched/control quasi-experimental design that involved 13 program and 13 matched control schools. The "matched pairs" of schools were formed according to the following criteria: locale, grade levels, number of students, percent qualified for free/reduced lunch, ethnicity, and achievement (elementary = reading and mathematics; middle school = algebra; high school = biology). The ETL data were collected in late spring. The same data collection instruments and procedures were used for the TCLF and ETL studies. Therefore, discussions regarding TLCF findings will refer to the timeframe: fall or spring, whereas ETL results will be referenced by group: program or control.

Context

Both the TLCF and ETL were targeted to high-need schools, as seen in the student demographics for the two programs (see Table 9.2). Collectively, a total of 30,722 students participated in study, the majority of which were Caucasian, however, approximately one-half of all students were classified as economically disadvantaged (TLCF = 55.2%; ETL Program = 48.4%, Control = 44.5%). The grades represented at the 52 schools ranged from PreK through 12. As shown in Table 9.3, the majority of the schools served elementary through middle school students, 7 served high school students, and 2 served grades K-12. Collectively the schools had a total of 2,114 teachers.

Table 9.2. TLCF and ETL Student Demographics

Factor	Detail	TLCFL N = 18,302	ETL Program N = 6,197	ETL Control N = 6,223l
Ethnicity	Caucasian	65.1%	84.3%	81.9%
	African American	31.6%	7.0%	7.6%
	Hispanic	2.1%	2.1%	2.8%
Economically Disadvantaged	—	55.3%	48.4%	44.5%

Table 9.3. TLCF and ETL School Information

Grade Range	TLCF	ETL Program	ETL Control
Elementary only (PK-5)	12 (46%)	5 (39%)	4 (31%)
Elementary and middle school (K-8)	3 (12%)	3 (23%)	2 (15%)
Middle school (5-8)	6 (23%)	3 (23%)	3 (23%)
Middle school and high school 6-12)	-	1 (8%)	1 (8%)
High school (9-12)	5 (19%)	1 (8%)	1 (8%)
All grades (K-12)	—	—	2 (15%)
Total schools	26	13	13
Total teachers	1,187	486	441

Instruments and Procedures

Although the initial studies involved a comprehensive research plan with multiple data collection instruments, the focus of this chapter is to examine actual classroom practices in high-poverty schools, Therefore, the instruments and procedures discussed will be those used for direct classroom observations.

Two instruments were used to descriptively, not judgmentally record observed classroom practices: the School Observation Measure (SOM) (Ross, Smith, & Alberg, 1999) and the Survey of Computer Use (SCU) (Lowther & Ross, 2001). Both instruments had been shown to be reliable and valid (Lewis, Ross, & Alberg, 1999; Sterbinsky, Ross & Burke, 2004). In addition, trained, unbiased site researchers conducted all data collection procedures.

Observation Instruments

The observation instruments were designed to collect a unique set of information, that when combined provide a rich, triangulated description of actual classroom practices. With that in mind, the School Observation Measure (SOM) (Ross et al., 1999) was designed to capture the frequency with which 24 instructional practices were implemented. The practices range from traditional (e.g., direct instruction and independent seatwork) to alternative, predominately student-centered methods associated with educational reforms (e.g., cooperative learning, project-based learning, inquiry, discussion, using technology as a learning tool). The strategies, which were identified through surveys and discussions involving policy makers, researchers, administrators, and teachers, were considered to be most useful in providing indicators of schools' instructional philosophies and implementations of commonly used reform designs (Ross et al., 2004). The final items on the SOM are used to record the level of student attention and/or interest and the amount of time focused on academics on a 3-point scale (low, moderate, high). Data from the SOM are reported on the basis of how frequently the strategies were observed using the following 5-point scale: 0 = Not Observed; 1 = Rarely; 2 = Occasionally; 3 = Frequently; 4 = Extensively.

The second instrument, the Survey of Computer Use (SCU) (Lowther & Ross, 2001) was designed to capture exclusively *student* access to, ability with, and use of computers rather than teacher use of technology. This distinction is of importance because student use of computers has been shown to be associated with more student-centered teaching practices (Inan, Lowther, Ross, & Strahl, 2005), which is directly aligned with our research interests. The SCU begins with space to record several factors that influence student ability to use technology: the number and types of available computers; student grouping during computer activities; and the computer literacy levels of students. Next, the researchers recorded observed computer activities by the software being used (16 types grouped by production tools, Internet/research tools, and educational software) and the subject area(s) addressed. The computer activities are summarized with the same scale used for the SOM (0 = Not observed and 4 = Extensively). For the final section, researchers use an "Overall Rubric" to rate the degree to which each computer activity reflected "meaningful use" of computers *as a tool* to enhance learning. The rubric has four levels (1 – Low-level use of computers, 2 – Somewhat meaningful, 3 – Meaningful, and 4 – Very meaningful).

Observation Procedures

Direct classroom observations were conducted via a *whole-school* approach. The intent of the whole-school observations was to capture routine classroom practices; therefore, they involved an extended timeframe in which multiple classrooms were observed. For instance, one whole-school observation consisted of a researcher spending 3 hours in a school conducting 15-minute observations in 10-12 randomly selected classrooms. At the conclusion of the visit, the researcher recorded the frequency with which the various instructional practices were observed. To better represent everyday teaching and learning in the schools, multiple whole-school observations were conducted for each program: TLCF = 6 per school (2 fall baseline observations; 4 spring observations); ETL = 5 spring observations per program and control school. The whole-school observations yielded a comprehensive sample of classroom practices collected by external researchers who spent 804 hours conducting 268 three-hour observations during which 2,590 classrooms were observed. Distribution of the data is as follows: TLCF (fall = 49 visits/490 classes; spring = 89 visits/890 classes) and ETL (Program = 65 visits/597 classes; Control = 65 visits/613 classes).

Research Designs

A pretest-posttest treatment only design was used for the TLCF study. Baseline measurements were collected in early falls when program implementation was at its earliest stages, followed by collection of "post" data in late spring. In contrast, ETL, which was funded through NCLB, utilized a more rigorous, quasi-experimental matched-control design. The "matched pairs" of schools were formed according to the following criteria: locale, grade levels, number of students, percent qualified for free/reduced lunch, ethnicity, and achievement (elementary = reading and mathematics; middle school = algebra; high school = biology) (Lowther et al., 2004).

Regardless of design employed, we computed effect sizes (*ES*) using Cohen's *d* formula (Cohen, 1988) to determine the educational importance of differences. An *ES* indicates the number of standard deviations by which the "treatment" group surpasses the "control" group. According to Cohen, an *ES* having an absolute value greater than .25 is considered to be educationally important.

HOW CLASSROOMS CHANGED

Our primary intent in this chapter is to explore how classrooms practices changed when technology was integrated effectively into the curriculum in an environment providing ongoing, embedded teacher support. Results reflect observations during random visits to 2,590 TLCF and ETL Program and Control classrooms.

SOM Results

The SOM results are first discussed by the most commonly occurring instructional practices and the significant differences found between the respective groups (TLCF = fall vs. spring; ETL = Program vs. Control). Significant differences for TLCF and ETL are reported in Table 9.4.

There was a common pattern observed across all groups in that traditional, teacher-centered activities such as direct instruction and use of independent seatwork, were the prominent means of instruction, being observed occasionally to extensively in over 80% of the classroom visits (Lowther et al., 2004; Ross et al., 2002). However, the TLCF teachers significantly reduced the frequency with which they utilized teacher-centered methodologies. Specifically, after a year of program implementation, there were fewer instances of teachers using *direct instruction* (*ES* = -0.61) and students were less frequently observed using *independent seatwork* such as worksheets or answering the end-of-chapter questions (*ES* = -0.54). Further reflecting the shift from traditional pedagogy, the next most commonly observed activity was *teachers acting as a coach or facilitator*, which occurred in approximately 60% of the TLCF and 86.1% of the ETL Program classes (Lowther et al.; Ross et al.).

Other student-centered practices, although seen less frequently, were observed significantly more during the TLCF and ETL end-of-program visits—suggesting that the technology interventions had a positive impact on changing classroom environments to better meet student needs. In particular, teachers in both programs significantly increased the use of *project-based learning, independent research/inquiry* on the part of students,

Table 9.4. Summary of SOM© Items Showing TLCF and ETL Significant Differences

TLCF

SOM Items	Fall (n = 49)		Spring (n = 89)		F (1, 136)	p	ES
	M	SD	M	SD			
Direct instruction	3.08	.812	2.52	.967	12.036	.001	-.61
Project-based learning	0.27	.491	0.67	.836	9.828	.002	.55
Independent seatwork	2.96	.789	2.51	.854	9.389	.003	-.54
Independent inquiry/research	0.24	.434	0.62	.776	9.637	.002	.56
Computer for instructional delivery	0.55	.738	1.40	1.052	25.336	.000	.89
Technology as a learning tool	0.57	.612	1.27	.986	20.239	.000	.80
High level of academically focused class time	2.65	.522	2.87	.343	8.233	.005	.53
High level of student attention/interest/engagement	2.37	.528	2.60	.516	6.075	.015	.44

ETL

SOM Items	Program(n = 65)		Control (n = 65)		F (1, 114)	P	ES
	M	SD	M	SD			
Technology as learning tool-resource	2.01	1.09	0.73	0.67	56.77	0.000	+1.40
Computer for instructional delivery	1.73	1.06	0.55	0.63	53.05	0.000	+1.36
Work centers	1.26	1.37	0.46	0.63	15.90	0.000	+0.74
Teacher acting as coach-facilitator	2.61	1.02	1.96	0.95	12.53	0.001	+0.66
Independent inquiry-research	0.61	0.71	0.25	0.43	10.91	0.001	+0.61
High level of student attention-interest-engagement	3.01	0.77	2.53	0.89	09.67	0.002	+0.57
Project-based learning	0.85	0.84	0.46	0.63	07.72	0.006	+0.52
High level of academically focused class time	3.38	0.66	3.01	0.75	07.71	0.006	+0.52

Scale: 0 = Not Observed, 1 = Rarely Observed; 2 = Occasionally; 3 = Frequently; 4 = Extensively.

and ETL students more often worked in *centers* specialized for specific learning tasks, for example, reading, science experiments, or technology.

The SOM data also yielded significant differences with regard to the observed classroom environments. Students in the TLCF classrooms had a significantly higher level of *student attention/interest* during the late spring observations as compared to the observations conducted in the fall ($ES = +0.44$). Spring data also revealed that the TLCF teachers had increased the level of *academically focused time* in their classes ($ES = +0.53$). Similar differences in student attention were seen between the ETL Program and Control classroom environments ($ES = +0.57$). The ETL teachers also maintained a higher level of time spent on academics than teachers in the matched-control classes ($ES = +0.52$).

Not surprisingly, two areas where additional significant differences were observed involved the use of computers. First, teachers and students in TLCF and ETL more frequently used computers as a means of *delivering instruction*. Examples observed include teachers presenting lecture notes with a digital projector, students completing computer-based reading assessments, and students using drill and practice software. The second technology-supported strategy was student use of *computers as a tool*, which represented the strongest effect for both programs (TLCF $ES = -0.80$; ETL $ES = +1.40$). This finding is promising because it is reflective of the highest level on the *en-Guage-Range of Use* model—teachers' implementation of authentic constructivist activities requiring student application of higher-order thinking skills (NCREL, 2004). Further support indicating a shift toward changed classroom environments is found in the SCU results.

SCU Results

The SCU data reflect the computer configuration of the observed classrooms, the frequency with which students used different computer applications, and the meaningfulness of the computer activities. Over 75% of the classrooms across all groups had at least 2 to 4 computers, while over 25% had from 5 to 10 computers (Lowther et al., 2004; Ross et al., 2002). The program schools understandably had a greater percentage of computers rated as being up-to-date (high speed processor and Internet capable). However, computer access in all schools could be considered adequate as only 1.5% of the TLCF and ETL Program, and 7.7% of the ETL Control computers were rated as being outdated. In addition, approximately 90% of all observed computers were connected to the Internet (Lowther et al; Ross et al.). Almost all (95%) of the students exhibited moderate to very good computer skills. Thus, it appears that most TLCF, ETL Program and ETL Control teachers had adequate access to computers and taught students with reasonable computer readiness (Lowther et al.; Ross et al.).

The SCU divides student computer activities into three groups based on how students used computers during the classroom observations, for example, as production tools, as research/Internet tools, or as educational software. Of note, the variety of software used by all the students was very limited, in that only four applications were observed in use occasionally or more in at least 20% of the visited classrooms: word processing, presentation, Internet, and drill, and practice (Lowther et al., 2004; Ross et al., 2002). Still, significant progress in the TLCF and ETL students was observed for each of these applications (Table 9.5). Not surprisingly, the most frequently observed tool was the *Internet* browser, which was seen occasionally or more in over 40% of the program classes and only 12% of the Control classes ($ES = +0.66$). Program students also more frequently used *word processing, presentation,* and *draw/graphics* applications. When looking at computers for delivery of instruction, *drill and practice* software was observed nearly as frequently as use of the Internet.

These results indicate that students in ETL and TLCF classes more frequently used computers, but were the activities meaningful? That is, a teacher could have students use word processing simply to copy notes from the white board, while other teachers could have students write their own step-by-step directions for dividing fractions, paraphrase the Bill of Rights, or use the thesaurus to simplify a downloaded copy of Preamble to the U.S. Constitution. All of the activities engage students in using word processing as a tool; however, the task of copying notes is clearly not as meaningful as the remainder of the activities. Through the meaningfulness ratings, the SCU results showed that the TLCF and ETL programs had positive impacts on teacher ability to implement high-level computer activities (see Table 9.5).

IMPLICATIONS FOR PRACTICE AND FUTURE RESEARCH

Our intent in this chapter was to show how schools serving many economically disadvantaged students could change classroom practices through the effective use of technology. We hypothesized that for these changes to occur, teachers would need to shift from traditional teaching to student-centered, constructivist approaches that have students use computers for authentic and challenging activities (Morrison & Lowther, 2005; NCREL, 2004). The reasoning underlying this approach is that learner-centered activities require students to use and develop higher-order skills through problem-solving, reflective thinking, and metacognitive activities (Brans-

Table 9.5. Summary of SCU© Items Showing TLCF and ETL Significant Differences

TLCF	*Fall (n = 52)*		*Spring (n = 104)*				
SCU ITEMS	*M*	*SD*	*M*	*SD*	*t (149)*	*p*	*ES*
COMPUTER ACTIVITIES							
Production Tools							
Word processing	0.34	0.848	0.83	1.184	2.621	.010	+0.45
Presentation	0.10	0.580	0.53	0.819	3.355	.001	.+0.58
Internet/research tools							
Internet browser	0.32	0.844	1.39	1.216	5.566	.000	+0.96
Educational software							
Drill and practice	0.76	0.960	1.25	1.184	2.538	.012	+0.44
MEANINGFULNESS OF ACTIVITIES							
Somewhat meaningful use of computers	0.68	1.133	1.44	1.255	3.624	.000	+0.63
Meaningful use of computers	0.34	0.823	0.93	1.145	3.238	.000	+0.56
Very meaningful use of computers	0.02	0.141	0.45	1.019	2.965	.004	+0.51

ETL	*Program (n = 65)*		*Control (n =65)*				
SCU ITEMS	*M*	*SD*	*M*	*SD*	*t (127)*	*p*	*ES*
COMPUTER ACTIVITIES							
Production Tools							
Word processing	0.70	0.99	0.16	0.41	4.02	0.000	+0.71

Presentation	0.73	0.98	0.16	0.65	3.86	0.000	+0.68
Drawing/paint/graphics/photo-imaging	0.31	0.69	0.03	0.17	3.43	0.001	+0.60
Internet/Research Tools							
Internet browser	1.40	1.29	1.26	0.99	3.78	0.000	+0.66
MEANINGFULNESS OF ACTIVITIES							
Meaningful use of computers	1.26	1.25	0.84	0.76	4.93	0.000	+0.88
Very meaningful use of computers	0.84	1.26	0.10	0.36	4.48	0.000	+0.79

Scale: 0 = Not Observed; 1 = Rarely Observed; 2 = Occasionally; 3 = Frequently; 4 = Extensively.

ford et al., 1999; McCombs & Whisler, 1997; NCREL, 1999). Additionally, when teachers use a student-centered approach, basic knowledge and skills are not taught through typical drill-and-practice activities, but rather are acquired during the completion of complex, authentic tasks (Means, Chelemer, & Knapp, 1991, Murnane & Level, 1996).

An expected result of the TLCF and ETL programs was increased student use of technology. However, teachers were also willing to step out of their "comfort zones" and implement student-centered strategies that were significantly different from classroom practices in "typical" U.S. schools – thus, suggesting a shift in teacher beliefs (CREP, 2005; Ertmer, 1999; Ertmer, 2001). Specifically, the teachers more frequently created and integrated student work centers into their lessons, engaged students in project-based learning and had students conduct independent research/inquiry. Within these student-centered environments, the teachers more often served as a facilitator of student learning and more frequently integrated effective and meaningful computer activities into their curriculum. Therefore, although the analyses of student achievement was beyond the scope of this chapter, the data did reveal significant increases in teacher use of research-based practices shown to improve student performance (Bransford et al., 1999; Bruner, 1996; Cradler et al., 2002; Lowther et al., 2003; Ross & Lowther, 2003).

These findings are encouraging, because technology can often serve as a catalyst for increased use of student-centered practices because it allows teachers to "optimize" the learning environment (Inan et al., 2005; Switzer, Callahan, & Quinn, 1999). In other words, when students use technology as a problem-solving tool, activities can be more challenging and complex, which often results in increased student engagement, motivation, and learning (Baker, Gearhart, & Herman, 1994; Means & Olson, 1995; Sandholtz, Ringstaff, & Dwyer, 1997). However, "Achieving such fundamental change ... requires a transformation of not only the underlying pedagogy (basic assumptions about the teaching and learning process), but also the kinds of technology applications typically used in classrooms serving at-risk students" (Means, 1997).

Even though our study results revealed promising progress toward changed classrooms in high-risk environments, the observation data indicated that the teachers' instruction represented a mixed approach that was predominately traditional, yet also included constructivist methods. Ertmer, Gopalakrishnan, and Ross (2001) suggest that teachers may not fully adopt a nontraditional approach due to contextual influences from administrators, parents or other teachers, and/or constraints related to curricular requirements. The findings also align with research that advocates that the adoption of new beliefs or use of innovations occurs on a personal, or teacher-by-teacher level and progresses through a variety of stages as confidence, knowledge, and skills increase (Hall, George, & Rutherford, 1998; Loucks, Newlove, & Hall, 1998; NCREL, 2004).

Since the release of *A Nation at Risk* (National Commission of Excellence in Education, 1983) over 20 years ago, extraordinary amounts of supplemental government, corporate, and foundational funding has been and is budgeted to be spent on "Improving the Academic Achievement of the Economically Disadvantaged" (U.S. DOE, 2004a). Yet, the majority of at-risk students continue to emerge from our educational system without the knowledge and skills (U.S. Department of Labor, 1992) to become successful members of today's global society (U.S. DOE, 2004b). In response to these issues, the No Child Left Behind Act of 2001 challenges our K-12 schools to identify and implement research-based approaches that meet the individual needs of each student, in high-risk and nonhigh-risk environments, and result in improved learning and performance (U.S. DOE, 2001). In turn, the overall goal of this research was to explore and describe how classrooms serving many economically disadvantaged students can be positively changed through student use of computers in a learner-centered environment. Although the study revealed trends of transformation, teachers need time, adequate resources, and ongoing support to ensure that the emerging positive changes in their beliefs regarding student use of technology become fully adopted and result in systemic reform of classroom practices (Pajares, 1992)

To achieve changed and improved classrooms in high poverty schools, further research is needed to identify means of assisting teachers to maintain and increase the use of research-based practices that result in improved learning and technological literacy. Specific areas of investigation could include examining the possible influence of these changes on student learning and motivation; determining if relationships exist between predominate teaching styles and how technology is used; and, comparing technology lesson plans to actual implementation to identify areas of disconnect.

As technology access is no longer considered a key barrier to achieving effective technology integration, effective teaching becomes critical in removing the environmental barriers hindering the academic progress of economically disadvantaged students.

REFERENCES

Baker, E. L., Gearhart, M., & Herman, J. L. (1994). Evaluating the Apple classrooms of tomorrow (SM). In E. L. Baker & H. F. O'Neil, Jr. (Eds.), *Technology Assessment in Education and Training* (pp. 173-198). Hillsdale, NJ: Erlbaum.

Bartlett, S. (1998). Does inadequate housing perpetuate children's poverty? *Childhood, 5*(4), 403-420.

Bloom, B., S., & Krathwohl, D, R. (1984). *Taxonomy of educational objectives, Handbook 1: Cognitive domain*. New York: Addison Wesley.

Bransford, J. D., Brown, A. L., & Cocking, R. R. (1999). *How people learn: Brain, mind, experience, and school*. Washington, DC: National Academy Press.

Bruner, J. S. (1996). *The culture of education*. Cambridge, MA: Harvard University Press.

CEO Forum (2001, June). *The CEO forum on school technology year 4 report:* Key *building blocks for student achievement in the 21st cent*ury. Retrieved July 7, 2005, from http://www.ceoforum.org/downloads/report4.pdf

Cohen, D. K. (1988). Educational technology and school organization. In R. S. Nickerson & P. P. Zodhiates (Eds.), *Technology in education: Looking toward 2020* (pp. 231-264). Hillsdale, NJ: Erlbaum.

Cradler, J., McNabb, M. F., & Burchett, R. (2002). How does technology influence student learning? *Learning & Leading with Technology, 29*(8), 46-56.

Center for Research in Educational Policy (CREP). (2005) School Observation Measure (SOM) National Norms for Elementary and Secondary Schools. Memphis, TN: Center for Research in Educational Policy, The University of Memphis.

Education Week. (2004). *Technology Counts 2004: United States*. Retrieved May 4, 2005, from http://counts.edweek.org/ sreports/tc04/ article.cfm?slug=35sos_notes.h23

Ertmer, P. A. (1999). Addressing first- and second-order barriers to change: Strategies for technology integration. *Educational Technology Research and Development, 47*(4), 47-61.

Ertmer, P. A. (2001). Responsive instructional design: Scaffolding the adoption and change process. *Educational Technology, 41*(6), 33-38

Ertmer, P. A., Gopalakrishnan, S., & Ross, E. M. (2001). Technology-using teachers: Comparing perceptions of exemplary technology use to best practice. *Journal of Research on Technology in Education, 33*(5). Retrieved June 2, 2005, from http://www.iste.org/inhouse/publications/ jrte/33/5/ertmer.cfm?Sec tion=JRTE_33_5

Evans, G. (2004). The environment of childhood poverty. *American Psychologist, 59*(2), 77-92.

Fox, E. (May, 2005). *Tracking U.S. trends. Education Week's technology counts 2005*, Marion, OH: Editorial Projects in Education.

Hall, G. E., George, A. A., & Rutherford, W. L. (1998). *Measuring stages of concern about the innovation: A manual for the use of the SoC Questionnaire*. Austin, TX: Southwest Educational Development Laboratory.

Hixson, J., & Tinzmann, M.B. (1990). Who are the "at-risk" students of the 1990s? Retrieved June 15, 2005, from http://www.ncrel.org/sdrs/areas/rpl_esys/ equity.htm

Holum, A., & Gahala, J. (2001). *Critical issue: Using technology to enhance literacy instruction*. Retrieved July 5, 2005 from, http://www.ncrel.org/sdrs/areas/issues/ content/cntareas/reading/li300.htm

Inan, F. A., Lowther, D. L., Ross, S. M., & Strahl, J. D. (2005, October). *Observation of technology use: Identifying instructional strategies used in K-12 schools*. Paper presented at 2005 Association for Educational Communications and Technology International Conference, Orlando, FL.

Jackson, A. P. (2003). The effects of family and neighborhood characteristics on the behavioral and cognitive development of poor black children: A longitudinal study. *American Journal of Community Psychology, 32*(1-2), 175-186.

Jonassen, D. H. (1994). Thinking technology: Toward a constructivist design model. *Educational Technology 34*(4), 34-37.

Lewis, E. M., Ross, S. M., & Alberg, M. (1999, July). *School observation measure: Reliability analysis*. Memphis, TN: Center for Research in Educational Policy, The University of Memphis.

Loucks, S. F., Newlove, B. W., & Hall, G. E. (1998). *Measuring levels of use of the innovation: A manual for trainers, interviewers, and raters*. Austin, TX: Southwest Educational Development Laboratory.

Lowther, D. L., & Ross, S. M. (2001). *Survey of computer use (SCU)*. Memphis, TN: Center for Research in Educational Policy, The University of Memphis.

Lowther, D. L., Ross, S. M., & Morrison, G. R. (2003). When each one has one: The influences on teaching strategies and student achievement of using laptops in the classroom. *Educational Technology Research and Development, 51*(03), 23-44.

Lowther, D. L., Ross, S. M., Strahl, J. D. Inan, F. A., Francescini, L., & Li, W. D. (2005). *Tennessee Department of Education EdTech Launch 1 2004-2005 Evaluation Report*. Memphis, TN: The University of Memphis, Center for Research in Educational Policy.

Lowther, D. L., Ross, S. M., Wang, L. W., Strahl, J. D., & McDonald, A. J. (2004). *Tennessee Department of Education EdTech Launch 1 2003-2004 Evaluation Report*. Memphis, TN: The University of Memphis, Center for Research in Educational Policy.

McCombs, B. L., & Whisler, J. S. (1997). *The learner-centered classroom and school*. San Francisco: Jossey-Bass.

Means, B. (1997). *Critical Issue: Using Technology to enhance engaged learning for at-risk students*. Retrieved May 18, 2005, from http://www.ncrel.org/sdrs/areas/ issues/students/atrisk/at400.htm

Means, B., Chelemer, C., & Knapp, M. S. (Eds.). (1991). *Teaching advanced skills to at-risk students: Views from research and practice*. San Francisco: Jossey-Bass.

Means, B., & Olson, K. (1995). *Technology and education reform: Technical research report. Volume 1: Findings and conclusions*. Menlo Park, CA: SRI International.

Morrison, G. R., & Lowther, D. L. (2005). *Integrating computer technology into the classroom* (3rd ed.). Englewood Cliffs, NJ: Merrill/Prentice Hall.

Moursund, D. (1996). *Increasing your expertise as a problem-solver: Some roles of computers* (2nd ed.). Eugene, OR: International Society for Technology in Education.

Murnane, R. J., & Levy, F. (1996). *Teaching the new basic skills: Principles for educating children to thrive in a changing economy*. New York: Free Press.

National Commission of Excellence in Education. (1983). *A nation at risk: The imperative for educational reform*. Washington, DC: U.S. Government Printing

Office. Retrieved July 12, 2005 from http://www.ed.gov/pubs/NatAtRisk/risk.html

Newman, H. (2002, February 26). Computers used more to learn than teach. *Detroit Free Press.* Retrieved, June 7, 2005 from http://www.freepress.com/news/education/newman26_20020226.htm

North Central Regional Educational Laboratory (NCREL). (1999). *Learner-centered classrooms, problem-based learning, and the construction of understanding and meaning by students.* Retrieved July 5, 2005 from http://www.ncrel.org/sdrs/areas/issues/content/cntareas/science/sc3learn.htm

North Central Regional Educational Laboratory (NCREL). (2000). *enGauge: A framework for effective technology use in schools* [Brochure]. Oak Brook, IL: Author.

Pajares, M. F. (1992). Teachers' beliefs and educational research: Cleaning up a messy construct. *Review of Educational Research, 62*(3), 307-332.

Partnership for 21st Century Skills. (2003). *Learning for the 21st century.* Washington, DC: Retrieved June 12, 2005 from http://www.21stcenturyskills.org/downloads/P21_Report.pdf

Ross, S. M., & Lowther, D. L. (2003). Impacts of the Co-nect school reform design on classroom instruction, school climate, and student achievement in inner-city schools. *Journal for Educational Research on Students Placed At Risk, 8*(3), 215-246.

Ross, S. M., Lowther, D. L., Walter, J. W., McDonald, A. J., & Wang, L. W. (2002). *Tennessee Technology Literacy Challenge Fund: Evaluation Report.* Memphis, TN: The University of Memphis, Center for Research in Educational Policy.

Ross, S. M., Smith, L. J., & Alberg, M. (1999). *The School Observation Measure (SOM©).* Memphis, TN: Center for Research in Educational Policy, The University of Memphis.

Ross, S. M., Smith, L., Alberg, M., & Lowther, D. (2004), Using classroom observations as a research and formative evaluation tool in educational reform: The school observation measure. In S. Hilberg & H. Waxman (Eds.), *New directions for observational research in culturally and linguistically diverse classrooms* (pp. 144-173). Santa Cruz, CA: Center for Research on Education, Diversity & Excellence.

Sandholtz, J. H., Ringstaff, C., & Dwyer, D. C. (1997). *Teaching with technology: Creating student-centered classrooms.* New York: Teachers College Press.

Sterbinsky, A., Ross, S. M., & Burke, D., (2004). *Tennessee EdTech Accountability Model (TEAM) Reliability Study.* Alexandria, VA: The CNA Corporation.

Switzer, T. J., Callahan, W. P., & Quinn, L. (1999, March). *Technology as facilitator of quality education: An unfinished model.* Paper presented at Society for Information Technology and Teacher Education, San Antonio, TX.

U.S. Department of Education (DOE). (2001). *No Child Left Behind Act.* Retrieved July 28, 2005, from http://www.ed.gov/nclb

U.S. Department of Education. (2003). *Federal funding for educational technology and how it is used in the classroom: A summary of findings from the Integrated Studies of Educational Technology.* Washington, DC: Office of the Under Secretary, Policy and Program Studies Service. Retrieved May 3, 2005, from http://www.ed.gov/about/offices/list/os/technology/evaluation.html

U.S. Department of Education (DOE). (2004a, October). *A guide to education and No Child Left Behind: Improving the academic achievement of the economically disadvantaged*. Washington D.C. Retrieved July 28, 2005, from http://www.ed.gov/nclb/overview/intro/guide/guide_pg13.html#disadv

U.S. Department of Education (DOE). (2004b, November). *U.S. Department of Education FY 2004 Performance and Accountability Report*. Washington DC: Retrieved July 28, 2005, from http://www.ed.gov/about/reports/annual/2004report/index.html

U.S. Department of Labor. (1992). *Secretary's Commission on achieving necessary skills (SCANS)*. Retrieved July 14, 2005, from http://wdr.doleta.gov/SCANS/

CHAPTER 10

KOREAN STUDENTS' REACTIONS TO PERCEIVED LEARNING ENVIRONMENT, PARENTAL EXPECTATIONS, AND PERFORMANCE FEEDBACK

Evidence for the Moderating Role of Performance-Approach Goals

Mimi Bong and Sung-il Kim

Imagine a teacher who assigns 100 points to every student in her class at the beginning of the semester. She takes away points from students who misbehave during class or do not turn in their homework on time. Another teacher in the next class does exactly the opposite. All students in her class start their new semester with zero points. They accumulate points for every good classroom deed and every assignment they submit

Effective Schools, 235–262

on time. Should there be a difference between these two classes in how much students enjoy schooling?

Now imagine parents who frequently express high expectations for their children. They let their children know that they deeply care about how the children are doing in school. They want their children to be successful in school, believe the children can achieve well academically, and are ready to provide assistance in every way possible to help their children perform better in school. Owing to their parents' strong support, the children feel confident about their capabilities to learn and perform in school and try their best to meet their parents' high expectations.... Or would they?

CHAPTER OVERVIEW

Recent developments in motivation theory and research have significantly advanced our knowledge of motivational phenomena in school. Investigators are now in a far better position to discuss which motivational beliefs and perceptions are important to students, how these beliefs and perceptions are created and maintained, and under what circumstances each of these beliefs and perceptions plays a critical role in determining students' cognitive, affective, and behavioral responses. Researchers have also discovered that students' motivational beliefs are heavily affected by contextual factors such as salient teaching and evaluation practices in the classroom or perceived parental expectations.

Whereas the general pattern of relationships between contextual factors and students' motivation is more or less clearly established with U.S. samples, direct applicability of the findings to students in other countries is yet to be tested. Evidence on the possible factors that could moderate motivation-context relationships is also currently lacking or inconsistent. For example, identical feedback from a teacher could engender positive feelings toward schooling in some students but neutral or even negative feelings in others. Parents' high expectations are generally known to boost children's confidence toward academic learning. However, there is a possibility that such high expectations produce unintended, detrimental effects for certain subgroups of children, especially when accompanied by conditional support or social comparative remarks.

In light of these observations and the general theme of the present volume, we pursued three objectives in this chapter. Our first objective was to test whether the pattern of relationships between learning environment and students' motivation and affect, obtained largely among U.S. students, could be replicated in Korean contexts. We thought it was essential to first check the comparability of these relations across countries because different relations would suggest different instructional implications for effective schooling. Our second objective was to discover potential moderators that either amplify or alleviate contextual influences on individual students' motivation and affect. Again, if there existed different relationships between the characteristics of learning environments and students' motivation in the presence of some moderators, it would be important to discover these moderators in order to be able to maximize the positive impacts and minimize the negative impacts of particular learning environments. Our final objective was to put one hypothesized moderator to the test by experimentally manipulating performance feedback, easily the most prominent factor in classroom teaching, and examining if its impact on subsequent motivation indeed differed across different types of the presumed moderator.

We begin this chapter with a brief overview of the relationships between student motivation and contextual factors, paying a particular attention to the types of perceived learning environments that either facilitate or harm students' motivation and learning. We then discuss the general characteristics of Korean classrooms and the unique role of parental expectations in Korean students' motivation in school. Finally, findings from two empirical studies follow, illustrating Korean students' responses to perceived learning environment, parental expectations, and performance feedback. Results suggest that students react differently to the same contextual influences according to the strengths of their personal performance-oriented achievement goals.

PERCEIVED LEARNING ENVIRONMENT AND STUDENT MOTIVATION

Among a host of motivational beliefs and perceptions that are deemed important to students' successful functioning in school, the following prove to be somewhat more useful than others for explaining and predicting students' achievement-related strivings.

Personal Motivational Beliefs

Academic self-efficacy refers to students' subjective convictions that they could successfully carry out given academic tasks at desired levels (Schunk, 1991). A strong sense of self-efficacy helps students to choose challenging tasks (Bandura & Schunk, 1981), demonstrate effort and resilience in accomplishing a given task (Bandura & Schunk; Schunk, 1982, 1983), and use more effective cognitive and self-regulatory learning strategies (Pintrich & De Groot, 1990; Zimmerman, Bandura, & Martinez-Pons, 1992; Zimmerman & Martinez-Pons, 1990). *Task value* refers to an incentive to engage in given tasks or activities, which encompasses perceived importance, perceived usefulness, and intrinsic interest in the tasks and activities (Wigfield & Eccles, 1992). Students' beliefs of self-efficacy and task value have been powerful predictors of the level and quality of their task performance and their subsequent task choice (Eccles, Wigfield, Schiefele, 1998; Multon, Brown, & Lent, 1991).

Another important set of motivational beliefs that are in the center of the current motivation research is achievement goals (Pintrich, 2003). *Achievement goals* refer to the underlying purposes or reasons for engaging in achievement-oriented behaviors (Ames, 1992; Dweck & Leggett, 1988; Nicholls, 1984; Urdan & Maehr, 1995). Whereas earlier conceptions of achievement goals distinguished between mastery and performance goals only, more contemporary views recognize three achievement goals, which are mastery, performance-approach, and performance-avoidance achievement goals (Elliot & Harackiewicz, 1996; Middleton & Midgley, 1997; Skaalvik, 1997).

Broadly speaking, students with *mastery goals* are primarily concerned with improving their competence through task mastery. They are little concerned about how they compare with others and instead focus on acquiring new skills and accomplishing given tasks. Students with *performance-approach goals*, though ostensibly similar to mastery-oriented students in their pursuit of academic excellence, express a strong desire to impress and outperform others, which is often a primary motivator of their task engagement. Yet for some other students, the main purpose of demonstrating achievement-related behaviors is not to confirm their superiority but to conceal their relative incompetence in front of others, so as to avoid the possibility of failure. These students are said to have taken up *performance-avoidance goals*. Like beliefs of academic self-efficacy and task value, achievement goals have been linked significantly to diverse indexes of learning and motivation (Elliot, 1999).

Perceptions of Learning Environment

Researchers have discovered that students' motivational beliefs are neither constant nor determined solely by the tasks at hand. Social cognitive theorists posit reciprocal determinism between person, environment, and behavior (Bandura, 1986; Zimmerman, 1989). Consistent with this notion, investigators have identified several contextual variables, more accurately, students' subjective understandings of their learning environment, which play a significant role in shaping students' self- and task-related beliefs and behaviors. Perceived goal structures in school and classrooms, teacher-student relations, peer relations, and parental expectations comprise the list of contextual variables that have been more actively researched.

Perceived school and classroom goal structures, in particular, have attracted much attention from researchers due to their purported direct impact on students' motivational beliefs. *Perceived school and classroom goal structures* refer to the typical ways with which tasks are presented and completed, important decisions are made, and students are treated and evaluated in school or classroom settings as perceived by the students in those settings. Students perceive *mastery-goal structures* in classrooms where task mastery, effort investment, and individual progress are valued and understanding of the material is emphasized over test scores. In classrooms with mastery-goal structures, students tend to personally adopt mastery achievement goals for themselves.

In contrast, students in classrooms with *performance-goal structures*, where teachers focus on test scores and evaluation, promote competition among students, and reward only the highest achievers, often pursue performance-oriented achievement goals themselves. The goal structure variables are shown to affect not only students' motivational beliefs such as personal achievement goals, academic self-efficacy, and task value but also students' use of self-regulatory and self-handicapping strategies and their affective reactions toward schooling (Ames & Archer, 1988; Church, Elliot, & Gable, 2001; Roeser, Midgley, & Urdan, 1996; Ryan & Patrick, 2001; Turner et al., 2002; Urdan, Midgley, & Anderman, 1998; Wolters, 2004).

CHARACTERISTICS OF KOREAN CLASSROOMS AND KOREAN PARENTS' EXPECTATIONS

Ames (1992) proposed six classroom dimensions that must be considered for designing motivationally adaptive learning environments. These dimensions include: Task; authority; recognition; grouping; evaluation; and timing and are widely known by their acronym T.A.R.G.E.T. According to Ames, students display motivated, mastery-oriented behaviors in classrooms where they could find meaningful reasons to engage in tasks and activities; are provided with adequate opportunities to choose among alternatives and participate in important classroom decision-makings; are recognized by their effort rather than their ability; work collaboratively with their peers; are evaluated on the basis of individual progress and improvement toward pre-specified goals and objectives; and are allowed sufficient time to learn and complete assigned tasks.

Bong (2003, 2004) contended that average Korean secondary classrooms do not meet these basic requirements for mastery-oriented learning environments. Indeed, there is a strong indication that the task dimension of Korean classrooms fails to invoke interest and curiosity among their learners. One of the national surveys conducted by the Korea Institute of Curriculum and Evaluation in 2000 showed that almost 70% of Korean students never found their homework to be interesting. Delegating authority to students is also a rare event in Korean classrooms. Classroom communication is usually one-way and dominated by the teacher. The teacher assigns convergent tasks to the whole class and students are seldom asked to choose the classroom activities and homework assignments that they prefer. Perhaps most important, the evaluation system is normative and extremely competitive. As such, students' relative standings among their peers largely determine the kinds of rewards and recognition they receive in the classroom.

By and large, Korean classrooms exhibit many of the features that typify classrooms with strong performance-goal structures. This might explain why Korean students display one of the lowest levels of interest and self-concepts in many international comparisons, despite their unquestionably outstanding and superior academic performance (e.g., Martin et al., 2001; Mullis et al., 2001). Still, the archetypal relationships between perceived school and classroom goal structures and student motivation in the existing literature mostly hold within Korean secondary classrooms, as demonstrated in previous studies (e.g., Bong, 2005) as well as later in this chapter.

Parental expectations, on the other hand, may serve a rather unique function in Korean students' psychology. Korean parents view education as an effective means for their children to realize future social and financial successes. Because East Asian cultures promote individuals' attentiveness to the members in their social network and feelings of obligation to please and not disappoint significant others (Heine, 2001; Markus & Kitayama, 1991; Oishi & Diener, 2001), parental expectations likely wield tangible influence on Korean students' school-related cognitions and affect. However, investigators do not agree on the exact nature of such influence. Several researchers claimed that Korean parents' excessively strong desire to expose their children to higher education places heavy pressure on Korean youth to the degree that it interferes with the children's stress coping (Chung, 1991; Kim, 1992). Others maintain that emotional and social support from parents and teachers are an important motivator for Korean children and they are positively motivated by parental achievement pressure and a sense of indebtedness toward their parents (Kim & Park, 2005; Kim, Park, & Park, 2000).

PERFORMANCE GOALS AS MODERATORS OF CONTEXTUAL EFFECTS?

It stands to reason that the nature and intensity of students' reactions to perceived school culture, parental expectations, and specific instructional treatments depend on individual characteristics and motivational profiles. We propose in this chapter that the strength of students' personal performance goals moderates the effects of contextual influences, especially when such influences render students' learning environment intimidating and unresponsive.

There is no doubt that heavy and ubiquitous performance-goal emphases in the environment, excessively high parental expectations, and negative performance feedback, commonly encountered in Korean classroom situations, are sources of debilitating motivation and learning for all students. However, their effects may be particularly consequential for students with strong performance-approach goals, who wish to publicly document their superior ability and hence constantly monitor their performance levels and other people's reactions for supporting evidence. The keen interest in and awareness of others' thoughts and feelings associated with Asian cultures (Heine, 2001; Markus & Kitayama, 1991) may further contribute to these students' insecurity in highly taxing learning environments. It is unclear whether the same moderation would occur with respect to performance-avoidance goals.

In the following section, we present results from two empirical studies conducted with Korean students that exemplify the trend of suggested moderation. In Study 1, the conventional relationships between contextual variables and student motivation are replicated, thereby confirming that the findings reported in the literature are indeed applicable to Korean contexts as well. On the same token, the successful replication of existing relationships leaves open the possibility that what we report in this chapter with Korean students may also turn out to be a universal phenomenon. We then examine if there is a difference in these context-motivation relationships according to students' performance-approach goal levels. In Study 2, we present evidence of interaction between types of performance feedback and levels of personal performance goals on students' interest and satisfaction on experimental tasks.

STUDY 1

Participants and Procedures

Participants were 389 girls at a public high school in Seoul, South Korea. Their ages ranged from exactly 16 years to 16 years and 11 months. The survey from which the present data came were administered during the second semester and the girls were believed to have acquired sufficient experience in their school setting to accurately respond to context-related questions in the survey. Portions of the data analyzed in this chapter were also used in Bong (2005).

Measures

Contextual variables.   Items for measuring students' contextual perceptions were adopted from the Patterns of Adaptive Learning Survey (PALS; Roeser et al., 1996). Five items each assessed perceived mastery-goal structures in school (e.g., "In this school, understanding the work is more important than getting the right answers") and perceived performance-goal structures in school (e.g., "In this school, teachers only care about the smart students"). Three items from Ethington (1991) were used to assess perceived parental expectations (e.g., "My parents want me to get a good grade in school").

Motivation and affect variables.   Students' self-efficacy for self-regulated learning, academic self-efficacy, task value, feelings of school belonging, and positive school affect were assessed, along with mastery, performance-approach, and performance-avoidance achievement goals. Self-efficacy for self-regulated learning was assessed with a scale used in Zimmerman, Bandura, and Martinez-Pons (1992; e.g., "I'm confident that I can study when there are other interesting things to do"). For assessing academic self-efficacy, five items were adopted from the self-efficacy subscale of the Motivated Strategies for Learning Questionnaire (MSLQ; Pintrich & De Groot, 1990) and PALS (e.g., "I'm certain I can master the skills taught in school this year"). Task value assessment consisted of three items, each referring to perceived importance, perceived usefulness, and interest in school learning.

As regards achievement goals, there were four *mastery goal* (e.g., "Understanding the schoolwork is more important to me than the grade I get") and three *performance-approach goal* items adopted from PALS (e.g., "I like to show my teachers that I'm smarter than the other students"). Among the three *performance-avoidance goal* items, two were from PALS (e.g., "The reason why I study is so that the teacher doesn't think that I'm not as smart as the other students").

Items on *positive school affect* were adopted from Wolters, Garcia, and Pintrich (1992, cited in Roeser et al., 1996; e.g., "I like being in school"). Three items were adopted from PALS for measuring *feelings of school belonging* (e.g., "I feel that I matter in this school"). All items referred to school learning in general rather than specific subject areas. Portions of the items originally referring to specific subjects were substituted with words such as "school" or "schoolwork." Table 10.1 reports the mean, standard deviation, and Cronbach's α of each scale.

RESULTS

Replicating existing relationships. The relationships between contextual variables and student motivation were first examined in a confirmatory factor analysis (CFA). Each item functioned as an indicator of the respective context or motivation latent variable. Self-efficacy for self-regulated learning and task value were too highly correlated with other

Table 10.1. Descriptive Statistics of Scales (N = 388)

Scale	M	SD	a
Perceived mastery-goal structures in school	3.21	.65	.73
Perceived performance-goal structures in school	2.74	.66	.78
Parental expectations	3.86	.70	.74
Mastery goal	3.51	.64	.61
Performance-approach goal	3.51	.86	.70
Performance-avoidance goal	2.66	.76	.65
Self-efficacy for self-regulated learning	2.97	.52	.81
Academic self-efficacy	3.56	.65	.84
Task value	2.80	.74	.75
Feelings of school belonging	3.03	.76	.81
Positive school affect	2.95	.86	.83

Table 10.2.   Correlation Coefficients Among Latent Variables

Latent Variable	1	2	3	4	5	6	7	8	9
1. Perceived mastery-goal structures in school	—								
2. Perceived performance-goal structures in school	−.36	—							
3. Parental expectations	.19	−.04	—						
4. Mastery goal	.43	−.23	.12	—					
5. Performance-approach goal	.11	−.07	.54	.23	—				
6. Performance-avoidance goal	.02	.28	.30	−.05	.60	—			
7. Academic self-efficacy	.37	−.09	.28	.56	.34	−.03	—		
8. Feelings of school belonging	.51	−.27	.18	.57	.30	−.03	.60	—	
9. Positive school affect	.48	−.20	.14	.54	.26	−.02	.67	.35	—

Note: Coefficients greater than .14 in absolute magnitude are significant at $p < .05$. χ^2 (490, $N = 388$) = 852.97, $p < .001$ (NNFI = .91, CFI = .92, average standardized residuals = .04).

variables and hence removed from the final model. Table 10.2 reports the correlation coefficients among the latent variables.

As can be seen, the pattern of relationships emerged from the present data resembled those reported in the literature. Perceived mastery-goal structures in school positively correlated with Korean high school girls' mastery goals, feelings of school belonging, academic self-efficacy, and positive school affect. Perceived performance-goal structures in school positively correlated with students' performance-avoidance goals and negatively correlated with students' mastery goal, feelings of school belonging, and positive school affect. Perceived mastery- and performance-goal structures in school correlated negatively to each other.

To further replicate previous findings, the predictive relationships among relevant variables reported in Roeser et al. (1996) were mapped onto the present set of variables in a structural equation model. This model was a simple rearrangement of the variables in CFA and hence shared the same fit indexes with the CFA model. Figure 10.1 presents statistically significant paths among the latent variables. Again, the predictive pattern was largely consistent with the existing literature. It is worth noting that perceived parental expectations were a significant predictor of these Korean girls' performance-approach as well as performance-avoidance goals.

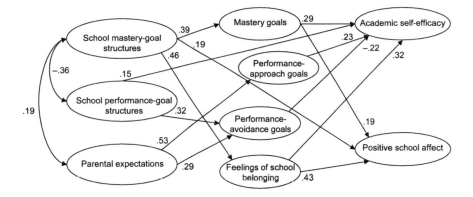

Figure 10.1. Replicating relationships between contextual perceptions and motivation.

Performance-approach goal moderation. We speculated earlier that students' personal performance-approach goals might moderate the relationships between contextual variables and personal motivational beliefs. To test this hypothesis, we divided the sample into high and low performance-approach goal groups by a median split and regressed each of the student motivation and affect variables on the set of contextual perception variables. If students' performance-approach goals moderated these relationships, different relationships would emerge in the high versus low performance-approach goal groups. Indeed, that was what we observed.

Table 10.3 displays the pattern of moderation by personal performance-approach goals when predicting students' positive school affect, feelings of school belonging, and task value beliefs from students' perceptions of the learning context. Regardless of the level of individual students' performance-approach goals, perceived parental expectations and mastery-goal structures in school were associated with predictive relations of similar nature and magnitude. In comparison, predictive relations demonstrated by perceived performance-goal structures in school differed by students' personal performance-approach goals. Perceptions of the performance-goal structures in school did not significantly predict students' motivation and affect-related beliefs in the low performance-approach goal group. However, the same contextual perceptions of the high performance-approach goal students significantly and negatively predicted their personal motivation and affect.

Consistent with the literature, as students perceived a stronger focus on ability and relative superiority in their learning environment, they tended to express more negative motivational beliefs. However, those

**Table 10.3.   Performance-Approach Goal Moderation of
Perceived Performance-Goal Structures in School**

Predictor	Total Sample (N = 387)	High Performance- Approach Goal (N = 193)	Low Performance- Approach Goal (N = 193)
On positive school affect			
Parental expectations	.06	.01	.06
Mastery-goal structures in school	.38***	.37***	.35***
Performance-goal structures in school	−.04	−.14*	.04
On feelings of school belonging			
Parental expectations	.09	.08	.03
Mastery-goal structures in school	.37***	.38***	.31***
Performance-goal structures in school	−.10*	−.19**	.01
On task value			
Parental expectations	−.02	−.10	.05
Mastery-goal structures in school	.32***	.32***	.29***
Performance-goal structures in school	−.15**	−.22**	−.07

*$p < .05$. **$p < .01$. ***$p < .001$.

with strong performance-approach goals appeared to be at particular risk because, as they perceived stronger performance-goal structures in their school, they also reported significantly more negative school affect, weaker feelings of school belonging, and lower task value beliefs toward school learning.

Table 10.4 presents another interesting set of findings regarding the performance-approach goal moderation. When students perceived higher parental expectations, they generally reported stronger self-efficacy for self-regulated learning and stronger academic self-efficacy. Parental expectations were also a positive predictor of students' personal performance-avoidance goals. However, when the students were divided into high versus low performance-approach goal groups, the positive motivational pattern associated with perceived parental expectations disappeared in the high performance-approach goal group yet the negative trend on their performance-avoidance goals remained. Those with high performance-approach goals felt more vulnerable as they perceived greater expectations from their parents, whereas those with low performance-approach goals became more confident as they perceived higher parental expectations.

Table 10.4.   Performance-Approach Goal Moderation of Perceived Parental Expectation

Predictor	Total Sample (N = 387)	High Performance-Approach Goal (N = 193)	Low Performance-Approach Goal (N = 193)
On self-efficacy for self-regulated learning			
Parental expectations	.17***	.01	.32***
Mastery-goal structures in school	.30***	.34***	.22**
Performance-goal structures in school	−.04	−.07	.02
On academic self-efficacy			
Parental expectations	.21***	.10	.20**
Mastery-goal structures in school	.28***	.24**	.30***
Performance-goal structures in school	.03	−.05	.08
On performance-avoidance goal			
Parental expectations	.24***	.23***	.13
Mastery-goal structures in school	.07	.05	.03
Performance-goal structures in school	.23***	.18*	.27***

$*p < .05. **p < .01. ***p < .001.$

STUDY 2

In this study, we explored whether the performance-goal moderation of contextual effects we observed with the correlational data in Study 1 could be replicated in an experimental setting.

Types of Performance Feedback

Among the many features that exist in any given learning environment, various verbal and nonverbal feedback from the teacher are arguably the most salient factor in students' perceptions of the learning environment. We thus experimentally manipulated performance feedback on experimental tasks and examined whether the effects of different types of feedback on subsequent motivation differed depending on the level of personal performance goals.

Performance feedback, when used under proper conditions, could improve learners' task performance by enhancing their intrinsic motivation. However, not all types of feedback are beneficial for developing learners' intrinsic motivation in the tasks. Research on intrinsic motivation has repeatedly ascertained that only the kinds of feedback that inform learners of the appropriateness and relevancy of their target performance demonstrate positive motivational influence. Performance feedback that either lacks such informational value or is uniformly provided to learners without consideration of individual differences will negatively affect learners' interest, task performance, or both (Kluger & DeNisi, 1996).

To date, most research on performance feedback has focused on the relationship between feedback type and intrinsic motivation or performance. However, studying the interactive effects between types of feedback, types of tasks, and learners' individual characteristics could generate results that may be more practical and instructive. For instance, McGraw (1978) suggested that extrinsic rewards or feedback could increase or maintain learners' interest in quantitative tasks (e.g., speed or algorithmic problems) but they might decrease learners' intrinsic motivation in qualitative tasks (e.g., heuristic problems involving problem-solving or divergent thinking). We examined the pattern of interaction between feedback type and learners' individual characteristics, namely, personal performance goals and perceived competence in the present experiment.

Perceived Competence Interaction

As described earlier, Korean students are under great pressure to perform well in an intensely competitive atmosphere. The highly performance-focused learning situations in most secondary classrooms tend to push students toward adopting performance goals in their own learning (Ames & Archer, 1988). As such, we speculated that perceived competence, along with personal performance goals, might also play a role in determining Korean students' motivation.

Perceived competence refers to expectations individuals hold regarding their own capabilities. Harackiewicz and Manderlink (1984) demonstrated that personal perceptions of doing well on the tasks mediated the effects of performance feedback on participants' intrinsic motivation. That is, learners whose level of perceived competence was high were not as affected by the negative feedback compared to those whose level of perceived competence was low. The latter participants exhibited significantly decreased interest in the task activity after receiving negative feedback. Similar episodes were documented in the classic study of Elliott and Dweck (1988). In their experiment, performance-goal oriented children with low perceived competence responded to failure in a highly maladaptive manner with deteriorated use of problem-solving strategies, negative affect, and attributions of failure to uncontrollable causes. In contrast, performance-goal oriented children with high perceived competence showed reactions to failure similar to those demonstrated by mastery-goal oriented children.

In addition to the performance feedback manipulation in the present experiment, we also manipulated levels of perceived competence within each performance-goal group. Therefore, it was possible to test whether the performance-goal moderation of feedback effects, if any, would play out differently for individuals with high versus low perceived competence. It should be noted that the approach and avoidance components of the performance-oriented achievement goals were not differentiated in this study. As a result, performance goals assessed in this experiment represented students' desires to document their superior ability by performing better than others and, at the same time, avoid potential failure by shunning challenging tasks and cutting down effort in the fear of displaying lower ability (Dweck & Leggett, 1988; Elliott & Dweck, 1988).

In sum, the purposes of this experiment were twofold. The primary purpose was to document the performance-goal moderation of feedback effects on subsequent motivation. The secondary purpose was to examine whether the pattern of such moderation differed by not only the feedback type but also the level of perceived competence.

Participants

The sample consisted of 174 seventh graders (89 girls and 85 boys) who were randomly assigned to one of three experimental conditions: Gain, lose, and combined. There were 55 students in the gain condition, 60 in the lose condition, and 59 in the combined condition of gain and lose.

Materials and Procedures

Experimental task. The experimental task was a spurious web-based critical thinking test. The test consisted of six subtests: Association; creativity; divergence; productivity; combination; and expression. For example, the productivity test asked students to write as many words as came to mind when seeing a given picture.

Performance feedback manipulation. There were three performance feedback conditions. In the *gain* condition, no medal was given to students initially. Two medals were then provided for each success trial.

Nothing was taken away for failure. In the *lose* condition, 12 medals were given initially. Two medals were taken away for each subsequent failure but no medal was provided for success trials. In the *combined* (gain + lose) condition, six medals were given initially. Two medals were provided for each success trial and two were taken away for each failure trial.

Although the feedback was predetermined regardless of students' actual performance levels, students were led to believe that the feedback was determined by comparing their task performance with the norm in a huge database system. All performance feedback conditions operated under the same contingency plan of three success and three failure trials, ending up with six medals.

Perceived competence manipulation.   To manipulate students' feelings of competence toward experimental tasks, a practice session was run. Students received test results that were predetermined according to the experimental condition to which they belonged. Students in the *high competence* condition received test results that showed that their performance earned 91-95 points and ranked in the top 7-9%. Those assigned to the *low competence* condition received test results of 55-66 points and a rank in the bottom 8-15% (see Figure 10.2 for an example of test result screen).

To check if the perceived competence manipulation was successful, students were asked the following question at the end of the experiment: "There were 100 students who performed the same task as you did in this experiment. Where do you think you rank in terms of your task performance?" Students in the high competence condition expected significantly better performance ($M = 47.4$) than did those in the low competence condition ($M = 68.4$), suggesting the manipulation was successful. Students also rated task interest and performance satisfaction at the end of the experiment.

Measures

Performance goals.   We used the Performance Goal Orientation scale of Kwon and Kim (2003), developed on the basis of Meece, Blumenfeld, and Hoyle (1988). This measure includes five items with response scales ranging from $1 = $ *strong disagree* to $5 = $ *strongly agree*. A reliability coefficient for this scale was $\alpha = .73$. Students were divided into high and low performance-goal groups by a median split.

Task interest and performance satisfaction.   We assessed students' interest in the task and satisfaction with their task performance with a scale originally developed by Kim, Kwon, Yoon, So, Kim, and Lee (2004). Several

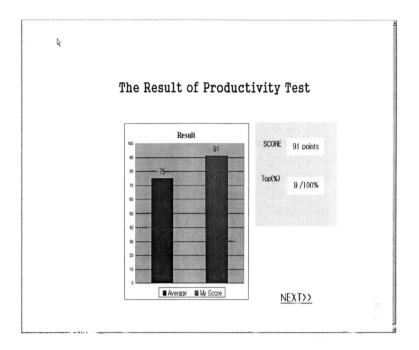

Figure 10.2.   Example practice test result for perceived competence manipulation.

items were adapted to better suit the purposes of the present experiment. Two factors, task interest and performance satisfaction, were extracted in an exploratory factor analysis, constituting evidence of construct validity. Cronbach's αs were .79 and .62 for task interest and performance satisfaction scales, respectively.

Design

A 3 (feedback type; gain, lose, and combined) × 2 (performance goal; high vs. low) × 2 (perceived competence; high vs. low) factorial design was used. Dependent variables were task interest and performance satisfaction scores.

RESULTS

In factorial design, interaction effects usually take primacy over main effects. When the interaction effects prove statistically significant, we describe the results mainly in terms of the interaction effects, although some main effects were also statistically significant. Table 10.5 and 10.6 present mean ratings of task interest and performance satisfaction, respectively, for each group.

Interaction between feedback type and performance goal on task interest. The interaction between feedback type and performance goal was significant, $F(2, 162) = 3.83$, $p < .05$. Students with low performance goals indicated significantly greater interest in the experimental tasks when presented with the gain type feedback than the lose or the gain + lose combined feedback. Those with high performance goals, on the other hand, expressed stronger task interest when the performance feedback included a "lose" component, with the difference between the

Table 10.5.   Mean Ratings of Task Interest
(Standard Deviations in Parentheses)

Perceived Competence	Performance Goal		Feedback Type			
			Gain	Lose	Combined	Total
High	High	(n = 42)	3.43 (.21)	3.91 (.20)	4.05 (.60)	3.79 (.17)
	Low	(n = 43)	3.81 (.21)	3.60 (.19)	3.36 (.21)	3.59 (.13)
	Total	(n = 85)	3.62 (.12)	3.75 (.13)	3.71 (.13)	3.69 (.15)
Low	High	(n = 46)	3.56 (.18)	3.85 (.21)	3.64 (.21)	3.67 (.12)
	Low	(n = 43)	3.75 (.27)	3.19 (.19)	3.58 (.18)	3.47 (.17)
	Total	(n = 89)	3.61 (.13)	3.48 (.17)	3.61 (.15)	3.57 (.11)
	Total (n = 174)		3.61 (.11)	3.62 (.11)	3.65 (.16)	3.63 (.13)

Table 10.6.   Mean Ratings of Performance Satisfaction
(Standard Deviations in Parentheses)

Perceived Competence	Performance Goal		Feedback Type			
			Gain	Lose	Combined	Total
High	High	(n = 42)	3.36(.22)	2.73(.20)	2.85(.22)	2.98(.20)
	Low	(n = 43)	3.62(.22)	3.23(.19)	2.85(.22)	3.15(.16)
	Total	(n = 85)	3.63(.13)	2.98(.17)	2.85(.19)	3.01(.15)
Low	High	(n = 46)	3.49(.18)	3.36(.21)	2.88(.22)	3.24(.17)
	Low	(n = 43)	3.50(.28)	2.69(.20)	3.58(.18)	3.26(.20)
	Total	(n = 89)	3.50 (.15)	3.01 (.16)	3.23 (.17)	3.25(.15)
	Total (n = 174)		3.49 (.17)	3.00 (.15)	3.04 (.16)	3.16(.17)

gain and the lose conditions reaching statistical significance (see Figure 10.3). This suggests that the high performance-goal participants might have been more interested in keeping the given medals and not losing them rather than gaining additional medals. The high performance-goal participants, who were keenly interested in social comparison, might have found the lose type of performance feedback more useful for gauging their relative superiority. As long as they lost less medals than did others, it would guarantee their winning.

Interaction between feedback type, performance goal, and perceived competence on performance satisfaction. There was a significant main effect of feedback type on performance satisfaction, $F(2, 162) = 6.06$, $p < .005$. As can be seen in Table 10.6, participants reported the highest level of performance satisfaction when they received the gain type of feedback ($M = 3.49$) than when they did the lose ($M = 3.00$) or the gain + lose combined feedback ($M = 3.04$). This adaptive effect of the gain type of feedback relative to the other two types of feedback was consistently demonstrated across the low and high performance goal groups as well as the low and high perceived competence conditions. It is noteworthy that the latter two feedback conditions both contained a "lose" component.

In addition to the significant main effect of feedback type, the three-way interaction between feedback type, performance goal, and perceived

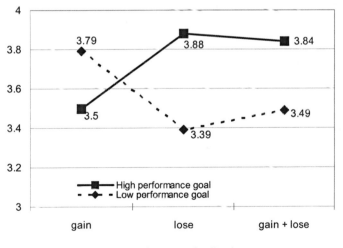

Figure 10.3. Interaction between feedback type and performance goal on students' task interest.

competence also proved significant, $F(2, 162) = 4.92$, $p < .01$. In the high competence condition, both the high and low performance-goal students rated their performance the most satisfactory when they received the gain type of feedback. Difference in the performance satisfaction scores was statistically significant only among the low performance-goal participants between the gain and the gain + lose combined conditions (see Figure 10.4).

The pattern was reversed in the low competence condition. Among the low-competence participants, those with low performance goals were significantly less satisfied with their performance when they received the lose type of feedback than the gain or gain + lose combined types of feedback. There was no significant difference in the performance satisfaction scores between the three feedback conditions among those with high performance goals (see Figure 10.5). The results suggest that the lose type of feedback, which is quite commonly used in school, should be avoided and it is particularly detrimental for students with low competence and low performance goals.

DISCUSSION

Debilitating Effects of Performance-Oriented Environments: A Common Finding

A universal thread across the two studies in this chapter was that students profited from an environment that emphasized task mastery, deep understanding of the learning material, and individual improvement and accomplishment. Students suffered in learning environments that instead stressed relative ability, competition, and evaluations and penalized them for their mistakes. The present results corroborate findings in the extant literature and highlight, once again, the importance of designing mastery-oriented learning environments for effective schooling.

Study 1 demonstrated that Korean high school girls' perceptions of the mastery-goal structures in their school were associated with many adaptive motivational outcomes. As these girls perceived a stronger emphasis on task mastery than test scores per se, their personal mastery goals, academic self-efficacy beliefs, feelings of belonging to their school, and positive affect while at school also became stronger. The opposite was true for perceived performance-goal structures. As the girls perceived heavier pressure on doing better than others and getting higher test scores, their positive motivation and affect plummeted gradually in the form of weaker personal mastery goals, stronger performance-avoidance

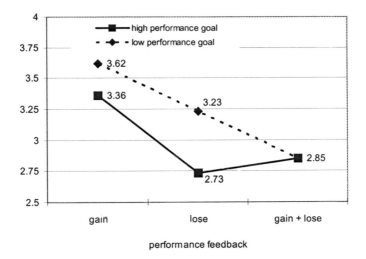

Figure 10.4.   Interaction between feedback type and performance goal on performance satisfaction in the high-competence condition

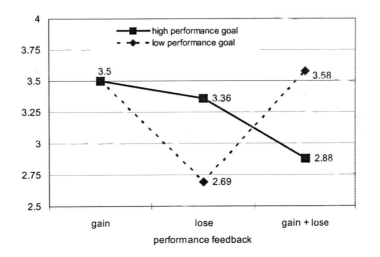

Figure 10.5.   Interaction between feedback type and performance goal on performance satisfaction in the low-competence condition

goals, weaker feelings of school belonging, and less positive affect toward school.

Analogous results emerged in an experiment. In Study 2, Korean middle school students felt the highest level of satisfaction about their task performance when they were presented with the gain type of feedback. In the "gain" feedback condition, students earned medals for every successful performance but were not punished for the mistakes they made. It is difficult to draw an exact parallel between the perceived learning environment in a natural school setting and artificially manipulated performance feedback in an experiment. Nonetheless, one may still see some resemblance between the attributes of perceived goal structures in Study 1 and performance feedback in Study 2, particularly between the performance-goal structures in school and the "lose" or the "gain + lose combined" feedback conditions. In those two feedback conditions, students were led to believe that they paid for every mistake they committed when they yielded two medals.

Whereas the lose type of feedback might have appeared more straight-forward and hence provided more useful information for social comparison purposes, the combined feedback of gain + lose, with which students ostensibly picked up medals when succeeded and lost them when erred, could have been construed as more controlling. Both feedback conditions, therefore, were strongly performance-oriented. It is not surprising that students in the lose and the combined feedback conditions reported substantially less satisfaction at the end of the experiment compared to those in the gain feedback condition, although there was no difference in the final number of medals remaining across all three feedback conditions.

Many students are confronted with performance-goal oriented environments where competition and social comparisons are constantly taking place. They compete for limited tangible rewards such as grades. As demonstrated in numerous studies in the field as well as the present chapter, students who receive controlling feedback in the form of directions, orders, deadlines, or possibility of losing points for the mistakes they make are bound to relinquish intrinsic motivation and exhibit less voluntary effort for learning new things. If controlling feedback cannot be avoided for whatever reason, we suggest that teachers and practitioners try to use "gain" types of feedback as much as possible. Since the gain type of feedback seems beneficial to positive motivation and affective reactions regardless of individual students' level of personal performance goals, it would likely prove effective in classrooms where diverse groups of students are learning together, each pursuing different goals and objectives.

Nature of Performance Goal Moderation: Some Conflicting Findings

Another common finding of this chapter was that students' personal performance goals moderated the effects of their learning environments. The nature of this moderation, however, was not consistent across the two studies. Korean high school girls in Study 1 were more vulnerable to external pressure such as performance-goal structures in school and perceived parental expectations when they held strong performance-approach goals. As these girls perceived a stronger emphasis on performance and ability in their school environment, they exhibited more negative feelings toward school, a weaker sense of belonging to their school, and lower task value toward school learning. These girls also demonstrated stronger orientations toward performance-avoidance goals, as they perceived higher parental expectations. The girls who did not endorse performance-approach goals as strongly, in contrast, appeared more resilient to the same achievement press in their learning environment. The motivation of these girls with relatively weak performance-approach goals was not affected by their perceptions of the harsh and competitive school environment. Further, their perceptions of stronger parental expectations enhanced their academic and self-regulatory self-efficacy beliefs.

In Study 2, Korean middle school students with high performance goals reported higher task interest when they received either the lose or the gain + lose combined feedback than when they did solely the gain type of feedback. Those with relatively weak performance goals showed the reverse pattern and reported the highest interest in the experimental tasks in the gain feedback condition. A similar pattern was observed with regard to students' performance satisfaction but only in the low perceived competence group. Specifically, even among those with low perceived competence, the taxing environment created by the lose type of feedback appeared especially harmful to students with low but not high performance goals because they displayed the lowest level of satisfaction with their task performance.

The seeming incongruity between the two sets of results may reflect differences in the nature of the two studies. Others' opinions and evaluations are believed to loom larger for students with strong performance goals. When these students perceive a heavy focus on their relative standings and strong achievement pressure from significant adults in their environment, they are bound to feel increasingly more insecure and anxious about the possibility of failure and letting others learn about their incompetence. This was demonstrated in Study 1, where only the students with high performance-approach goals significantly lowered their positive affect and feelings of belonging to their school and significantly raised their performance-avoidance goals as they perceived a greater performance press in their school environment.

Results of Study 2, however, suggest a possibility that when the results of task performance do not carry much tangible consequence (i.e., grades), these students might actually crave for information that could be used to more accurately evaluate their performance in comparison to others in their immediate reference group. In the "gain" type of feedback condition, performers were not punished for their mistakes, whereas they did pay for every seeming failure by having their points deducted in the "lose" type of feedback condition. If individuals wished to compare their own performance capabilities to those of their peers, the "lose" type of feedback would appear to provide more useful information. Nevertheless, teachers and practitioners should keep in mind that there is a danger that students may end up with stronger dissatisfaction with their performance when the results of comparisons are not favorable and eventually turn to performance-avoidance goals (see, e.g., Bong, 2005).

CONCLUSION AND DIRECTIONS FOR FUTURE RESEARCH

It is worth noting that the conflicting pattern across the two studies regarding students' performance goals bears similarity to the current argument in the achievement goal literature on the adaptive role of performance goals in highly competitive and taxing situations (see, e.g., Harackiewicz, Barron, Pintrich, Elliot, & Thrash, 2002; Kaplan & Middleton, 2002). More specifically, research with K-12 populations has repeatedly demonstrated the motivationally maladaptive nature of performance-goal structures in the learning environment as well as learners' personal performance goals, including both performance-approach and performance-avoidance. In contrast, studies conducted with college samples have demonstrated that performance-approach goals can have some positive effects such as improved performance and thus should not be actively discouraged without first considering the type of learning situations in which students are asked to function (Harackiewicz et al.; McGregor & Elliot, 2002).

Often, the adaptive nature of performance goals most clearly materializes in experimental settings that involve competition but no serious consequence, just like the one in Study 2. Future research should examine tenability of the present conjecture that performance goals might operate as a positive short-term motivator for trivial tasks but will ultimately lead students to motivationally unhealthy paths as the stakes of performing poorly become increasingly high. Longitudinal studies in naturalistic settings seem best suited for answering questions on the performance-goal moderation observed in this chapter.

It is premature to reach any definitive conclusion regarding the moderating role of performance-oriented achievement goals on the basis of only two studies. Nevertheless, the particularly negative reactions of the high performance-goal students to various environmental presses in actual Korean classrooms make us wonder, contrary to the arguments by some, if adopting such goals can ever prove truly beneficial for students' motivation, learning, and performance under the normal learning circumstances.

ACKNOWLEDGMENT

This work was supported by the 2004 Ewha Womans University Research Grant awarded to Mimi Bong and the Basic Research Program of the Korea Science & Engineering Foundation (R0120030001170002005) awarded to Sung-il Kim. Correspondence concerning this chapter should be sent to mimibong@ewha.ac.kr

REFERENCES

Ames, C. (1992). Classrooms: Goals, structure, and student motivation. *Journal of Educational Psychology, 84,* 261-271.

Ames, C., & Archer, J. (1988). Achievement goals in the classroom: Students' learning strategies and motivation processes. *Journal of Educational Psychology, 80,* 260-267.

Bandura, A. (1986). *Social foundations of thought and action: A social cognitive theory.* Englewood Cliffs, NJ: Prentice Hall.

Bandura, A., & Schunk, D. H. (1981). Cultivating competence, self-efficacy, and intrinsic interest through proximal self-motivation. *Journal of Personality and Social Psychology, 41,* 586-598.

Bong, M. (2003). Choices, evaluations, and opportunities for success: Academic motivation of Korean adolescents. In F. Pajares & T. C. Urdan (Eds.), *Adolescence and education: Vol. 4. International perspectives* (pp. 323-345). Greenwich, CT: Information Age.

Bong, M. (2004). Classroom culture as a source for the mismatch between Korean students' performance and motivation. *East West Education, 21,* 1-18.

Bong, M. (2005). Within-grade changes in Korean girls' motivation and perceptions of the learning environment across domains and achievement levels. *Journal of Educational Psychology, 97*(4), 656-672.

Chung, W. S. (1991). The dynamics of Korean youth in family and community. *International Journal of Adolescence and Youth, 3*(1-2), 99-116.

Church, M. A., Elliot, A. J., & Gable, S. L. (2001). Perceptions of classroom environment, achievement goals, and achievement outcomes. *Journal of Educational Psychology, 93,* 43-54.

Dweck, C. S., & Leggett, E. L. (1988). A social-cognitive approach to motivation and personality. *Psychological Review, 95,* 256-273.

Eccles, J. S., Wigfield, A., & Schiefele, U. (1998). Motivation to succeed. In W. Damon & N. Eisenberg (Eds.), *Handbook of child psychology: Vol. 5. Social, emotional, and personality development* (5th ed., pp. 1017-1095). New York: Wiley.

Elliott, E. S., & Dweck, C. S. (1988). Goals: An approach to motivation and achievement. *Journal of Personality and Social Psychology, 54,* 5-12.

Elliot, A. J. (1994). Approach and avoidance achievement goals and intrinsic motivation: A mediational analysis. *Journal of Personality and Social Psychology, 70,* 461-475.

Elliot, A. J. (1999). Approach and avoidance motivation and achievement goals. *Educational Psychologist, 34,* 169-189.

Elliot, A. J., & Harackiewicz, J. M. (1996). Approach and avoidance achievement goals and intrinsic motivation: A mediational analysis. *Journal of Personality and Social Psychology, 70,* 461-475.

Ethington, C. A. (1991). A test of a model of achievement behaviors. *American Educational Research Journal, 28,* 155-172.

Harackiewicz, J. M., Barron, K. E., Pintrich, P. R., Elliot, A. J., & Thrash, T. (2002). Revision of achievement goal theory: Necessary and illuminating. *Journal of Educational Psychology, 94,* 638-645.

Harackiewicz, J., & Manderlink, G. (1984). A process analysis of the effects of performance-contingent rewards on intrinsic motivation. *Journal of Experimental Social Psychology, 20,* 531-551.

Heine, S. J. (2001). Self as cultural product: An examination of East Asian and North American selves. *Journal of Personality, 69,* 881-906.

Kaplan, A., & Middleton, M. J. (2002). Should childhood be a journey or a race? Response to Harackiewicz et al. (2002). *Journal of Educational Psychology, 94,* 646-648.

Kim, S., Kwon, E., Yoon, M., So, Y., Kim, W., & Lee, S. (2004). The effects of types of concept map and science self-efficacy on interest and comprehension: A comparison of 4th and 5th graders. *Korean Journal of Educational Psychology 18*(4),17-31.

Kim, Y. –H. (1992). Social class and parents' demand for children's education. *Korean Journal of Educational Research, 30*(4), 173-197.

Kim, U., & Park, Y. S. (2005). Integrated analysis of indigenous psychologies: Comments and extensions of ideas presented by Shams, Jackson, Hwang and Kashima. *Asian Journal of Social Psychology, 8*(1), 75-95.

Kim, U., Park, Y. S., & Park, D. (2000). The challenge of cross-cultural psychology: The role of the indigenous psychologies. *Journal of Cross Cultural Psychology, 31,* 63-75.

Kwon, E. J., & Kim, S. (2003). The effect of achievement goals and types of feedback on intrinsic motivation and perceived competence. *Korean Journal of Educational Research, 41*(4), 341-364.

Kluger, A. N., & DeNisi, A. (1996). The effects of feedback interventions on performance: A historical review, a meta-analysis, and a preliminary Feedback Intervention Theory. *Psychological Bulletin, 119*(2), 254-284.

Markus, H. R., & Kitayama, S. (1991). Culture and the self: Implications for cognition, emotion, and motivation. *Psychological Review, 98,* 224-253.

Martin, M. O., Mullis, I. V. S., Gonzales, E. J., O'Connor, K. M., Chrostowski, S. J., Gregory, K. D., et al. (2001). *Science benchmarking report: TIMMS 1999—eight grade.* Chestnut Hill, MA: Boston College, International Study Center.

McGraw, K. O. (1978). The detrimental effects of reward on performance: A literature and a prediction model. In M. R. Lepper & D. Greene (Eds.), *The hidden cost of rewards* (pp. 30-60). Hillsdale, NJ: Erlbaum.

McGregor, H., & Elliot, A. J. (2002). Achievement goals as predictors of achievement-relevant processes prior to task engagement. *Journal of Educational Psychology, 94,* 381-395.

Meece, J. L., Blumenfeld, P. C., & Hoyle, R. H. (1988). Students' goal orientations and cognitive engagement in classroom activities. *Journal of Educational Psychology, 80,* 514-523.

Middleton, M. J., & Midgley, C. (1997). Avoiding the demonstration of lack of ability: An underexplored aspect of goal theory. *Journal of Educational Psychology, 89,* 710-718.

Mullis, I. V. S., Martin, M. O., Gonzales, E. J., O'Connor, K. M., Chrostowski, S. J., Gregory, K. D., et al. (2001). *Mathematics benchmarking report: TIMMS 1999—eight grade.* Chestnut Hill, MA: Boston College, International Study Center.

Multon, K. D., Brown, S. D., & Lent, R. W. (1991). Relation of self-efficacy beliefs to academic outcomes: A meta-analytic investigation. *Journal of Counseling Psychology, 38,* 30-38.

Nicholls, J. G. (1984). Conceptions of ability and achievement motivation. In R. Ames & C. Ames (Eds.), *Research on motivation in education: Vol. 1. Student motivation* (pp. 39-73). Orlando, FL: Academic Press.

Oishi, S., & Diener, E. (2001). Goals, culture, and subjective well-being. *Personality and Social Psychology Bulletin, 27,* 1674-1682.

Pintrich, P. R. (2003). A motivational science perspective on the role of student motivation in learning and teaching contexts. *Journal of Educational Psychology, 95,* 667-686.

Pintrich, P. R., & De Groot, E. V. (1990). Motivational and self-regulated learning components of classroom academic performance. *Journal of Educational Psychology, 82,* 33-40.

Roeser, R. W., Midgley, C., & Urdan, T. C. (1996). Perceptions of the school psychological environment and early adolescents' psychological and behavioral functioning in school: The mediating role of goals and belonging. *Journal of Educational Psychology, 88,* 408-422.

Ryan, A. M., & Patrick, H. (2001). The classroom social environment and changes in adolescents' motivation and engagement during middle school. *American Educational Research Journal, 38,* 437-460.

Schunk, D. H. (1982). Effects of effort attributional feedback on children's perceived self-efficacy and achievement. *Journal of Educational Psychology, 74,* 548-556.

Schunk, D. H. (1983). Ability versus effort attributional feedback: Differential effects on self-efficacy and achievement. *Journal of Educational Psychology, 75,* 848-856.

Schunk, D. H. (1991). Self-efficacy and academic motivation. *Educational Psychologist, 26,* 207-231.

Skaalvik, E. M. (1997). Self-enhancing and self-defeating ego orientation: Relations with task and avoidance orientation, achievement, self-perceptions, and anxiety. *Journal of Educational Psychology, 89,* 71-81.

Turner, J. C., Midgley, C., Meyer, D. K., Gheen, M., Anderman, E., Kang, Y., et al. (2002). The classroom environment and students' reports of avoidance strategies in mathematics: A multimethod study. *Journal of Educational Psychology, 94,* 88-106.

Urdan, T., & Maehr, M. L. (1995). Beyond a two-goal theory of motivation and achievement: A case for social goals. *Review of Educational Research, 65,* 213-243.

Urdan, T., Midgley, C., & Anderman, E. M. (1998). The role of classroom goal structure in students' use of self-handicapping strategies. *American Educational Research Journal, 35,* 101-122.

Wigfield, A., & Eccles, J. S. (1992). The development of achievement task values: A theoretical analysis. *Developmental Review, 12,* 265-310.

Wolters, C. A. (2004). Advancing achievement goal theory: Using goal structures and goal orientations to predict students' motivation, cognition, and achievement. *Journal of Educational Psychology, 96,* 236-250.

Zimmerman, B. J. (1989). Models of self-regulated learning and academic achievement. In B. J. Zimmerman & D. H. Schunk (Eds.), *Self-regulated learning and academic achievement* (pp. 1-25). New York: Springer-Verlag.

Zimmerman, B. J., Bandura, A., & Martinez-Pons, M. (1992). Self-motivation for academic attainment: The role of self-efficacy beliefs and personal goal setting. *American Educational Research Journal, 29,* 663-676

Zimmerman, B. J., & Martinez-Pons, M. (1990). Student differences in self-regulated learning: Relating grade, sex, and giftedness to self-efficacy and strategy use. *Journal of Educational Psychology, 82,* 51-59.

CHAPTER 11

EFFECTIVE DISCIPLINE IN MULTICULTURAL SCHOOLS IN SOUTH AFRICA

Two Case Studies

Jan Heystek

As an academic, researcher, parent, and member of a school governing body, I am involved in schools across the entire educational spectrum in South Africa. I was a teacher in several former White-only schools in South Africa until 1994. Thereafter I joined a university and have since undertaken research in the former Black-only schools.

This chapter analyses disciplinary issues in two (now) multicultural schools in South Africa. I selected the two schools involved in this research project because they represent two points on the continuum from apparently good discipline to apparently poor discipline. They also represent two points on the continuum between, at the one extreme, being opposed to any social and cultural change and, at the other extreme, accepting the social, political and cultural changes occurring in the broader South African society without question. The analysis indicates

Effective Schools, 263–281
Copyright © 2006 by Information Age Publishing

that racism still exists in some schools. However, an understanding of the attitudes of the individuals involved provides an important context for the racism and its associated disciplinary issues.

Effective education is a high priority for the government of South Africa, because the government aspires to establish South Africa as a significant participant in the international arena. This aspiration entails a core belief that South Africa should develop from its current status of being a developing country to achieving recognition as a developed country. In order to fulfil this aim, schools should be effective, and should equip their students with all the skills and knowledge that will enable them to compete successfully in the global (developed) village.

Effective discipline should contribute to effective education and effective schools. While various meanings can be attributed to the term effective school, in this chapter an effective school, and its accompanying effective discipline, implicates a situation in which quality teaching takes place to initiate and support ongoing learning at a high level. This chapter specifically considers discipline and its potential influence on effective schooling in multicultural schools in South Africa. The disciplinary problems scrutinized in this chapter do not include serious or life-threatening problems related to drugs, gangs and sexuality. They do include, however, disciplinary problems that occur daily in classrooms especially those which may affect the effectiveness of day to day teaching and learning in the classroom. It should be born in mind that the evolving democracy in South Africa is an integral part of the classroom situation. Thus, power relations and the dominance of cultures have a decisive affect on discipline in the classroom situation.

Discipline in schools should not be equated with punishment in the sense that schools should have a rule for every possible aberrant activity and a related punishment for the transgression each of the rules. This would represent a negative approach to discipline. A positive approach, in contrast, entails a focus on the acquisition of self-discipline, which in turn is based on respect and values that provide the basis for acceptable behavior (Beckmann & Nieuwenhuis, 2004; De Klerk & Rens, 2003).

The analysis in this chapter considers the perceptions of teachers and students from different cultural groups with respect to disciplinary issues in their schools. The research problem posed for the research was: Does the multicultural situation in South African schools have an impact on effective education? This question was investigated through the eyes of the teachers and students in the selected schools. Research questions probed how teachers and students perceive their school; what is considered to be unacceptable behavior in a school; and what students and teachers would like to change, especially in regard to the codes of conduct and the demerit systems in the schools.

SOCIOCULTURAL CONTEXT OF THE RESEARCH

South Africa is a young democracy. In 1994, all citizens of the country were able to participate in national elections for the first time. Until then, the South African population was officially divided into four racial groups, namely White, Black, Colored, and Indian, and only White citizens could participate in elections for the national government. Separate schools were also established for each of the designated racial groups. After the acceptance of the new constitution in 1996, new legislation abolished the previous racial definitions. Moreover, unfair discrimination based on, for example, race, sex, religion, or language was no longer permissible and any child could therefore be enrolled in the school of their parents' choice.

Although racial classification has been abolished in South Africa, the former racial classification concepts are used in this chapter to elucidate the situation that continues to prevail in South African schools and society. There are eleven official languages in South Africa, namely Afrikaans (which is spoken by the majority of the White population), English and nine other languages that are spoken in the Black population. Thus, the Black population (about 35 million of the 42 million inhabitants) is linguistically divided into nine groups, which makes the multicultural situation in South Africa especially complex.

South African Schools

There were approximately 4,000 White-only schools and 27,000 Black-only schools in South Africa in 1994. Before 1994, all the teachers in the White schools were White. After 1994, the composition of the staff in the new multicultural schools did not change significantly. One of the main reasons for the limited change was that many of the Black parents who enrolled their children in the former White-only schools did not want Black teachers in these schools. These parents said that Black teachers were not professional, lacked self-discipline, and were not well qualified. The schools referred to in this chapter are predominantly former White-only schools. However, these schools currently enroll students from all racial groups. In the spirit of the transformation and democratization of the country, these schools are referred to as multicultural schools in the ensuing analysis (Shields, Bishop, & Mazawi, 2005).

The historical role of schools in the struggle to abolish apartheid in South Africa is related to the emphasis on effective schooling in this volume. From the middle of the 1970s, the slogan "liberation before education" had a (perhaps paradoxically) *detrimental* effect on the effectiveness of the Black schools. Students and teachers disrupted schools by means of strikes, damaged school buildings and destroyed learning materials, resulting in ineffective schools in many Black communities. Moreover, the post-1994 government has had limited success with its numerous campaigns and policies to restore the culture of teaching and learning in the former Black schools. The dearth of effective schools motivates many Black parents, especially those living in and near the rural towns and cities, to enroll their children in the former White schools. These Black parents perceived, and still perceive, the education provided in the former White schools to be superior to education in the Black schools. The trend is still that Black children enroll in White schools, but not vice versa.

The migration of Black students to White schools has made many White communities nervous, because the White communities were and still are afraid that the perceived culture of poor discipline (that existed in the era of "liberation before education") will permeate the White schools that enroll Black students. Poor discipline, parents perceive, could affect the academic standards of schools, depriving their children of the opportunity of becoming active participants in the global village. This fear has caused many White parents to remove their children from the multicultural schools and enrol them at the few schools that have remained predominantly White and that use Afrikaans as the medium of instruction.

An additional with respect to the multicultural schools is that the media and the government often use incidents that have occurred between Black and White students, or between White teachers and Black students in multicultural schools, to illustrate that these schools still practice racism or apartheid. An example is: a boy hits another boy in an argument about a girl. Just add the adjectives, "Black" boy and "White" boy and it is not a discipline issue anymore but a racial issue. The small number of incidents of this nature that actually occur, such as fighting, threats, and verbal abuse, receive disproportionate attention from the media and the government and makes discipline a thorny issue in schools. This difficult situation implicates what Skiba, Michael, Nardo, and Peterson (2002) and Gregory and Mosely (2004) identify concerning the influence of perceived racial issues on normal school activities. Thus, the interpretation or perspective of the observer(s) determines many times if a situation is construed as a normal disciplinary situation or a racial issue.

Most of the former White schools use Afrikaans as the medium of instruction. However, because of the new political situation that prevails in South Africa, Black students and their parents now often demand that the Afrikaans schools should change their medium of instruction to English, or at least make provision for Black children who prefer (or whose parents prefer) to have English as their medium of instruction. This demand often leads to an increase in the workload of White Afrikaans-speaking teachers, because they often have to prepare and present lessons in Afrikaans and in English and use Afrikaans and English in the same classroom for instruction. This complicating factor often impedes the improvement of the quality of education in these schools.

DISCIPLINE AND DEMOCRACY

Ensuring effective discipline in multicultural schools in South Africa is seen as part of the process of integrating students from all cultures into a united South African nation. Thus, for the purposes of this analysis, the emphasis is placed on discipline as a relational activity rather than as a rules-driven, legislative activity. This emphasis to discipline emphasizes the attitudes and behaviors of a person (Beck, 2000), motivational factors in their behavior (Beck; Pintrich & Schunk, 2002), as well as the organizational climate which influences the human activity and values of the persons involved in that activity (Van Der Westhuizen, 2002). Moreover, an given disciplinary regime can be represented as a point on a continuum that varies between very strict, rule-bound, autocratic approaches on the one hand, and self-discipline on the other. Motivationally, rule-based discipline is aligned with extrinsic motivation, while self-discipline inclines towards intrinsic motivation (Pintrich & Schunk).

In a democratic and transforming society, the ideal situation occurs when all the role players in the school participate in decision-making processes, such as in drafting rules or codes of conduct (Dieltiens, 2000). Thus, consensus, group control over decisions and group ownership of decisions are essential in pluralistic societies (English, 2005). In the present case, democratic decision making would be expected to lead to a situation in which all groups in multicultural schools are more willing to accept "the rules" and to adhere to them. If so, it would then not be nec-

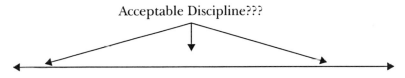

Figure 11.1.   Acceptable discipline.

essary to enforce the rules by means of autocratic processes. Divergent value systems, however, also become important in a multicultural situations. Thus, according to Kochan and Reed (2005), prevailing values should bind groups together, but should also provide groups with sufficient freedom so that no group is forced to strictly conform to the values of the dominant group.

Discipline is associated with power. Power does not necessarily mean exercising physical force, but refers to any process or activity in which a dominant group or individual can influence others to do what the dominant group/individual wants them to do (Adams & Waghid, 2005). Power is not necessarily linked to a particular value system or based on any particular ethical code. However, when power (e.g., in the form of a disciplinary system) is linked to a value system, power is strengthened and its exercise may become even more autocratic. Thus, in a culturally diverse society such as South Africa, and especially in schools, factors such as values, power and dominant culture become very important in the determination of the criteria for discipline and in the determination of rules in a school that will be acceptable to "everyone."

Discipline is also a social and situational issue. What is acceptable discipline in one family or organization (school) may not be acceptable discipline, or seen to be acceptable discipline, in another family or organization. It is therefore not possible to lay down precise rules or guidelines for effective discipline for all schools. It is essential that each school should determine its own codes of conduct and rules, while taking into consideration the values of the school community and the broader society. This approach to discipline draws on both systems theory and contingency theory in which schools are considered to be open structures that are influenced from outside and which also influence the communities and societies they serve (Owens, 1981). Thus, schools may be considered to be systems that function within the wider culture and values of the community (English, 2005). More specifically, contingency theory suggests that schools adapt and accommodate key features of the prevailing sociocultural situations in which they are embedded (English). This implies that leaders and teachers in these schools take salient sociocultural features into consideration when deciding on actions to be taken— including actions regarding disciplinary matters.

RESEARCH DESIGN

This chapter discusses two case studies that were undertaken in two multicultural schools in South Africa. School 1 is situated near a rural town, while School 2 is located in a large city. The schools were selected on the grounds that the disciplinary situations in them differ significantly. The purpose of the specific case studies was not to make a direct comparison between the two schools per se, but rather to provide a wider perspective on two schools that have very different cultures and climates. Moreover, although the primary purpose of undertaking the case studies was not to generalize the findings, other schools in South Africa (and perhaps even more broadly) may be able to learn from the results of the analyses.

Qualitative methods were used in the project, namely focus-group interviews with students and teachers as well as open-ended questionnaires that were completed by students and teachers. The specific aim of the investigation at both the schools was to determine how the students and teachers felt about the disciplinary situation that prevailed in their particular school. Some key questions put to the participants in the course of the interviews were: What is the purpose of a school? Why are you in this school? What do you like and what do you dislike about the school? What is considered to be unacceptable behavior in the school? What would you change at the school if it were possible for you to make changes? What changes have occurred at the school during the past few years? The questionnaires consisted of open-ended questions similar in intent to the above. At both schools the focus-group interviews followed the completion of the questionnaires in order that the questionnaire data could be used to help guide the direction of the focus group questions.

School Sample

School 1 is located a few kilometers from a medium-sized rural town. Three of the 23 staff members are not White. (The typical situation that prevails in the majority of the previously White-only schools is that there are no, or only a few, non-White teachers.) The former stream of White students that enrolled at the school has declined as a result of urbanization and the declining number of young White farmers in the area. The students at the school come from a wide geographical area, up to 300 kilometers from the school. The majority of them travel by bus from two big cities. Currently the student population consists of 75% Black students and 25% White students. Most of the Black students stay in the school residences, while most of the White students live in the surrounding area. The majority of the teachers have been at the school for many years.

Most of the teachers at School 1 live on the school premises and often do not have regular contact with people outside the school. The geographical and social isolation of the staff members who live on the school premises could have an effect on their attitude towards, and perceptions of, the school and the world beyond the school. Specifically, this isolation could be a reason for the apparent lack of change in their attitudes towards the transformation that is occurring in the country.

School 2 is an urban school of which about 50% of the students are Black and all the members of staff are White. The majority of the Black students live in the township that is located 15 kilometers from the school. These students typically travel by bus to the school. The White students all live in the immediate geographical area of the school. Although there are also White English-speaking students in the school, there is a tradition at this school, and in similar schools, to refer to the Black students as the "English" students, because they represent the greater majority of English-speaking students in the school.

There have not been any serious disciplinary problems involving the various cultures, which the parents, teachers or students have attributed to being race related. However, teachers referred to the disciplinary problems at the school as constituting "low-scale terrorism," because a continuous stream of small problems occur in the classroom. The problems are not of a sufficient magnitude to result in the suspension of a child or to request that the child's parents to come to the school for a discussion. The problematic activities typically relate to classroom disturbances that occur during lessons.

STUDENT/TEACHER SAMPLE AND METHODOLOGY

The samples at the two schools were selected from the entire student enrolment with the assistance of the principals concerned. School 1 is an English-medium school. The research groups and methods involved at this school are indicated in order in Table 11.1.

In somewhat more detail, the Grade 8 and Grade 9 students initially answered oral questions that were put to the whole group in the hall. The purpose of these questions was to gain an overview of the issues regarding discipline in the school. After answering questions in the whole-group setting, discussions were held with individual students who requested such a discussion. Thereafter separate meetings were held with the student representative council (LRC) for Grades 10 to 12, and teaching-staff members. Each LRC member and staff member answered questions that were similar to those answered by the grade eight and grade nine students.

The research methods employed for the various groups at School Two are indicated in order in Table 11.2.

More specifically, the research process at School 2 commenced with each learner answering survey questions during register periods. (The students were divided into Afrikaans-medium and English-medium regis-

Table 11.1.   Methods and Samples Used in School 1

Sample	Method
School management team, including the principal, five heads of department and four senior staff members acting as heads of department or subject heads (SMT) (10 people)	Focus group interview
All the grade eight students in the hall (131)	Open-ended questionnaires and informal discussions
All the grade nine students (111)	Open-ended questionnaires and informal discussions
Student representatives of grades 10, 11 and 12 (LRC) (20 in the group)	Open-ended questionnaires and focus-group interviews
The remainder of the staff (13 members)	Open-ended questionnaires and focus-group interviews

Table 11.2   Methods and Samples Used in School 2

Sample	Method
Grades 8 to 12	Open-ended questionnaires
Teachers	Open-ended questionnaires
Grade 10 students. Four groups, namely White and Black obedient group; Black and White disobedient group	Focus-group interview
Grade 11 students. Four groups, namely White and Black obedient group; Black and White disobedient group	Focus group interview

ter classes.) After the completion of the survey process, focus-group interviews were conducted with Grade 10 and Grade 11 students. Purposeful sampling was used to select students who could provide data-rich information. The principal rendered assistance in the selection of the students in accordance with specific criteria, that is, there should be both boys and girls in each of the eight focus groups; each grade should have a group of Black students and a group of White students; the Black group and the White group per grade were further divided into students who were identified as "good" (or typically obedient) students and as "bad" (or often disobedient) students on the basis of school records. Only Grade 10 and Grade 11 students were selected for the focus-group interviews. These students had all been in the school for at least 3 years and therefore have significant experience of the codes of conduct and disciplinary issues in the school.

RESULTS

The results reported here are indicative rather than comprehensive, and focus on those finding of most relevance to the issue of school discipline in the context of effective schooling in a diverse sociocultural climate. The results are organized around three key questions relating to: (a) participants' perceptions of the purposes of schooling in general, (b) reasons for choosing to attend their particular school, and (c) participants' specific perceptions of discipline and related issues at their school. I also report on an analysis of a specific disciplinary structure used at both schools: namely a demerit system.

What is the Purpose of Schooling?

The aim of this key question was to determine the attitudes of students and teachers towards school and education in general terms. Attitudes to school are an important determinant of prevailing school climates, and therefore also of the disciplinary situation in any school. Indicative results from School 2 are reported in Table 11.3.

Table 11.3 indicates that the most important perceived purposes for school revolve around issues relating to preparation for the future, the transfer of knowledge; social involvement; and learning to develop morality and self-discipline.

Why Did You Choose Your School?

The students in School 2 indicated broad satisfaction with their school. Students typically echoed the following comment made by a Grade 11 student in School Two: "I am in this school, because it is the only school I like. The schools near my home are corrupt. I have to travel 90 minutes by bus, but this is the only bilingual school that is not corrupt." (According to the members of the Grade 11 "disobedient" group, a corrupt school is one in which there is "no discipline" and where students "drink alcohol and use drugs." It also appeared from the interviews that the majority of the Black students attend School 2 because they and/or their parents consider this school, and the former White-only schools in general, to be "better" than the Black schools.

The situation in School 1 differs from that in School 2. Students at School 1 said that their parents think that it is a good school, but they (the students) do not agree with this view. The disciplinary problems in the school are reflected in the students' reluctance to accept that it is a "good"

Table 11.3.   The Purpose of School?

	Gr 10 Eng.	Gr 10 Afr.	Gr 11 Eng.	Gr 11 Afr.
Builds my future (To get a good job)	37	34	30	30
For my education	24	18	26	21
Being with friends, having fun	17	13	22	23
Attitudes and morals such as responsibility (to friends and schools)	11	6	10	2
Discipline, a place to learn rules	15	6	14	9
Learn how to live with other people	16	14	9	3
Meet new people (that have a positive or a negative influence)	3	4	6	4
A safe place, keeps one away from serious crimes such as murder	5	4	16	5

school. According to the principal, however, the parents prefer this school to other alternatives because it has high academic standards, its medium of instruction is English, and it has boarding facilities.

The teachers in School 1 said they are "the right people in the wrong place." This remark is indicative of a negative attitude towards the prevailing situation in the school. The principal explained the teachers' attitude by stating that the teachers want to maintain the English traditions at the school and expect the students to conform to the climate of the school. However, although the parents selected the school on the grounds of its tradition and climate, the students, who have been influenced by the evolving culture of democracy and individual rights in the country, do not accept the traditional climate of the school without question. Hence, conflict between students and teachers arises.

At School 1, the students were asked to draw a picture that reflects their feelings about their school. They produced some pictures that reflected happiness, either general happiness or the happiness of being with friends. There were also some pictures that reflect intermediate perspectives, that is, pictures that reflect that the students are happy sometimes and sad sometimes. In general, however, students expressed more negative feelings than positive feelings. Their negative feelings were expressed in images such as a broken heart; drawings of an unhappy and boring school; anger and hatred expressed by depicting themselves as being in prison; and the prospect of a bleak future that was expressed by means of dilapidated buildings, knives, an arrow piercing a heart and various types of monsters. Several students associate the school with actions such as bombing, gunfire, the throwing of material into a dustbin, a fire occurring in the school and jumping from a high building. When asked to explain the significance of the prison that they had drawn, some students explained that it indicated a plea to get out of the school and to go home. The pictures revealed may of the same attitudes that were expressed in the interviews. The students in this school are not happy and their unhappiness gives rise to disciplinary problems. The teachers are intent on enforcing the rules whereas the students challenge the rules.

Unacceptable Behavior in the Classroom

A third key question was "what is considered to be unacceptable behavior in the classroom," is related to the first question regarding what a school is. As an indicative set of results, Table 11.4 reflects what the students in School 2 indicated as being unacceptable behavior in and outside their classrooms.

The unacceptable types of behavior mentioned most frequently include talking while the class is in progress; arriving late; intimidation of other students; failure to do homework; walking about the class without obtaining permission to do so; and arrogance towards teachers and other students. Reasons given for undisciplined behavior in School 1 include poor relations between the students and the teachers; between teachers and the school management team; and between the school governing body and the school (teachers). These relations were typically characterized by a lack of trust and respect.

Demerits as part of the Disciplinary System: Problems and Potential Solutions

Unacceptable behavior cannot continue without consequences. The next section focuses on a particular disciplinary structure that is in operation in the schools to (ostensibly) maintain discipline and ensure obedience to the rules.

The abolition of corporal punishment in 1996 created a problem for many schools, as corporal punishment formed the backbone of the disciplinary system of many schools until 1996. In the past, it was possible for teachers to control the "low-scale terrorism" of class disruption through a controlled system of corporal punishment. Teachers used threats of corporal punishment, then students who continued to disrupt the classroom were caned.

Table 11.4.   Unacceptable Behavior

	Grade							
	8	8	10	10	11	11	12	12
	Eng	Afr.	Eng.	Afr.	Eng.	Afr.	Eng.	Afr.
No. Students per Class	35	31	31	25	25	25	30	42
1. Not doing homework	8	2	6	2	2	2	1	6
2. Talking while a teacher/ child is explaining work	18	12	16	20	1	7	6	21
3. Back-chatting teachers and classmates	5	3	8	7	1	3	9	1
4. Disrupting the class, misbehaving, clowning	13	5	12	12	3	12	9	7
5. Showing disrespect to teachers, challenging teachers	12	8	8	6	1	5	7	7
6. Showing disrespect to RCL members or students	3	7	5	4	4	4	6	7
7. Making a noise in free periods	5	4	5	3	2	4	3	3

At present, teachers in the study reported, there is nothing with which the teachers can threaten disruptive students. As a result, extended arguments between teachers and students may occur, which is detrimental to effective learning and teaching. It is understandable in the South African context that teachers would continue to equate discipline with punishment and especially corporal punishment. The South African government is, however, currently attempting to find alternatives for corporal punishment in order to assist schools with disciplinary problems. Nevertheless, the findings regarding the two schools in this case study (discussed below) suggest that more rules or more forms of punishment will not solve the problem.

School 1 and School 2 both used a demerit system as part of their disciplinary process. The demerit system is based on the allocation of marks for certain transgressions, followed by detention, and the performing of specific duties. If a child commits a transgression of a serious nature, or accumulates a particular number of demerits, he or she could appear at a disciplinary hearing of the school's governing body.

At both schools, teachers are not satisfied that the demerit system assists them sufficiently to maintain discipline and to enhance the effectiveness of teaching and learning. The demerit process, especially in respect of minor transgressions, or "low-scale terrorism," takes too long and frustrates the teachers. A disciplinary hearing may result in the suspension of the student from the school for a maximum of 5 days or expulsion of the student from the school upon the endorsement of the measure by the provincial head of department. A significant allegation made by teachers in both schools is that the provincial department does not support them in regard to serious offences and that it takes too long to react upon a disciplinary hearing. In School 2, for example, students had been found guilty of using drugs and the department agreed with the recommended expulsion, but nevertheless changed the punishment to a suspended sentence. As a result of acts of this nature, the students gain the impression that nothing will happen to them and that they can continue with their unacceptable behavior. The disciplinary process is also tedious, because the disciplinary hearing requires the teachers and members of the parental governing body to have legal-type expertise, which they normally do not have. Teachers in School 1 stated that: "We are not lawyers, but the students bring lawyers to these hearings, which makes it almost impossible to get rid of students who are guilty of misbehaving in class."

The students also hold the opinion that the demerit system does work as a punishment and especially as a deterrent to disciplinary transgressions. Moreover, in School 1, the students specifically stated that they challenge the rules because they were not involved in the rule-making process. It is therefore not surprising that the teachers have difficulty in maintaining order in the classroom.

Table 11.5 provides an indication of the demerits that are allocated for the transgressions of specific rules. The most demerits are allocated for serious offences, but these offences do not occur frequently in the schools. Activities that occur daily typically receive few demerits. As a result, students who disrupt classroom, even on a regular basis, may continue to exhibit this behavior for a long time before they are taken to the next level of disciplinary activity, for example detention. The demerit example provided below is from School 2. School 1 has a similar format and structure for its demerit system.

Demerits Assigned

An analysis of the demerit lists and discussions with the principal revealed that only a few teachers assign demerits. The limited use of the demerit system is problematic for the teachers because students gain the impression that disruptive behavior is acceptable and that it is those teachers who do assign demerits who are out of touch with what is acceptable and what is not.

Table 11.5.   Number of Demerits per Transgression

Transgression	Points
1. Use or possession of alcohol: possession of drugs; drunkenness; immoral behavior; theft; possession of weapons.	150
2. Forgery; trading in examination material	75
3. Discriminatory behavior; dishonesty, lying or copying work; disrespectful to teacher; gambling; smoking or in possession of cigarettes	50
4. Not attending detention; hate speech, sexism, and racism	40
5. Crude language; denial of other students' right to education; disruption of classroom; homework repeatedly not done; disruptive walking around; leaving school without permission; disobeying code of conduct	30
6. Poor behavior; noisy during free periods	15
7. Entering area out of bounds; late for school; repeatedly late for class; transgressions of rules regarding appearance	10
8. Disruption of class; talking while teacher is teaching, continuously arguing with teacher, not working in classroom; back-chatting, showing disrespect; verbal aggression	0

The students, on the other hand, are of the opinion that some teachers misuse the demerit system, because they cannot control their students. Students perceive that teachers use the demerit system to threaten the students, but that they lack the foundational respect and trust of the students. This perception provides a "breeding ground" for the escalation of disciplinary problems: the teacher threatens and then allocates demerits, followed by students' unhappiness and more challenges to the "power" of the teacher to allocate demerits, because the demerits are seen to be a misuse of power, which results in more threats and demerits being allocated. As soon as the students realize that the demerits do not have any real effect, however, they can continue to challenge the teacher and the situation gets out of hand. The net result is that effective teaching diminishes.

Improving the System

Teachers indicated that the schools may have two options to increase the effectiveness of the demerit system. In the shorter term, they could allocate higher demerit marks for misbehavior in class. This adaptation could be accompanied by stricter steps when the student reaches the maximum number of demerits. Furthermore, even stricter measures, for example expulsion, could also be introduced earlier in the discipline process. It is also seen as a fundamental prerequisite that the parents and community support the proposed stricter enforcement of discipline. In the longer term, schools should also promote the value of education and its importance for the students and the community both for its intrinsic value and as a means of promoting pro-social behaviors among students.

DISCUSSION

Some of the more salient points arising from the research are discussed below. One of the most interesting aspects of this investigation of discipline in two South African schools is that race did not appear to be a significant reason for, or an important contributing factor to, disciplinary problems School 2, but did appear to be so in School 1. In School 2 only one student mentioned racism or a negative attitude towards them as a Black person, as a reason for class disruption. In School One, however, race is a more prominent factor. All the student groups interviewed in this school mentioned teacher's attitudes, which included racial attitudes, as possible reasons for disciplinary problems in classrooms. Thus, the school-specific context appears to be an important factor when examining the perceived causes of disciplinary problems.

Attitudes play an important part in a school's disciplinary system. In School 2, the students have a generally positive attitude, because they want to be in that school. In School 1, the negative attitude of the teachers towards the students, and vice versa, creates disciplinary problems. These problems are difficult to solve, because the participants may not realize that their *own* attitudes can hamper the cooperative maintenance of discipline in their school. It is clear from the findings of the research that relations between teachers and students at School 1, as well as the attitudes of particular individuals, may require specific attention.

It is understandable that teachers differ with respect to the way they deal with disciplinary problems in their classrooms. However, an important issue is that teachers should at least maintain roughly comparable standards and criteria when making disciplinary judgements. Teachers should, thus, discuss accepted norms of behavior among themselves before interpreting them to the students. For examples, teachers may deal with students arriving late in their own way, but each teacher should clearly signal to the students that arriving late is not acceptable. When teachers use very different approaches to disciplinary actions, the students become confused and it is difficult for other teachers to follow a uniform disciplinary process.

The teachers mentioned that students' disrespectful behavior towards them presents many problems. Yet this behavior did not appear to be punished as frequently as may be expected. One possibility for this apparent under-reporting is that teachers who react to disrespect with disciplinary measures often leave themselves vulnerable to criticism. Should a teacher allocate demerits or send a child to the principal for disrespect or for disruption, this act may be interpreted as indicating that that teacher is not able to earn the respect of the students or is not able to maintain order in the classroom. Thus, teacher need to be reassured that referring discipline problems "up the tree" is not interpreted by school leaders as indicating incompetence on behalf of the teacher.

A key recommendation for improving the demerit system described in the research would be to increase the demerit marks allocated for frequently occurring transgressions. A child should experience that it is unacceptable to disrupt a classroom. A related problem that arises in this regard, however, is that there should be sufficient and appropriate methods for punishing the child whose demerits reach the maximum set limit. These methods should exceed punishment by means of detention. Expulsion may be the next step, but school governing bodies have limited powers in this regard. They may only expel a child for a maximum of five days. Moreover, expulsion is problematic, because the child who is expelled can probably least afford to be absent.

Active and genuine participation by all the role players in a school, namely the students, teachers, and parents, is important to ensure acceptance of the disciplinary process. Students and parents should participate in the drafting of codes of conduct and rules for the school. This participation should not be cursory. It should involve genuine cooperation in which the perspectives of the parents and the students are positively considered and incorporated in the new code and rules. Cooperation, in turn, implies that a school fosters an effective communication process. The students and the teachers, for example, may both oppose certain forms of "unacceptable" behavior, but they may not discuss and explain their judgements to one another. Discussions held during grade meetings or during register periods once a week may provide the best opportunity to have an open discussion about these matters. The holding of such discussions will also require the teachers discuss these matters amongst themselves. Furthermore, teachers should be receptive to the students' suggestions and be willing to incorporate students' ideas in disciplinary policies and practices. Disregarding students' inputs does not contribute to a relationship of trust or a more effective teaching and learning climate.

CONCLUSION

Although White people are in the minority in South Africa, and Black people are in the majority, Black children are still in the minority in many of the new multicultural schools—including those schools examined in this study. The prevailing situation is therefore one in a sociocultural minority attempts to maintain effective schools with high academic standards, which often includes specific approaches to discipline within a specific school climate and culture. On the other hand, members of the Black community, who are politically and culturally dominant in the country, also want the most effective schooling for their children and therefore seek to enroll their children in the multicultural schools. After enrolling their children in these schools, however, the Black parents (and their children) often demand a new culture in these schools, which includes English as the only medium of instruction, as well as a new, "democratic" climate and culture that accommodates Black children. These background features of education in South Africa are closely related to the disciplinary situations that are discussed in this chapter. However, despite the importance of the sociocultural context of South African schools, this study found that school-level and individual-level factors are at least as important in determining the nature of disciplinary issues and the relationship of these issues to the effectiveness of schooling. Thus, it is important to incorporate a multilevel perspective on discipline and school effectiveness when examining schools in the South African context, and probably in other diverse sociocultural contexts as well.

REFERENCES

Adams, F., & Waghid, Y. (2005). In defence of deliberative democracy: challenging less democratic school governing practices. *South African Journal of Education*, *25*(1), 25-33.

Beck, R. C. (2000). *Motivation: Theories and principles*. Englewood, Cliffs, NJ: Prentice Hall.

Beckmann, J. L., & Nieuwenhuis, J. (2004). *The education manifesto about values and democracy in education: A founding or flirtation with values?* [Die Onderwysmanifes oor waardes en demokrasie in die onderwys: 'n fundering of flirtasie met waardes?]. *South African Journal of Education*, *24*(1), 55-63.

De Klerk, J., & Rens, J. (2003). The role of values in school discipline. *Koers*, *68*(4), 353-371.

Dieltiens, V. M. (2000). *Democracy in education or education for democracy? The limits of participation in South African school governance*. Unpublished MEd dissertation, University of Witwatersrand, South Africa.

English, F. W. (Ed). (2005). *The SAGE handbook of educational leadership. Advances in theory, research and practices.* London: SAGE.

Kochan, F. K., & Reed, C. J. (2005). Collaborative leadership, community building and democracy in public education. In English, F. W. (Ed.), *The SAGE handbook of educational leadership.* London: SAGE.

Owens, R. G. (1981). *Organizational behaviour in education.* Englewood, Cliffs, NJ: Prentice Hall.

Pintrich, P. R., & Schunk, D. H. (2002). *Motivation in education. Theory, research and application.* Englewood, Cliffs, NJ: Prentice Hall.

Shields, C. M., Bishop, R., & Mazawi, A. (2005). *Pathologizing practices. The impact of deficit thinking on education.* New York: Peter Lang

Skiba, R. J., Michael, R. S., Nardo, A. C., & Peterson, R. L. (2002). The color of discipline: Sources of racial and gender disproportionality in school punishment. *The Urban Review, 34*(4), 317-342.

Van der Westhuizen, P. C. (Ed.). (2002). *Schools as organisations.* Pretoria, South Africa: Van Schaik.

ABOUT THE AUTHORS

Eric Anderman is the associate dean for research and graduate studies at the University of Kentucky, Lexington, Kentucky. He received his PhD in educational psychology from the University of Michigan in 1994. His current research examines motivation during adolescence (both academic motivation and motivation to avoid engaging in risky behaviors), and academic cheating. Dr. Anderman is associate editor of the *Journal of Educational Psychology,* one of the official journals of the American Psychological Association. Dr. Anderman is principal investigator on an NIH/NINR grant examining methods of motivating adolescents to avoid situations that might lead to pregnancy or HIV infection. He is also a coinvestigator on several other federally funded grants examining the prevention of risky behaviors in adolescent populations. Dr. Anderman serves on the editorial boards of *Educational Psychologist, Child Development,* and *Contemporary Educational Psychology.* E-mail: eande1@uky.edu

Mimi Bong is associate professor in the Department of Educational Technology at Ewha Womans University, Seoul, Korea. She received her PhD from the University of Southern California in 1995, and was associate professor of educational psychology, research, and technology at the University of South Carolina from 2000-2004. Her research and scholarship focus on student motivation and learning with particular emphases on academic self-efficacy beliefs and achievement goal orientations, theoretical and empirical comparisons of diverse motivational constructs, and cross-domain/cross-cultural generalizability of motivational processes. Her recent research interests include the impact of perceived learning environments and sociocultural factors affecting Korean adolescents' motivation. Mimi Bong was recognized as the eighth most productive educational psychologist in the world for the period of 1997-2001. She currently serves on the editorial boards of *Journal of Educational Psychology, Contemporary Educational Psychology,* and *Educational Researcher* and as Consulting Editor of *Child Development* and *Journal of Experimental Education*. E-mail: mimibong@ewha.ac.kr

Bert P. M. Creemers is professor in educational science and Dean of the Faculty of Psychology, Education and Sociology at the University of Groningen, The Netherlands. Until September 2002, he acted as director of GION, the Groningen Institute for Educational Research. He is member of several national and international scientific organizations and founder and corresponding editor of the journals *School Effectiveness and School Improvement,* and of *Educational Research and Evaluation*. He is also a member of the editorial board of other scientific and professional journals. He is involved as a researcher and/or as an advisor in the improvement and evaluation of education in the Netherlands, and is invited frequently as expert for educational research and evaluation in other countries. His main research interests are in the evaluation of teaching, educational effectiveness and improvement, and change processes and policies at the different levels of educational systems. E-mail: b.p.m.creemers@rug.nl

Martin Dowson is postdoctoral research fellow in the SELF Research Centre, UWS, and adjunct associate professor at the Asia Graduate School of Theology and the Sydney Obesity Research Clinic. He received his PhD in educational psychology from the University of Western Sydney in 2000, and has other degrees in education, philosophy, and theology. He is the author of more than 100 peer-refereed publications in psychology and education, including publications investigating the relationship of motivation to self-concept, cognitive processing, and academic achievement. More recently, Martin has pursued studies in religion, religious self-identify, and the psychology of ministry from both motivational and psychometric perspectives. Martin also maintains a strong background and interest in multivariate statistical modeling with latent variables. E-mail: mdowson@unisurf.com.au

R. Trent Haines is a doctoral candidate at the University of Kentucky in the Department of Educational and Counseling Psychology. His current research interests are in the effects of social influences on African American adolescent development and in the use of culturally relevant pedagogy in public school classrooms. He holds a master's degree in public administration from Eastern Kentucky University and a bachelor's degree in sociology from Asbury College.

Jan Heystek is senior lecturer in education management and at the University of Pretoria, South Africa. Jan has a strong interest in school management and governance and has published extensively in the field school governance and management with the emphasis on school improvement and school effectiveness. His textbook, *Human Resource Management In Education* is used widely at different universities and schools in South Africa. Jan's latest publications cover topics such as working relationships between principals and their governance teams, effective school governing bodies, an overview of school governance in South Africa, and using parents as governors and partners in school management and organization. E-mail: jheystek@up.ac.za

Mike Horsley is senior lecturer in the Faculty of Education and Social Work at the University of Sydney, where he directs the Teaching Resources and Textbook Research Unit (TREAT). He is the chief judge of the Australian Awards for Excellence in Educational Publishing, managed in partnership between TREAT and the Australian Publishers Association. Mike is the vice president of the International Association for Research on Textbooks and Educational Media (IARTEM), and a leading expert in observation studies used to investigate teaching and learning materials in the classroom. E-mail: m.horsley@edfac.usyd.edu.au

Fethi A. Inan is a member of the instructional design and technology program at the University of Memphis. Currently, Fethi is responsible for research design and data analysis pertaining to various research and evaluation projects for the Center for Research in Educational Policy. He also teaches technology integration courses at the University of Memphis. His recent research focuses on the effects of individual and contextual factors on the quality of instruction and student outcomes in K-12 schools. E-mail: finan@memphis.edu

Sung-il Kim is professor in the Department of Education at Korea University. He received his bachelor's degree in psychology from Korea University and his master's and PhD in cognitive psychology from Utah State University. He has held positions at the University of Nebraska-Lincoln, Kwangwoon University in Seoul before joining the faculty of Korea University in 2002. He received the Edwin B. Newman Award for Excellence in Research from the American Psychological Association/Psi Chi in 1992 and the Distinguished Teaching Award from Korea University in 2004. Although his earlier research focused on memory and discourse comprehension, his recent research interests revolve around interdisciplinary approaches on interest and motivations to learn. His current research projects include modeling interest-based learning, investigating neural bases of interest and motivation, developing a motivationally adaptive tutoring agent, and designing fun and exciting learning environments. He has published over 50 journal articles and has presented over 100 research papers at various professional meetings. E-mail: sungkim@ korea.ac.kr

Leonidas Kyriakides is assistant professor in educational research and evaluation at the University of Cyprus. He obtained first degrees from the Pedagogical Academy of Cyprus (Teacher's Diploma, 1988) and the State University of New York (BSc., 1990, Mathematics). He attended graduate studies at the University of Warwick (MA., 1991 and PhD, 1994 in educational research and evaluation). His main research interests concern the development of generic and differentiated models of educational effectiveness, the evaluation of student progress and teacher effectiveness, the application of effectiveness research to the improvement of educational practice, and the methodology of validation studies. He is member of the editorial board of the journal *School Effectiveness and School Improvement* and is author of more than 50 research papers in international journals, 7 books and 15 chapters in books. His most recent book (with Campbell, Muijs, and Robinson) is *Assessing Teacher Effectiveness: Developing a Differentiated Model* (2004). E-mail: kyriakid@ucy.ac.cy

Deborah L. Lowther is associate professor of instructional design and technology at the University of Memphis. She received her PhD in Educational Technology from Arizona State University in 1994. She has coauthored *Integrating Computer Technology* into the Classroom (3rd ed.), several book chapters and refereed journal articles, and is currently a member of the editorial board for the journal *Educational Technology Research and Development*. Her scholarly activities also include numerous presentations at national and international educational conventions, coguest editing a special edition of a national journal, working with multiple grants focused toward technology integration, and providing professional development to educational institutions across the United States. E-mail: dlowther@memphis.edu

Dennis M. McInerney is professor of educational psychology at the University of Western Sydney, Australia and associate director of the Self-concept Enhancement and Learning Facilitation Research Centre. Dennis has a strong interest in motivation research, has published extensively in refereed international journals, and has written numerous book chapters and conference papers, particularly in the area of motivation and achievement from a cross-cultural perspective. His textbook *Educational Psychology: Constructing Learning* (4th ed, 2006, Pearson Australia) is widely used as a standard text in Australian universities. Dennis's latest texts are *Helping Kids Achieve Their Best: Understanding and Using Motivation in the Classroom* (Allen & Unwin, 2001, Information Age Publishing, 2005), *Publishing Your Psychology Research: A guide to writing for journals in psychology and related fields* (Sage, 2001), *Research on Sociocultural Influences on Motivation and Learning Vols. 1-5* (Information Age Publishing), *International Advances in Self Research Vols. 1 & 2* (Information Age Publishing) and *Developmental Psychology for Teachers* (Allen & Unwin, in press). E-mail: d.mcinerney@uws.edu.au

Daniel Muijs holds the Chair of school leadership and management in the School of Education, Communication and Language Sciences, University of Newcastle, UK. He has previously worked at the Universities of Warwick, Exeter, and Loughborough. His main research interests include school leadership, school and teacher effectiveness, and quantitative research methods, and he has published widely in these areas. Daniel's current projects include leadership in extended schools, leading edge leadership, a longitudinal study of gifted and talented youth, the meta-analysis of teacher effectiveness factors, evaluation of the UK's Federations policy, evaluation of e-registration systems, and development of international system of teacher observation forms. E-mail: daniel.muijs@manchester.ac.uk

Steven M. Ross received his doctorate in educational psychology from Pennsylvania State University. He is currently a Faudree professor and executive director of the Center for Research in Educational Policy at the University of Memphis. He is a noted lecturer on school programs and educational evaluation. Dr. Ross is the author of six textbooks and over 120 journal articles in the areas of educational technology and instructional design, at-risk learners, and educational reform. He is editor of the research section of the journal *Educational Technology Research and Development*. In 1993, he was the first faculty recipient of the University of Memphis Eminent Faculty Award for teaching, research, and service and recently held the Lillian and Morrie Moss Chair of Excellence in Urban Education. He has testified on school restructuring research before the U.S. House of Representatives Subcommittee and is a technical advisor and researcher on current federal and state educational initiatives. E-mail: smross@memphis.edu

Robert Rueda is professor in psychology in education at the Rossier School of Education at the University of Southern California. He completed his doctoral work at the University of California at Los Angeles in educational psychology and special education, and completed a postdoctoral fellowship at the Laboratory of Comparative Human Cognition at the University of California, San Diego. His research has focused on the sociocultural basis of motivation and instruction, with a focus reading and literacy in English learners, students in at-risk conditions, and students with mild learning handicaps. His most recent work examines motivational and sociocultural aspects of reading comprehension, including how para-educators mediate instruction and provide cultural scaffolding to English-learners, and issues surrounding reading engagement among inner-city immigrant students in a central city community. E-mail: rueda@usc.edu

La Tefy Schoen began her career in 1982 as a director of an early childhood program and as an elementary school teacher. While working on her PhD at Louisiana State University, she became interested in school effectiveness and school improvement, and wondered why many well conceived, research-based reform initiatives had inconsistent results. Her research has taken her into numerous schools—interviewing and/or observing dozens of teachers, students, parents and several levels of administrators. The more different school contexts she became familiar with, the more she became convinced that school culture makes a difference in terms of school effectiveness and school improvement. Dr. Schoen now works as a student achievement facilitator for a PK-12 school, and runs a private consultation company entitled *School Works*, in which she uses her knowledge of school culture to assist with school improvement efforts at the state, district and school level. E-mail: latefy@cox.net

J. Dan Strahl, Jr. received a bachelor's degree in psychology from Memphis State University, and his master of science degree in instructional design and technology from the University of Memphis. Dan is a project coordinator at the Center for Research in Educational Policy (CREP) at the University of Memphis. He is responsible for the management of several state and local research and evaluation projects primarily focused in the area of technology integration into K-12 schools. Previously Dan spent several years as a corporate manager of training, marketing, and project logistics. E-mail: jstrahl@memphis.edu

Kenneth M. Tyler earned his PhD in developmental psychology (2002) from Howard University. He has served as a postdoctoral research associate at the Center for Research on the Education of Students Placed At-Risk (CRESPAR), a 10-year federally funded collaborative research and development center between Howard and Johns Hopkins University. Kenneth's research focus pertains to the influence of culture on the cognitive development, identity development, and school learning of elementary students from minority populations. He has published research on culturally-based learning activities and their effects on student performance outcomes. His current research involves homeschool cultural practices and beliefs, and students' classroom motivation and academic performance.

Shawn Van Etten received his PhD from the State University of New York, Albany. Shawn is currently the director of institutional research and assessment at the State University of New York, Cortland, and is a member of the National Association for Institutional Researcher's Higher Education Data Policy Committee. Shawn is a member of SUNY Cortland's administrative team and plays a key role in numerous projects that cut across the SUNY System, College Divisions, Schools, and other academic and administrative units. He is the coeditor of *Research on Sociocultural Influences on Motivation and Learning* and has made many presentations on a variety of education and fiscal topics. Prior to assuming administrative roles in higher education, Shawn was a teaching-research faculty member at multiple institutions and has a strong record in academic publication, the production of technical reports, and grant work. E-mail: VanEttenS@cortland.edu

Richard Walker teaches educational psychology at the undergraduate and postgraduate levels in the Faculty of Education and Social Work at the University of Sydney. He obtained his PhD from the University of Sydney in 1995. Recent publications in the sociocultural area include chapters in *Practice, Knowledge and the Health Professions* (2001), *Sociocultural Influences on Motivation and Learning* (2002), *Sociocultural Influences and Teacher Education Programs* (2003). Richard's current interests include the application of Vygotskian sociocultural understandings to student motivation, and schooling for marginalized and homeless youth from a sociocultural perspective. E-mail: r.walker@edfac.usyd.edu.au

David Watkins David Watkins is professor in the Faculty of Education at the University of Hong Kong where he has taught and researched for almost 20 years. His main research interests are in student learning, approaches to teaching, and self-concept—all from a cross-cultural perspective. He is a former executive committee member of both the International Association of Applied Psychology and the International Association of Cross-Cultural Psychology. Some of David's most recent publications deal with issues such as teachers as scholars of their students' conceptions of learning, measurement invariance in cross-cultural settings, and conceptions of teaching held by school science teachers. E-mail: hrfewda@hkucc.hku.hk

Qunying Zhang is currently a PhD candidate in the Faculty of Education at the University of Hong Kong. Her present research explores conceptions of a good tertiary EFL teacher in the People's Republic of China. Her broader research interests include conceptions of teaching and learning, EFL/ESL teaching and learning, and second language acquisition. E-mail: candace5@hkusua.hku.hk